Political restructuring in Europe

This book provides the theoretical background to the re-structuring of Europe that is currently under way. It attempts to situate the ethical debates in a historical, legal and constitutional context, considering important and topical issues such as the rights to secession and self-determination of minorities in Eastern Europe, and the question of whether national movements are justified in using force to achieve their ends.

The contributors number distinguished legal and constitutional scholars, political philosophers and international relations theorists from East and West, including Michael Walzer, Charles Beitz, Cass Sunstein, Onora O'Neill and David Miller.

Chris Brown is Senior Lecturer in International Relations at the University of Kent.

Political restructuring in Europe

Ethical perspectives

Edited by Chris Brown

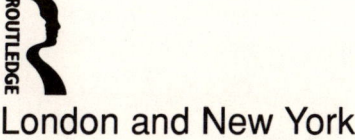

London and New York

First published 1994
by Routledge
11 New Fetter Lane, London EC4P 4EE

Simultaneously published in the USA and Canada
by Routledge
29 West 35th Street, New York, NY 10001

Typeset in Baskerville by
Ponting–Green Publishing Services, Chesham, Bucks
Printed and bound in Great Britain by
T.J. Press (Padstow) Ltd, Padstow, Cornwall
Printed on acid-free paper

British Library Cataloguing in Publication Data
A catalogue record for this book is available from the British Library.

Library of Congress Cataloging-in-Publication Data
has been applied for.

ISBN   0–415–09638–3

Contents

9   Notes on the new tribalism   187
    Michael Walzer

10 The moral basis of political restructuring   201
    Zarko Puhovski

Part IV   Conclusions

11 Cosmopolitans and communitarians –   223
    A commentary
    Ryszard Legutko

12 Comments and conclusions   239
    Hidemi Suganami

    Select bibliography and guide to further reading   253
    Index   256

Notes on contributors

Charles R. Beitz is Dean for Academic Affairs at Bowdoin College, Brunswick, Maine. His publications include *Political Theory and International Relations* (1979) and *Political Equality* (1989).

Chris Brown is Senior Lecturer in Politics and International Relations at the University of Kent at Canterbury. He is the author of *International Relations Theory: New Normative Approaches* (1992) and numerous articles on international political philosophy and international political economy.

Murray Forsyth is Professor of Politics and Head of the Centre for Federal Studies at the University of Leicester. His publications include *Unions of States* (1981) and, as editor, *Federalism and Nationalism* (1989).

Ryszard Legutko is Associate Professor at the Institute of Philosophy, Jagellonian University, Krakow, Poland, and President of the Centre for Political Thought. Under communism he edited an underground journal, *ARKA*, and is the author of **Capitalistic Dilemmas** (1985) and *Plato's Critique of Democracy* (1990).

David Miller is Official Fellow in Social and Political Theory at Nuffield College, Oxford. Among his most recent publications are *Market, State and Community: Theoretical Foundations of Market Socialism* (1989) and, as editor, *Liberty* (1991). His research interests include theories of justice and equality and ideas of nationality and citizenship.

Onora O'Neill is Principal of Newnham College, Cambridge: her most recent books are *Faces of Hunger: an Essay on Poverty, Development and Justice* (1986) and *Constructions of Reason: Explorations of Kant's Practical Philosophy* (1989). She was Professor of

Philosophy at Essex University from 1977 to 1992, is a past president of the Aristotelean Society, and has a particular interest in the reconstruction of links with philosophers in Eastern Europe and in Russia.

Thomas Pogge teaches philosophy at Columbia University in New York City. The author of *Realizing Rawls* (1989) and of various essays in moral and political philosophy as well as on Kant, he is currently writing a book on moralities and their effects.

Zarko Puhovski is Professor of Political Philosophy at the University of Zagreb, Croatia: he has published several books in Croatian (on Marx, critical theory, liberalism and the theory of culture) and articles in German and English. He was co-founder of the first Yugoslav alternative civic movement in 1988.

Hidemi Suganami is Senior Lecturer in International Relations at Keele University. His publications include *The Domestic Analogy and World Order Proposals* (1989) and he is currently completing a book entitled *Reasoning about War.*

Cass R. Sunstein is Karl N. Llewellyn Professor of Jurisprudence in the Law School and Department of Political Science at the University of Chicago, and co-Director of the Center for Constitutionalism in Eastern Europe. His publications include *After the Rights Revolution* (1990), *The Partial Constitution* (1993) and *Free Speech Now* (1993).

Michael Walzer is Professor of Social Science at the Institute for Advanced Study, Princeton, New Jersey. He is co-editor of *Dissent* and author of, amongst many volumes, *Just and Unjust Wars* (1977, second edition, 1992), *Spheres of Justice* (1983) and, most recently, a collection of essays entitled *What it Means to be an American* (1993).

The Ethikon Institute. The Berlin conference on which this volume is based was a project of the Ethikon Institute's Intersocietal Relations Programme, which studies the ethical dimensions of relations between states and between distinct communities within multinational states. A major objective of the Intersocietal Relations Committee is to develop a comparative literature on ethics and international affairs. The Ethikon Institute was established to promote mutual understanding and greater tolerance among peoples of different moral traditions. Focusing on issues of broad public concern, it aims to explore the unifying prospects of ethical consensus, where it can be found, and to identify grounds for the peaceful accommodation of irreducible differences. As a facilitator of dialogue, the Ethikon Institute takes no position on the issues which divide its participants. It serves not as an arbiter but as a forum for the amicable exchange of diverse and sometimes contending views.

Acknowlegements

This volume has its origins in a conference on 'The Restructuring of Political and Economic Systems' organized by the Ethikon Institute, in collaboration with the California Institute of Technology and the OstWestWirtschaftsAkademie, made possible by a grant from The Pew Charitable Trusts and held at the Villa Walther, Berlin, in January 1991. We are grateful to each of these institutions and their staff, and especially to Ethikon's Phil Valera, without whom neither conference nor book would have been possible. Ethikon is a institution which exists to promote dialogue between different ethical traditions, and the chapters in this book by Forsyth, Beitz, Pogge, Miller were presented in earlier forms at the Berlin conference – at which O'Neill, Brown and Puhovski were also present. The chapters by Sunstein and Walzer were first published elsewhere – in *The University of Chicago Law Review* and *Dissent* respectively – but were so obviously germane to our project that we are most grateful to the authors for allowing us to reprint them here. It is part of the Ethikon tradition to employ discussants and commentators to review the similarities and differences between the different ethical approaches represented under its auspices, and Legutko and Suganami performed this task with distinction.

The editor would like to add personal thanks to Phil Valera, to the conference's chairpersons, Brian Barry and Terry Nardin, to Routledge's Caroline Wintersgill and Diane Stafford, to Elizabeth Dorling and her colleagues in the Keynes College Secretarial Office, to Jarrod Wiener for help at the proofs stage – and to all the contributors, who put up with continual harassment with a reasonably good grace.

Chris Brown
Keynes College, November 1992

Chapter 1

Introduction

Chris Brown

The political structures of Europe have undergone an extra-ordinary level of change over the last few years – most obviously in Eastern and Central Europe, where the collapse of the Soviet empire in 1989 was followed by German unity in 1990 and the collapse of the Soviet Union itself in 1991. This has been a sequence of change unmatched by any other two-year period in the *peacetime* history of Europe. Throughout the region new states are emerging out of the rubble of the old regime, sometimes, as in Poland, Hungary, Bulgaria and Romania, occupying (at least for the time being) the same territory as their predecessors, but in other cases – the majority – within new boundaries. Each of these new political systems must carry out the fundamental economic changes required to replace the discredited communist command economy; almost all are attempting to establish liberal democratic political institutions; and in every case nationalist sentiments threaten these new countries with internal divisions and external conflicts. 'Eastern Europe' – a term now politically suspect, given its association with the old divisions of Europe, but as yet irreplaceable – is facing a desperate crisis: widespread political unrest, economic hardship, malnutrition, even mass starvation in some areas, are possibilities in the autumn of 1992, perhaps realities by the time these words are read.

The situation in Western Europe is, of course, nowhere near as potentially catastrophic. However, by all usual standards, the changes here are of great significance. In the late 1980s the European Community (EC) launched itself towards a much higher level of economic co-operation than before with its plans for a 'Single Market' by 1993 – a process which has led to a *higher* level of regulation and a more active role for the Commission within the Community than was previously the case, stoking fears of excessive bureaucracy. Meanwhile, the emergence of a unified Germany in 1990 reawakened old fears; the reaction to this event in some quarters – including Germany itself, where, amongst the political elite at least, fear of the power of the new state was as great if not greater than elsewhere – was to intensify the scale and speed of steps towards *European* unity, locking the new power firmly into a safe, European, identity. The combination of these two forces – opposition to bureaucratization and a desire to contain the new Germany – created complex pressures for change, which the Maastricht Treaty of December 1991 was designed to meet.

This treaty embodied the creation of an (ill-defined) European Union and a rough-and-ready timetable for the establishment of a common currency, but also contained a number of provisions designed to restrict the powers of the Commission and to prevent the emergence of supranationalism. This compromise appears to be satisfying no one. A Danish referendum narrowly rejected the treaty in June 1992; in Britain ratification by the House of Commons is uncertain. However, attempts to satisfy these critics by solemn declarations stressing the limits on Union contained in the treaty meet with opposition from the smaller and poorer members of the Community, who regard supranationalism as their best defence against the power of large states such as Germany, France and Britain. Reconciliation of these different interests seems impossible.

It is clear that in the new, post-communist world, the problems of East and West cannot be considered in isolation. Those who used to be 'East Europeans' want to become, in a socio-economic and political sense, 'West Europeans'; they see eventual membership of the European Community as a way of stabilizing their own political systems and promoting economic development. However, the nationalism of these societies seems incompatible with this ambition. Meanwhile, in the West, many EC members give rhetorical support for the extension of the Community to the East ('widening' in the jargon of Community discussions), while also supporting extensions of its scope and competence ('deepening') that make it implausible that this will happen in the foreseeable future.

These contradictions between policies and rhetoric might

suggest that the problems of the regions will remain separate, but the course of events suggests that this is highly implausible. Western Europeans cannot isolate themselves from the dramas of the East. The internal War of the Yugoslav Succession has forced West European countries to engage in mediation and peace-keeping, and some are already experiencing political problems as a result of an influx of refugees generated by the conflict – this latter, perhaps, but a foretaste of the problems which large-scale migration of labour will create if the disparity between basic living standards in East and West Europe remains as high as it currently is. In the medium run, the unpalatable choice may be between extensive aid to encourage Easterners to stay in the East, reluctantly provided and politically unpopular relief programmes for those who come west, or draconian controls on movement to keep out the dispossessed.

To summarize the implications of this thumbnail sketch of Europe in the early 1990s, it seems likely that the countries of Eastern and Western Europe are on the verge of achieving the impossible – a situation in which large numbers of Europeans will yearn for the 'good old days' of the Cold War, with even many Eastern Europeans, who had to suffer the hardships of communism directly, looking back with some nostalgia to the relative political and economic stability of the old regime. The political restructuring of Europe remains unavoidable – however, the kind of restructured Europe that will emerge at the end of the process is still, just, open to debate. The danger is that without a change in thinking it will be a Europe in which the West will be in the midst of economic depression, politically divided, and united only in its determination to exclude from its borders the millions who will be fleeing from political, social and economic collapse in the East. That this nightmare scenario could come to pass is a measure of just how serious the situation is – and just how important it is to understand the deeper forces and issues brought to the surface by the processes of political restructuring currently under way in Europe.

This volume is composed of essays which address this agenda, and in particular the *moral* and *ethical* forces which are shaping the new Europe. As will become apparent, its authors disagree on many counts, but one point of agreement is that the ethical dimension of change in Europe has not received the attention that it deserves. It is clear to us that ethical considerations have been major sources of change, in particular in Eastern Europe, where the moral bankruptcy of the old order was as apparent as its economic and political failures. Equally, the policies which will be, and are being, adopted in East and West to cope with change will not succeed in avoiding catastrophe unless they respond to this ethical dimension. Policies guided only by considerations of *Realpolitik* will not succeed in establishing a legitimate order in Europe. New structures will neither merit nor receive public acceptance unless they are seen as ethically defensible. That this is so is tacitly acknowledged by the attempts of the governments of Europe to provide moral justifications of their policies before their own, and European, public opinion.

However, it is clear that thinking about moral and ethical matters is often confused and unfocused. Many of the categories conventionally employed in moral discourse about the new political structures of Europe seem, in practice, to be singularly unhelpful. Neither the right to national self-determination, nor the concept of sovereignty, for example, seems to provide satisfactory guidelines in specific cases – where what needs to be decided is usually, say, not so much the existence of a right to self-determination as which of several competing groups should exercise it. Should *any* minority have a right to secede irrespective of the consequences? This seems impracticable, but if not, which minorities ought to have such a right? Under what circumstances is outside intervention in the affairs of a sovereign state legitimate? For that matter, how does a state achieve legitimacy in Europe today? How are just boundaries established?

The broad-brush ideas characteristically employed in public discourse to provide answers to these questions are insufficiently refined to perform the task. General principles need to be embedded in a wider set of ideas which would help us to give specific answers to the all-important 'who', 'where' and 'when' questions. However, it is unlikely that there will be simply *one* wider set of ideas that could provide these answers. Instead, it is clear that there are radically different perspectives on these problems, with different starting points and different kinds of reasoning, even if – as will become apparent later in this volume – these perspectives sometimes generate similar conclusions. There is an apparent paradox here. It might have been thought that the end of communism as an effective political force would lead to some kind of moral consensus, but, in fact, exactly the opposite has occurred. Moral arguments that were damped down under communism now take on a significance not seen since the late 1940s.

At the heart of this collection are a series of essays which address this debate, seen here in terms of a clash between 'cosmopolitan' and 'communitarian' views of the world. These perspectives offer competing views of the sources of value in social life, and the proper relationship that ought to exist between the individual and the polity. On the one hand, there are those who approach contemporary problems by assigning primary significance to the interests and values of individuals: on the other hand, there are those who see communities as the prime source of value. This is a very broad distinction – each perspective encompasses a range of views almost as different from one another as the difference between the two root positions – but, nonetheless, as we hope to demonstrate, it makes sense to organize consideration of contemporary moral debates in Europe in these terms.

It is not simply *moral* considerations that are a source of confusion in contemporary debate – it is also the case that *constitutional* matters do not receive the sort of attention they deserve. The legal implications of the act of secession are often taken for granted by both moral philosophers and current affairs commentators when discussing self-determination, while the language of federalism and confederalism is freely employed in both Western and Eastern Europe. In both cases, as contributors to this volume argue, a more sophisticated analysis would aid understanding. Moreover, it is too often taken for granted that nationalism – the single most important *political* force in Europe today – is a phenomenon whose origins and prospects are well understood. Again contributors argue that a more nuanced approach brings dividends.

The structure of this volume is shaped by the desire to place the moral and ethical debates generated by political restructuring in Europe within the framework of these other political and legal considerations. *Part I* examines the legal and constitutional aspects of restructuring. The American constitutional lawyer Cass Sunstein, drawing on both past American and current European experience, examines the legal side of secession and self-determination, arguing strongly against the superficially attractive idea of recognizing a right to secession in the new constitutions of Europe. In a companion chapter, Murray Forsyth explores the language and grammar of federalism in the new Europe, again examining current practice in the light of past experience elsewhere. A theme of both chapters is the unwisdom of imagining that there are legal or constitutional solutions to political and moral problems.

In *Part II*, at the heart of this volume, five authors offer contrasting views on the central debate between cosmopolitanism and communitarianism. Onora O'Neill opens this section with a cosmopolitan challenge to the absence of political writings on justice and boundaries, while Thomas Pogge and Charles Beitz continue the cosmopolitan theme in a wider context – demonstrating in the process that cosmopolitans can differ on quite central issues such as the moral basis of self-determination. David Miller and Chris Brown complete this section with studies from a communitarian perspective, again demonstrating that this broad approach covers a wide range of views.

Part III consists of two essays on contemporary European politics which establish different positions on the origins and prospects of nationalism. Michael Walzer's 1991 account of the 'new tribalism' is essentially – albeit guardedly – optimistic that the new tribes will eventually re-establish civilized relations, while Zarko Puhovski, writing from Croatia, is less optimistic, tracing the force of nationalism to the communist past and arguing the necessity for democratic self-restraint in the new states of the East.

In *Part IV*, two scholars present overall assessments of the debates. Ryszard Legutko concentrates on the cosmopolitan/communitarian divide, arguing that both parties fail to live up to the Aristotelean conception of politics, while, in a conclusion to the volume, Hidemi Suganami surveys the collection as a whole, bringing out agreements and disagreements and common themes.

The chapters that make up this volume come from scholars with different intellectual and national backgrounds, and reflect a number of different *genres*. In Part I the necessary detail that accompanies Sunstein's legal reasoning contrasts with Forsyth's panoramic overview of contemporary federalism. There is an obvious contrast in style between the chapters in Part II, which were for the most part written for the scholarly conference at which the idea for this volume originated, and the essays of Part III, produced for a different audience or under different conditions. This eclecticism is not a source of weakness: it is highly unlikely that the project of understanding our troubled times can be forwarded by work produced within one academic format, or by the methods of one discipline or by scholars from one part of the world and one intellectual tradition. What is needed is an exchange of ideas, a (friendly) confrontation of perspectives, philosophies, disciplinary skills and national viewpoints – and it is in this spirit that we offer this volume to the contemporary debate.

Part I

Constitutionalism, federalism and confederalism

Chapter 2

Approaching democracy: a new legal order for Eastern Europe

Constitutionalism and secession

Cass R. Sunstein

The Soviet Constitution guaranteed a right to secede.[1] The American Constitution does not. Although some secessionists in the American South, invoking state sovereignty, claimed to find an implicit right to secede in the founding document, it was more common to invoke an extratextual and non-justiciable 'right to secede' said to be enshrined in the Declaration of Independence.[2] In any case, no serious scholar or politician now argues that a right to secede exists under American constitutional law.[3] It is generally agreed that such a right would undermine the Madisonian spirit of the original document, one that encourages the development of constitutional provisions that prevent the defeat of the basic enterprise.[4]

Eastern European countries are now deciding about the contents of proposed constitutions. They are often doing so in the context of profound cultural and ethnic divisions, both often defined at least roughly in territorial terms. These divisions have propelled claims for local self-determination that could readily be transformed into attempts to guarantee a right to secede or even into secession itself. In Eastern Europe in particular, debates over the right to secede have already played an extraordinarily important role in discussions of new institutional arrangements.[5] Active secession movements have played a central role in current efforts to establish democratic governance. Such movements have led to claims for a constitutional right to secede, paralleling the Soviet right but to be respected in practice. A draft of the Slovak constitution, for example, creates a right to secede.[6]

It is likely that these claims will be asserted all the more vigorously in the future. The claims for secession, or for a right to secede, raise exceptionally large questions about the theory and practice of constitutionalism. It is therefore an especially important time to explore the relationship between secession claims and constitutionalism in general.

My principal claim in this chapter is that whether or not secession might be justified as a matter of politics or morality, constitutions ought not to include a right to secede.[7] To place such a right in a founding document would increase the risks of ethnic and factional struggle; reduce the prospects for compromise and deliberation in government; raise dramatically the stakes of day-to-day political decisions; introduce irrelevant and illegitimate considerations into those decisions; create dangers of blackmail, strategic behaviour, and exploitation; and, most generally, endanger the prospects for long-term self-governance.[8] Constitutionalism, embodying as it does a set of pre-commitment strategies, is frequently directed against risks of precisely this sort. Political or moral claims for secession are frequently powerful, but they do not justify constitutional recognition of a secession right.

The principal argument for recognition of a right to secede is that it would operate as a powerful deterrent to oppressive and discriminatory practices, and also serve as an effective remedy for these practices. Usually, however, these goals can be promoted through other, more direct means. If they cannot be, a negotiated agreement embodying secession or a right of revolution – also not recognized in founding texts – is a preferable safeguard. The opportunity for a negotiated agreement or a right of revolution would provide a remedy against most of the relevant abuses without raising the continuous risks to self-government that would be created by a constitutional right to secede.

In the process of making this argument, I hope also to disentangle the various possible grounds for a moral claim to secession and to indicate which of those grounds have force in different contexts. Some of the discussion will provide support for the view that secession is often justified as a matter of political morality. In such cases I argue against national efforts to stop secession through military or other action.

In Part I, I discuss constitutions as pre-commitment strategies, designed to foreclose debate over certain fundamental questions. These strategies should often be seen as enabling rather than constraining, that is, as devices not only for limiting government, but also for facilitating the difficult process of self-government. This argument has powerful roots in the American constitutional tradition and applies with particular force in the context of secession. The argument also has general implications for the theory of what does and does not belong in constitutions. This theory remains in a surprisingly primitive state, and I will venture some preliminary remarks on the subject.

In Part II, I discuss reasons why a sub-unit of a nation might want to secede, and provide a brief assessment of those reasons as a matter of political morality. My conclusion is that those reasons often create a strong moral claim for secession. Even when this is so, however, the creation of a right to secede in a founding document is usually unjustified. Part III discusses qualified rights to secession, arguing that even though these are superior to a general right of exit for sub-units, they are inferior to an across-the-board waiver of that right by all sub-units in a nation.[9]

CONSTITUTIONS AS PRE-COMMITMENT STRATEGIES

In general: notes on constitutionalism

It is often said that constitutionalism is in considerable tension with democracy. Thomas Jefferson was emphatic on the point, arguing that constitutions should be amended by each generation in order to ensure that the dead past would not constrain the living present.[10] Many contemporary observers echo the Jeffersonian position, claiming that constitutional constraints often amount to unjustified, anti-democratic limits on the power of the present and future.[11] Responding to Jefferson, James Madison argued that a constitution subject to frequent amendment would promote factionalism and provide no firm basis for republican self-government.[12]

Madison envisioned firm and lasting constitutional constraints as a precondition for democratic processes, rather than a check on them. This vision captures a central goal of American constitutionalism: to ensure the conditions for the peaceful, long-term operation of democracy in the face of often persistent social differences and plurality along religious, ethnic, cultural, and other lines. This goal is highly relevant to constitutional developments in Eastern Europe, where religious and ethnic hostilities are especially intense. Madison saw differences and diversity as strengths rather than weaknesses, if channelled through constitutional structures that would promote deliberation and lead groups to check, rather than exploit, other groups. It may be possible for Eastern European countries to replicate this approach, although they face far more profound differences of language, ethnicity, history, and religion than those that confronted the framers of the US Constitution.

To approach the question of secession, it will be useful to provide a brief outline of some of the reasons for entrenching institutional arrangements and substantive rights.[13] On such questions, constitutional theory remains in a surprisingly primitive state.[14] I begin by examining what sorts of considerations might lead people forming a new government to place basic rights and arrangements beyond the reach of ordinary politics. The crucial idea here is that, for various reasons, people in a newly formed nation might attempt to do so as part of a pre-commitment strategy.

Some rights are entrenched because of a belief that they are in some sense pre- or extra-political, that is, because individuals ought to be allowed to exercise them regardless of what majorities might think. Some of these rights are entrenched for reasons entirely independent of democracy. Here constitutionalism is indeed a self-conscious check on self-government, attempting to immunize a private sphere from public power. Plausible examples include the rights to private property,[15] freedom from self-incrimination, bodily integrity, protection against torture or cruel punishment, and privacy.

But many of the rights that are constitutionally entrenched actually derive from the principle of democracy itself. Their protection from majoritarian processes follows from and creates no tension with the goal of self-determination through politics. The pre-commitment strategy permits the people to protect democratic processes against their own potential excesses or misjudgements. The right to freedom of speech and the right to vote are familiar illustrations. Constitutional protection of these rights is not at odds with the commitment to self-government but instead a logical part of it.[16]

Institutional arrangements can also be understood as an

effort to protect a private sphere from majoritarianism. Often this effort stems from a fear of democratic processes. A decision to divide government among the legislative, executive, and judicial branches might be regarded as an effort to check and limit government by requiring a consensus among all three before the state could interfere with the private sphere.[17] Private liberty flourishes because government is partially disabled. So, too, a federal system may ensure that the nation and its sub-units will check each other, generating a friction that enables private liberty to flourish.[18]

Structural provisions of this sort limit the political power of present majorities (or minorities), and in this sense raise difficulties for those who believe that the only or principal purpose of constitutionalism is to provide a framework for democratic governance. But if structural provisions are generally seen as pre-commitment strategies, some of them can be enabling as well as constraining.[19] We can understand both individual rights and structural provisions in this way. Like the rules of grammar, such provisions set out the rules by which political discussion will occur, and in that sense free the participants to conduct their discussions more easily.

The system of separation of powers, for example, does not merely constrain government, but also helps to energize it, and to make it more effective, by creating a healthy division of labour. This was a prominent argument during the framing period in America.[20] A system in which the executive does not bear the burden of adjudication may well strengthen the executive by removing from it a task that frequently produces public opprobrium. Indeed, the entire framework may enable rather than constrain democracy, not only by creating an energetic executive[21] but, more fundamentally, by allowing the sovereign people to pursue a strategy, against their government, of divide and conquer. So long as it is understood that no branch of government is actually 'the people', a system of separation of powers can allow the citizenry to monitor and constrain their inevitably imperfect agents. In general, the entrenchment of established institutional arrangements enables rather than merely constrains present and future generations by creating a settled framework under which people may make decisions.

Thus far I have suggested that constitutions may create rights and institutions that follow from some independent theory of what individuals are owed, that are a natural corollary of the commitment to democracy, or that help to facilitate the democratic process by establishing the basic structures under which political arrangements can take place. Constitutional provisions may be facilitative in quite another sense: a decision to take certain issues off the ordinary political agenda may be indispensable to the political process.[22]

For example, the initial decision to create a system of private property places severe constraints on the scope of any political deliberations on that fundamental issue, and often serves to keep issues of private property off the political agenda completely. Indeed, Madison understood the protection of rights of property largely as a mechanism for limiting factional conflict in government, not as a means of protecting 'rights' and much less as a means of ensuring against redistribution.[23] The removal of the issue from politics serves, perhaps ironically, to ensure that politics may continue.

So, too, a nation may protect questions of religion against resolution by democratic processes, not only because there is a right to freedom of religious conscience, but also because the democratic process works best if the fundamental and potentially explosive question of religion does not intrude into day-to-day decisions. More narrowly and no doubt more controversially, the decision to constitutionalize the right to abortion might be justified because it minimizes the chances that this intractable and polarizing question will intrude into and thus disable the political process.

Yet another set of facilitative constitutional pre-commitment strategies includes provisions that are designed to solve collective action problems or prisoners' dilemmas, that is, situations in which the pursuit of rational self-interest by each individual actor produces outcomes that are destructive to all actors considered together, and that could be avoided if all actors agreed in advance to coercion, assuring co-operation.[24] People who are creating their government may voluntarily waive a right whose existence would rematerialize, and create serious risks, without the waiver. A decision to relinquish an otherwise available right advances the interests of all or most who are involved.[25]

This idea has played a large role in the American constitutional experience. The leading example is the Full Faith and Credit Clause,[26] which requires each state to enforce judgments rendered in other states. Every state might have an incentive to refuse to enforce the judgments of other states; if Massachusetts chooses not to honour the judgment of a New York court against a Massachusetts citizen, then Massachusetts receives a short-term gain because the resources its citizen needs to satisfy any judgment remain within the borders of Massachusetts. But all states would be better off if the law bound each of them to respect the judgments of others. The Full Faith and Credit Clause ensures precisely this outcome, effectively solving a conventional prisoners' dilemma.

Another illustration is the Commerce Clause.[27] The Supreme Court has consistently interpreted the clause as disabling the states from regulating interstate commerce.[28] In the period between the Articles of Confederation and the Constitution, battles among the states produced mutually destructive tariffs and other protectionist measures. The adoption of each of these measures may well have furthered the interest of each state considered in isolation.[29] Collectively, this system proved disastrous.[30]

Especially in light of the strong emotional attachments that fuel perceptions of state self-interest, a system in which each state can choose whether to initiate protectionist measures might well lead many states to do so. But an agreement by all states to refrain from protectionism, and thus to waive their antecedent right under the Articles of Confederation, should further the collective interest. The constitutional decision to remove control of interstate commerce from state authority solves the problem.[31] In this case, as with the Full Faith and Credit Clause, a relinquishment of what appears to be state sovereignty very likely furthers the interest of all states concerned. This example illustrates both the importance of pre-commitment strategies in resolving prisoners' dilemmas, and the potential value of judicial review in a healthy constitutional system. The Supreme Court's conclusion that the Commerce Clause contains an implicit limitation on state power over interstate commerce – a 'negative' federal power – was controversial at first and still raises thorny problems for the Court from time to time.[32] The Commerce Clause on its face provides the federal government with only the positive power to regulate, and locates this power in the legislature, not the courts. But the negative commerce power follows naturally from the structural logic of the Constitution. Its enforcement by the judiciary has been an important means of remaining faithful to that logic.[33]

Finally, constitutional pre-commitment strategies may serve to overcome myopia or weakness of will on the part of the collectivity, or to ensure that representatives follow the considered judgments of the people. Protection of freedom of speech, or from unreasonable searches and seizures, may represent an effort by the people themselves to provide safeguards against the impulsive behaviour of majorities. Here the goal is to ensure that the deliberative sense of the community will prevail over momentary passions.[34] Similarly, a constitution may represent a firm acknowledgement that the desires of the government, even in a well-functioning republic, do not always match those of the people.[35] Constitutional limits, introduced by something like the people themselves, therefore respond to the agency problem created by a system in which government officials inevitably have interests of their own. This problem arises in all systems of government, including democracies. In countries emerging from communist rule, without established principles of democratic representation, it is likely to pose a special danger, against which constitutional provisions should guard.

In all of these cases, the decision to take certain questions off the political agenda may be understood as a means not of disabling but of protecting politics, by reducing the power of highly controversial questions to create factionalism, instability, impulsiveness, chaos, stalemate, collective action problems, myopia, strategic behaviour, or hostilities so serious and fundamental as to endanger the governmental process itself. In this respect, the decision to use constitutionalism to remove certain issues from politics is often profoundly democratic.

We can also see many constitutional provisions as mechanisms for ensuring discussion and deliberation oriented towards agreement about the general good rather than factionalism and self-interested bargaining. The states' relinquishment of their pre-existing sovereign right to control the entry and exit of goods is the most prominent example. But the institutions of representation and checks and balances have frequently been designed to promote general discussion and compromise, to diminish the influence of particular segments of society, and to produce the incentives for and possibility of agreement. These principles largely guided the development of the United States Constitution. They bear directly on the attempts of Eastern European countries to meld constitutionalism with democracy in the midst of extraordinary diversity and pluralism.[36]

Secession

Eastern Europe: a brief note

Secession has become an extremely prominent issue in Eastern Europe. As of this writing, the situation is highly fluid, indeed changing almost daily. Anything said here about the situation will likely be significantly out of date by the time of publication. But some brief notes on the current situation will serve as a useful prelude to the discussion.

In an astonishingly short time, secession movements have fundamentally altered the map of Europe. Of course, the Soviet Union no longer exists. Moreover, the various republics that are now independent nations are far from stable, in part because they face secession movements of their own. It is not altogether clear that Russia and Ukraine will be able to maintain their current forms. The old Yugoslavia can be found only in history books; in the midst of civil war it is impossible to know what will happen to its former republics. After a series of efforts to reach compromise the Czechs and Slovaks have gone their separate ways. International borders in Eastern Europe are thus changing at an extremely rapid pace.

For many observers of the disintegration of communism, the rise of secession movements has been one of the most important, unanticipated and alarming developments. It was widely understood that, without a strong Soviet Union, ethnic and religious tension would increase, but most people did not anticipate the intensity of these tensions, and the extent to which they would distract attention from the crucial tasks of creating democratic institutions and the foundations of a market economy.

It is here that the secession movements have been especially dangerous, eliminating opportunities that, once lost, may be lost for a long time. The disintegration of communism furnished an extraordinary occasion for the creation of effective constitutional regimes, providing the preconditions for free markets and democratic institutions. But active secession movements – or *de jure* or *de facto* secession rights – can make it impossible to carry out these tasks. I return to this point in several places below.

Pre-commitment and secession

For the moment I will not speak to the issue of whether and when secession is desirable or just. Instead I want to ask whether a Constitution ought to recognize a right to secede. I will understand a constitutional right to secede as encompassing (1) an explicit textual provision guaranteeing such a right or (2) an implicit understanding that the constitution creates that right, accompanied in either case by (3) a willingness to enforce that right by a court with the power of judicial review – that is, a court capable of granting and enforcing a sub-unit's request to secede despite the objections of the central government. As the Soviet experience has shown in the context of individual rights as well as the context of secession, constitutional guarantees on paper often mean nothing without institutions available to vindicate them.[37]

At first glance, the argument for a right to secede seems straightforward. If a sub-unit no longer wants to exist within the nation, why should it have to do so? This initial challenge draws strength from a number of arguments, spelled out below, including the need for local self-determination, the history of unjust acquisition in Eastern Europe and elsewhere, the claims of ethnic and cultural integrity, and the threat of curtailment of basic rights and liberties.

The issue of secession is, however, an unusually good candidate for an analysis that stresses the use of constitutionalism as a pre-commitment strategy. Indeed, the problem of secession closely parallels the problems solved by the Full Faith and Credit Clause and the Commerce Clause, and in some respects follows naturally from those examples. The initial point is that constitutional recognition of a right to secede may well have a range of harmful consequences for democratic politics. In the face of such a right, a threat to secede could under certain conditions be plausible at any given time, allowing the exit of the sub-unit from the nation to be a relevant factor in every important decision. It is not difficult to imagine circumstances in which it will be in a sub-unit's interest to issue that threat. Rather than working to achieve compromise, or to solve common problems, sub-units holding a right to secede may well succumb to the temptation of self-dealing, and hold out for whatever they can get.[38] It is quite possible that some such self-dealing has already occurred in Eastern Europe.[39]

A right to secede will encourage strategic behaviour, that is, efforts to seek benefits or diminish burdens by making threats that are strategically useful and based on power over matters technically unrelated to the particular question at issue. Sub-units with economic power may well be able to extract large gains in every decision involving the geographical distribution of benefits and burdens. A constitutional system that recognizes and is prepared to respect the right to secede will find its very existence at issue in every case in which a sub-unit's interests are seriously at stake. In practice, that threat could operate as a prohibition on any national decision adverse to the sub-unit's interests.

A temporarily disaffected sub-unit could, in short, raise the stakes in ordinary political and economic decisions simply by threatening to leave. The threat would be especially credible and therefore disruptive if the sub-unit could or might prefer to exist on its own. The recognition of a right of exit on the part of the sub-unit could thus prevent fair dealing on the nation's part, by allowing the sub-unit to veto policies that were justified on balance.

It might also lead to undue caution. The threat to secede might deter the government from taking action that offended a sub-unit but was on balance justified. Consider, for example, the issue of taxation. A tobacco-growing sub-unit equipped with the right to secede might be able to veto a decision to raise taxes on (say) cigarettes even if that decision would further the nation's long-term interest. Similar considerations apply to the decision to enter into war, to enact environmental regulation, or to increase or decrease aid to agriculture. A secession right cannot plausibly be justified on the ground that it is a necessary check on national policies designed to ensure that those policies are in the general interest; the fact that a state wants to secede is neither a necessary nor a sufficient reason to believe that the general interest is being violated.

Family law supplies a helpful analogy. In a marriage, the understanding that the unit is not divisible because of current dissatisfaction, but only in extraordinary circumstances, can serve to promote compromise, to encourage people to live together, to lower the stakes during disagreements, and to prevent any particular person from achieving an excessively strong bargaining position. A decision to stigmatize divorce or to make it available only under certain conditions – as virtually every state in the United States has done – may lead to happier as well as more stable marriages, by providing an incentive for spouses to adapt their behaviour and even their desires to promote long-term harmony.[40] I intend to make no sweeping comment here on the structure of divorce law; I argue only that in the secession context there are strong reasons for making exit difficult.

Recognition of a right to secede would also ensure that any sub-unit whose resources are at the moment indispensable, and that might be able to exist on its own, is in an extraordinary position to obtain benefits or to diminish burdens on matters formally unrelated to its comparative advantage. Moreover, the shared knowledge that the nation is terminable at the option of any sub-unit would promote instability.

In these circumstances, we might understand a waiver of the right to secede as a solution to a collective action problem or a prisoners' dilemma. For each sub-unit, acting individually, recognition of the right might increase its authority to obtain a large share of the collective assets during any general allocation. But if the right to secede exists, each sub-unit will be vulnerable to threats of secession by the others. If the considerations marshalled thus far are persuasive, all or most sub-units are quite plausibly better off if each of them waives its right to secede. More generally, the difficulty or impossibility of exit from the nation will encourage co-operation for the long term, providing an incentive to adapt conduct and even preferences to that goal.

Of course, the existence of a right to secede will have few such consequences if a threat to secede is not credible. Under some conditions, however, the threat will be a real one. Some sub-units might well find it in their economic interest to exist on their own. If independence is economically preferable, the threat of secession will be fully plausible. Other sub-units will suffer some economic loss if they secede, but still find independence worthwhile because of gains in terms of cultural or geographical autonomy or capacity for self-governance. Here a threat of secession might be credible even if the seceding sub-unit would be an economic loser.

In the context of secession, the practical political problem goes especially deep. The right to secede is different from other potential vetoes on national legislative action precisely because it raises fundamental and often emotional issues having to do with the claims of ethnicity, territory, and history to separation and self-determination. These issues have a peculiar tendency to inflame both sub-units and those who want them to remain part of the nation. They tend to raise the emotional stakes in such a way as to make the ordinary work of politics – not to mention day-to-day interactions in other spheres – extremely hard to undertake.[41]

In Eastern Europe, divisions of this kind promise to be among the most important questions for constitutional resolution in the next generation.[42] Those divisions threaten not only to split nations into sub-units – which may or may not be good – but also to paralyse national and local governments and to deflect them from dealing with the enormous current social and economic problems. Deliberation is often an inadequate check, and it comes at a high price. A waiver of the right to secede protects against inflamed or impulsive behaviour.[43] On some occasions, the emotional stakes should be raised in precisely this way. But constitutional recognition of a right to secede accomplishes the relevant goals at great risk to the fundamental task of creating healthy, long-term constitutional structures.

The large destabilizing effects of a right to secede may also disrupt expectations whose existence is indispensable to both economic prosperity and democratic self-determination. After secession, it will be extremely hard to disentangle the contributions of the sub-unit and the nation in order to decide who should be paying whom for what. The sheer volume of the costs of allocation provide at least a consideration against recognition of a right to secede. Much more fundamentally, a nation whose sub-units may secede will be far less likely to engage in long-term planning. Interdependence will be both threatening and risky, and thus will be discouraged.

For Eastern European countries, it is imperative to develop institutions that can ensure confidence in the long-term health of the newly democratized governmental systems. Without such institutions, the emerging market economies will fail.[44] A waiver of the right to secede should be seen as part of a set of strategies designed to bring about stable institutional arrangements. In this light it should be unsurprising to observe proposed institutional reforms designed to foster stability in the face of separatist appeals, such as the Czechoslovakian plan to allocate much more power to the republics and the 'union treaty' proposal in the Soviet Union.[45]

There is an analogy here in the history of the American Constitution. The framers deemed it necessary to protect contractual agreements against state impairment, not to help creditors as a class, but to ensure that commercial interactions would occur in the first place.[46] A system in which states can impair contracts will discourage their formation in the first instance, and thus have harmful long-term effects on the economy as a whole. So, too, legal protection of national unity should have an important co-ordinating effect, creating expectations of long-term interaction indispensable to national self-government.

Thus far I have argued that a waiver of the right to secede is a sensible pre-commitment strategy, one that is likely to remove a serious threat to democratic processes. There are at least two possible responses to this line of argument. The first is that if the existence of the nation confers mutual benefits – an assumed precondition for its continuation – then sub-units will rarely threaten to secede even if constitutionally authorized to do so, and the threat will rarely be credible even if made. The costs of secession will usually be at least as large for the sub-unit as for the nation. On this view, recognition of a right to secede would never or rarely have the adverse effects claimed for it. A well-functioning nation simply will not face serious secession threats; sub-units will invoke the right only in the most extraordinary circumstances. Indeed, in those circumstances the right is a necessary corrective to the status quo.

This rejoinder may be correct. Under certain circumstances, recognition of a right to secede would probably make little difference. But the rejoinder seems too optimistic. Sometimes secession may well further the economic interest of the sub-unit, or the threat may be credible because an economic loss would be counteracted by gains in terms of symbolism or sub-unit autonomy. Moreover, national politics affecting multiple sub-units are subject to unpredictable and often highly emotional factors. Technocratic rationality does not characterize deliberations in which the spectre of secession is involved. The mere possibility of secession may prevent calm negotiation.[47]

There can be no assurance that secession will not be threatened simply because things are generally going well and there is mutual interdependence. Inflamed sub-unit sentiments have been a characteristic feature of recent developments in constitution-making, in Eastern Europe and elsewhere.[48] And in Eastern Europe in particular, social, economic, and environmental problems – many demanding strong action from the central government – have been quite severe, further fuelling ethnic and regional conflicts. In these circumstances a right to secede would be especially dangerous.

The second response would generalize the first, claiming that the case against a constitutional right to secession is simply too speculative. All the harmful effects are possible, but there is no good reason to think that they will occur. Perhaps a right to secede is a necessary inducement to persuade sub-units to enter the nation at all. Perhaps sub-units will rarely invoke the right to secede, because social and political norms will deter them from doing so. Perhaps the costs of secession to all sub-units will be so high as to make the threat implausible. The greater the degree of interdependence and cohesion, of course, the higher the costs of secession. Perhaps strategic behaviour will be collectively punished, so that it will occur rarely if at all. Perhaps the right to secede will be invoked only in cases in which it is an important safeguard.

These suggestions are plausible. Under certain conditions, the right to secession would have few deleterious effects, and it may prevent serious harms. This is especially so in cases involving a weak or loose confederation without substantial interdependences – the very concept now gaining popularity in Yugoslavia, Czechoslovakia, and the Soviet Union. In such cases, the risks posed by strategic behaviour and inflamed ethnic and other passions will be less severe. For the European Community, for example, a right to secede may therefore be more sensible, and indeed it will provide a greater incentive to join in the first instance.

For those deciding on the contents of a constitution, the questions are which scenarios are most likely and which provide the worst case. The most that one can do here is to point to the often large emotional attachments to sub-units, the possibility of financial gains from strategic behaviour, the familiar frailties of human nature, the rational and irrational factors that can make sub-units press secession claims, and the potentially debilitating effects of such claims on sub-unit and national processes of self-government.

In view of these considerations, it seems highly likely that recognition of a constitutional right to secede would create serious difficulties. In Eastern Europe, where strong nationalist passions persist and threaten to infect daily politics if given an explicit constitutional home, a right to secede would be especially damaging to the prospects for democratic government. All this suggests a strong presumption against a constitutional right to secede.

REASONS FOR SECESSION

Even if a constitutional right to secede would create risks for democratic politics, the case against such a right has hardly been completed. It may well be that the countervailing considerations, justifying a right to secede, outweigh any such adverse effects.

To explore this question, it will be useful to examine why a sub-unit of a country might want to secede. The reasons fall into five basic categories. All of them have played a prominent role in discussions of this subject in Eastern Europe. Thus, for example, infringement of civil liberties has played a role in Yugoslavia, where the fear of Serbian oppression partly motivates Slovenian and Croatian secessionism, and in the Ukraine, where Soviet suppression of the Ukrainian Church has played a similar role. Economic self-interest has been a motivating factor in the wealthier republics of Yugoslavia and also in the former Soviet Union.[49] Economic exploitation has been relevant in the Ukraine.[50] The injustice of the original acquisition was of special importance for Lithuania, Estonia, and Latvia. Claims of cultural and ethnic integrity played a role in the former Soviet

Union, Yugoslavia, and the Czech and Slovak Federative Republic.[51]

Many of these arguments provide plausible grounds for secession as a matter of political morality.[52] I evaluate them briefly here, with special attention to their relationship to a claimed constitutional right to secede.

Abridgement of civil rights or civil liberties

A sub-unit may want to secede because its people are being oppressed, according to (let us assume) traditional liberal understandings of oppression.[53] In the Soviet Union, for example, the history of widespread curtailment of free speech, of political liberty as a whole, and of basic guarantees of individual independence and security might well have supported a claim to secede, certainly before the increasing freedom encouraged by the Gorbachev regime in the late 1980s.

Governmental oppression of this sort may be limited to a sub-unit, or it may be part of a general pattern of governmental abuse. For example, the government may have limited the right to freedom of speech in only one part of the nation. Alternatively, the oppression may be quite general, and the sub-unit may want to secede because it sees itself as subject, like other sub-units, to an intolerable regime.

In this latter case, something other than the fact of oppression must also be at work in order to justify secession as distinct from, say, civil disobedience or revolution. If the oppression is general, some independent factor – like cultural homogeneity or a claim to territorial integrity based on history – is necessary to unite one of the many sub-units that are, by hypothesis, being oppressed. For this reason, I focus here on the case of a sub-unit that is singled out for injustice, in the form of curtailment of civil liberties or civil rights.

When oppression is pervasive, and not otherwise remediable, secession is a justified response; it is fully plausible to say that a sub-unit is entitled to leave a nation that is oppressing it. Standing alone, however, injustice or oppression does not provide a powerful case for creating a constitutional right to secede. If the central government suspends civil rights and civil liberties, the preferable response is to restore rights and liberties through the pressure of domestic or international law. A selective curtailment of the right of free speech is far more naturally countered by a restoration of that right than by permitting exit from the nation. Abridgement of civil rights or civil liberties appears to provide no good argument for a constitutional right to secede, but instead furnishes reasons for a constitutional order that makes abridgement unlikely.

If restoration is for some reason impossible, of course, secession might be necessary. In Eastern European nations without a recent history of protection of civil rights and civil liberties, such novel institutions as checks and balances and judicial review may take a long time to develop, and provide weak safeguards, especially at first.[54] In such cases a constitutional right to secede could be understood as an indirect, second-best means of reducing the risk of oppression. The oppression is not by itself a sufficient ground for secession, but the secession right is necessary to forestall it, buttressing the other constitutional safeguards. A possible preliminary conclusion, then, is that the risk that a central government will curtail the liberties of members of a sub-unit, or a history of such curtailment, combined with the infeasibility of eliminating the oppression, can justify both secession as a matter of political morality and the creation of a right to secede.

The implications for constitutional practice are twofold. The first and most obvious is that constitutional systems should contain powerful safeguards against the curtailment of civil rights and civil liberties. The most important such safeguards are checks and balances, federalism, a specification of protected rights, and judicial review. If the constitution establishes these safeguards and the central government observes them, this ground for secession will disappear altogether. This is admittedly a large task in Eastern Europe, but it is far more likely than a secession right to produce sound long-term results.

The second and more complex implication is that a constitutional right to secede may be necessary to deter the curtailment of civil rights and civil liberties. This argument has foundations in the work of Thomas Jefferson, who favoured both small political units and occasional therapeutic rebellions – views that led him to endorse a right to secede. Thus Jefferson wrote in 1816, 'If any State in the Union will declare that it prefers separation . . . to a continuance in union . . . I have no hesitation in saying, "Let us separate."'[55]

We can find a parallel to this argument in the continuing debates over federalism and rights of interstate mobility. Any society that constitutes its government through a federal system – one that embodies a decision to allow movement among states and to limit the scope of national law – necessarily creates a built-in safeguard against political or economic oppression. A government that oppresses its citizenry will eventually find itself without citizens at all. In Eastern Europe, for example, the existence of national controls that could not be escaped through rights of exit served as an extremely powerful check against change. The denial of the right to travel was therefore the denial of a crucial political right, one that belongs on the same plane as voting.[56] The recent history of Germany powerfully illustrates this proposition.

In a healthy federal system, states will often compete to attract citizens by offering better services. The result should be a beneficial 'race' to provide a mix of laws and regulations that maximize liberty and security. Indeed, the fact of interstate mobility in the United States is probably a far more powerful check against many forms of state tyranny than the existence of judicial review. Of course, there is a dark side to this process. The 'race' can be harmful as well as beneficial. Consider cases in which states compete for revenue-providing industry by eliminating environmental or occupational regulation that would in fact be optimal; here the competition is destructive, and the national government accordingly must be authorized to impose uniform regulation on its sub-units. But there can be no doubt that the right of exit operates as a powerful check on tyranny of various sorts. It may follow that a right to secede could be justified as a similar and quite valuable mechanism for insuring against oppression by the national government. The fact that the method is indirect does not mean that it is not extremely effective.

In some contexts, a right to secede might well be justified on this ground. Especially when it seems clear that other institutions cannot protect civil rights and civil liberties, a secession right might be justifiable. But in general, it is doubtful whether the argument overcomes the considerations against a constitutional right traced on pp. 19–26. I have noted that there are far more direct and less dangerous means of protecting against the curtailment of civil rights and civil liberties. A good constitution will contain those means. Rights of interstate mobility and a federal structure will operate as additional safeguards.

At least most of the time, a constitutional right to secede will create severe risks without at the same time conferring benefits that cannot be largely or entirely achieved through other strategies. In Eastern Europe in particular, secession movements have arisen at a time when the curtailment of civil rights and liberties has been drastically decreased, a point that suggests that the secession right is usually not founded on this form of oppression at all. Secession was not a feasible option in Eastern Europe as long as central governments consistently denied civil rights and liberties. For this reason, an attempted justification of a secession right based on those grounds seems unpersuasive.

Economic self-interest

A sub-unit may want to secede because economic self-interest suggests it ought to proceed on its own. The sub-unit may be subsidizing other people of the nation in various ways; for example, it may have valuable natural resources that are being used by outsiders at costs lower than the sub-unit would like to charge, or its members may be especially productive. Members of the sub-unit may come to believe that they will be financially better off if they create their own country.

In Eastern Europe, this sort of argument appears to have played at least some role in recent discussions. In Yugoslavia, the comparatively rich and developed northern republics of Slovenia and Croatia have sought to secede. Many Slovaks appear to fear that the Czechs will take a disproportionate share of the benefits of Western investment, and that the government of President Havel will not protect Slovakian economic interests.

Whether or not economic self-interest justifies secession as a matter of political morality is a complex question. The answer will turn, at least in part, on whether there is a justification for the economic harms faced by the sub-unit. This judgment will depend in turn on theories about what the state may do. For example, some appealing to the rule of the state attempt to justify redistribution from rich sub-units to poor ones. If such redistribution is indeed justified, then the fact that the economic self-interest of the rich sub-unit has been jeopardized is not a good basis for secession.

Regardless of one's view of the propriety of redistribution, however, the fact that secession might further a sub-unit's economic self-interest provides insufficient reason to create a right to secede. At any given time a sub-unit may be contributing more than what seems its fair share, and perhaps some sub-units will be doing so for very long periods. But unless there is some kind of injustice, the mere fact that secession is in a sub-unit's self-interest does not justify creation of that right. Self-interest is usually a controversial ground for political action at the individual level, unless translated into terms that invoke reasons other than self-interest alone; it is all the more difficult to support secession of sub-units on this ground.

This is especially so in light of the fact that to allow self-interest to be a justification would produce a range of risks, canvassed above, to the successful operation of the polity. Economic self-interest is an especially weak basis for creating a constitutional right to secede in light of the multiple deleterious effects that such a right would have for the process of national self-government, which may well be in the long-term interest of all sub-units of the country. A pre-commitment strategy is therefore appropriate.

Economic exploitation

A more serious argument for a right to secession would stress economic exploitation. By this term I mean not that a sub-unit is simply losing, but that it can claim, with reason, that the central government is treating it unfairly. We might hypothesize that the nation is systematically depleting the sub-unit's resources for the general good, thus reducing the sub-unit's wealth far below what it would be if the sub-unit stood alone; or the nation might be unfairly discriminating against the sub-unit in the distribution of general benefits and burdens. A claim for secession might well be based on this sort of behaviour from the nation's centre. Indeed, a right to secede – as in the case of curtailment of civil liberties and civil rights – might be justified as a means of deterring economic exploitation of sub-units. In Yugoslavia, this idea has played an important role. Slovenia and Croatia are economically advantaged, and they fear that they will have to submit to a Serbian-controlled national government, which they will have to subsidize.

In some cases, economic exploitation might indeed justify secession as a matter of political morality. But does the prospect of exploitation argue for a constitutional right to secede? There are several possible answers here. The first is that it is hard to define the baseline against which to measure a claim of exploitation; the term itself is a placeholder for ideas that must be substantively defended. No sub-unit has an antecedent right to a stream of welfare identical to what it would have received if it had not been a member of the nation. Moreover, it is extraordinarily difficult to calculate benefits and burdens, especially over long periods of time. In many cases the question of exploitation will be hard to assess in light of the many links by which sub-units in a nation become economically interdependent.

Suppose that in some cases we might agree that a sub-unit is being exploited by the nation. In such cases, a good constitution will provide both structural and rights-based provisions designed to prevent discrimination against certain sub-units, and these provisions will make a right to secede unnecessary. The sub-unit should, for example, be granted full representation in the legislature; this is a built-in, if partial, corrective. (It is only partial because other parts of the nation may unite against the sub-unit – hardly an unfamiliar phenomenon.) The United States Constitution achieves this goal in part through the establishment of a bicameral legislature in which all states, regardless of size, have equal representation in one house. This requirement is, in fact, the only element of the Constitution specifically protected by the document itself against amendment without the consent of the affected state.[57] The constitution could also ban discriminatory taxation, or require unanimous consent to certain measures raising a risk of exploitation.

These strategies pose dangers as well. Perhaps discriminatory taxation is justified as a redistributive strategy or as a means of taking account of differences in initial endowments. Perhaps discriminatory taxation is a reasonable response to the nature of the object of the tax. Suppose, for example, that a nation decides, out of concern for the environment and the public health, to limit through taxation the growing of tobacco or the mining of high-sulphur coal. Those regions that produce the relevant commodities will bear the brunt of the tax, but this disparate impact does not necessarily make the tax bad or secession justifiable. Moreover, a unanimity or supermajority requirement may forestall desirable national action. In this sense such a requirement poses some of the risks of a secession right. But the basic point is that a right to secede is a second-best and highly indirect remedy, one that creates a range of problems independent of economic exploitation and whose purposes might be accomplished through other means.

History and territory: the injustice of the original acquisition

Secession may be sought by a sub-unit that claims that its membership in the nation originally resulted from unjustified aggression, and that sees itself as having territorial integrity as a matter of history and international law, properly construed. Often some understanding of this kind plays a role in secession claims. Suppose sub-unit A existed as an independent entity at an earlier period. The larger unit absorbed sub-unit A through war or aggression. The sub-unit now seeks to separate from the nation as a way of undoing an historical wrong.

In Eastern Europe, of course, ideas of this sort have surfaced prominently and provided an important impetus for secession movements, especially in the Baltic states. Formerly independent Lithuania was forcibly incorporated into the Soviet Union in 1940 as a result of the Nazi–Soviet Pact, and the incorporation was clearly unlawful. Latvia and Estonia claim, plausibly, that they too were forcibly and illegally incorporated as a result of the same agreement. For these states, the Soviets were an occupying power, and their inclusion in the union resulted from duress in the form of a threatened Soviet attack.

Arguments of this kind may well provide a sufficient moral reason for secession. Certainly, if little time has passed since the original aggression, a right to secede seems self-evident; it corrects the original injustice. But, for three reasons, it is doubtful whether the existence of historic abuses is a sufficient reason to create a constitutional right to secede.

The first is that a well-functioning system of international law is the best, most direct way to prevent and to respond to aggression.[58] A right to secede is too general, applying in cases when there has not been aggression at all. At most the phenomenon of aggression justifies a moral right to secede in some narrowly defined class of cases in which membership in the nation was originally involuntary. Something like that right already exists as a matter of international law.[59] A generalized constitutional right to secession is unnecessary to recognize a right to exit from a union created by force.

The second problem is a practical one. A nation that takes other countries by force, and incorporates them, is unlikely to respect any right to secede that it has formally recognized. The former Soviet Union was at least a partial example.[60] In the event of incorporation by force, a right to secede is especially prone to becoming an ineffectual 'parchment barrier'.[61]

The third problem is that the origins of many, perhaps most, nations often involve aggression and abuse at some point in the past, and it is not easy to decide which such abuses provide a sufficient basis for a right to secede. The category of cases in which secession could plausibly be justified on such grounds is simply enormous, and if secession were generally to be permitted, the result would be an intolerable disruption of established arrangements. This consideration suggests that while the injustice of the original acquisition will often provide a good basis for a secession right, a system that would allow secession in all such circumstances would be hard to defend.[62]

In cases of sub-units absorbed through aggression, then, the preferable remedy is a system of international law, including an internationally recognized right to restore original borders when sufficiently little time has passed and when exercise of that right would not unduly disrupt existing arrangements.[63] Sometimes a right to secede is in fact justified on this ground as a matter of political morality, and this factor argues in favour of some secession movements now occurring in Eastern Europe, especially in the Baltic states. But a domestic constitutional provision guaranteeing the right to secede is both too small and too large a way to deal with this problem.

Cultural integrity and self-determination

Often a claimed right to secede is built on an understanding that the sub-unit has a cultural integrity that entitles it to self-determination. The sub-unit perceives itself as both homogeneous and substantially different in terms of basic norms and commitments. The very fact that it is governed by a broader entity appears to be a form of tyranny or an unjustifiable absorption by foreigners. Rule by outsiders eviscerates the sub-unit's distinct identity.

Ideas of this sort have frequently fuelled secession movements in Eastern Europe and elsewhere. Slovakia, for example, is more agricultural and devoutly Roman Catholic than is the Czech Republic, and the cultural difference certainly plays a role in the secession movement. Often a claim to cultural integrity is accompanied by a perception that the sub-unit had territorial integrity in the past, and was the object of unjustifiable aggression. As a practical matter, the two arguments tend to go hand in hand.

Whether a claim to cultural integrity justifies secession as a matter of political morality is a complex matter. Certainly ethnic homogeneity can make rule by outsiders impossible or oppressive. Just as certainly, productive interactions among heterogeneous groups can make for an especially successful democracy. History offers examples of both phenomena. It is therefore impossible to say, in the abstract, whether secession can be justified on this ground. Much will depend on how culturally homogeneous groups are treated by the larger nation, the nature of the differences between the sub-unit and the nation, and the forms their homogeneity takes. For example, a cultural group that oppresses others in its region can hardly make a powerful moral claim for a right to self-governance if the larger nation prizes civil liberties.[64]

Here, as before, any legitimate claims that underlie a right to secession may be accommodated by narrower and less dangerous strategies – in particular, federalism and representation mechanisms. A system of federalism often guards against precisely the problem of rule by remote leaders having insufficient identification with or knowledge of sub-units. In the American experience, federalism was designed to ensure local self-determination while at the same time providing and thus benefiting from governance at the national level. Federal systems can allow a large degree of governance by sub-units claiming cultural and territorial integrity. Indeed, the national constitution may restrict the central government to certain enumerated powers, including provision of national defence or regulation of interstate commerce,[65] or it may expressly reserve certain powers of internal self-governance to the sub-units. It may well be that, through these routes, federal systems can accommodate many of the concerns that underlie claims to secession based on cultural integrity.

Systems of representation might also supply a corrective here. Seats in the national legislature might be set aside for sub-unit representatives, to ensure that the views of sub-units are expressed on an ongoing basis during the deliberative process. Such seats might provide a form of proportional or even super-proportional representation. Perhaps a minority veto should be ensured on certain issues.

In some circumstances, however, these solutions will be inadequate. Sometimes nationhood demands interference with local self-determination, as in regulation of intrastate commerce having interstate effects. Sometimes the claim for self-determination is largely an emotional one, coming from a group affronted by the very fact of national incorporation and national rule. Sometimes nationhood involves an inevitable surrender of components of sovereignty claimed by sub-units. If full self-determination is the goal, the only remedy will be secession, enabling the sub-unit to escape entirely from the legal authority of the nation.

It may be that this argument is sufficient, as a matter of political morality, to justify secession in some contexts. It is surely strengthened if the argument from cultural integrity is accompanied by a claim to territorial integrity in the past. But it is doubtful that, standing alone, the argument from cultural integrity justifies a constitutional right to secede. In such cases, we are often dealing, by hypothesis, with sub-units that voluntarily agreed to enter the nation at some earlier time.[66] In such cases, the claim of cultural integrity will frequently be inadequate, because sufficient commonalities with the nation will likely exist, justifying the original agreement. Whether or not this is so, recognition of a right to secede, based on grounds of cultural integrity, will probably pose dangers to national self-determination that are not counterbalanced by the advantages to the various sub-units themselves. Whether or not the interest in cultural integrity provides a good moral justification for secession, it does not support a decision to place a right to secede in a founding document.

Indeed, cultural integrity is a particularly weak reason to constitutionalize the right to secede in so far as it is precisely the cultural integrity of sub-units that most dramatically threatens processes of national self-determination. In the most extreme cases, revolution or a negotiated settlement may be justified. But constitutional recognition of a right to secede would be a cure worse than the disease.

The right to revolt differs in interesting ways from the right to secede. It would be plausible to constitutionalize the former right as, in a sense, the United States Constitution has done through the right of amendment,[67] which in theory could be used by Congress and the states to rewrite the founding document in fundamental ways. But since the point of a revolution is to reject the established order, it is unclear why constitutionalization of any such right would be a useful step at all. If the argument above is persuasive, however, it is even less plausible to constitutionalize the right to secede. The latter right is usually defined in the discrete terms of some sub-unit – geographical, ethnic, or religious, or some combination of these – and these features of the relevant right pose the distinctive risks of strategic bargaining or an inflamed polity. A right of revolution does not create these risks in an even vaguely similar fashion.

Nor does a negotiated settlement pose the difficulties involved in a right to secede. The whole point of such a right is that there is no need for the approval of others in order for the right to be exercised. A negotiated settlement can be brought about without a constitutionalized secession right.[68]

A QUALIFIED RIGHT TO SECEDE?

A possible response to the discussion thus far would be that the right to secede should indeed be constitutionalized, but hedged with qualifications and limitations that minimize the risk of strategic behaviour. At least four possibilities seem plausible. One strategy would allow secession if and only if a large majority of the sub-unit sought it. Another would allow secession only under certain enumerated circumstances, as, for example, in cases of suspension of civil liberties or economic exploitation. Yet another would create a requirement of prolonged deliberation before secession would be lawful. Such a system might involve, for example, multiple popular votes, with substantial waiting periods between votes.[69] A fourth approach would create a right to secede, either absolute or qualified, but make it non-justiciable. Each of these possibilities raises difficult and general questions about constitutionalism. I deal with them only briefly here.

All these routes have large advantages over an unqualified right to secede, but it is doubtful whether the advantages justify constitutionalization of even a qualified right to secede. A requirement of a supermajority would certainly limit the occasions for, and seriousness of, secession threats. But in cases in which the sub-unit can be energized – for reasons of economic self-interest or ethnic and territorial self-identification – the protection would be inadequate. It is true that a sub-unit may want to secede for good reasons, but, as discussed above, there are better and less disruptive means of ensuring that the good motivations that sometimes underlie secession movements can be addressed. These involve, above all, federalism, checks and balances, entrenchment of civil rights and civil liberties, and judicial review. If these protections are inadequate, it is highly doubtful that a qualified right to secede will do the job.

There is something to be said in favour of a secession provision that would be limited to specified causes. Such a provision might be treated as ancillary to the non-discrimination principles and basic protections of liberties. It would furnish a powerful and self-enforcing mechanism against violation of the relevant rights. But to accomplish these purposes, the right to secede is probably too blunt and dangerous an instrument. One might hope that the direct provisions discussed above would be sufficient. More fundamentally, the recognition on paper of a right to secede is unlikely to be a useful supplement if they are not. A state that violates its textual commitments to civil rights and liberties will probably not respect its textual commitment to secession.

A right to secede after an extended period of deliberation would probably be the best of the various alternatives. Through this route it would be possible to reduce some of the risks of an inflamed polity. Indeed, the very difficulty of obtaining secession would deter efforts to seek that remedy unless it seemed necessary, and would diminish the possibility that any threat of secession could disrupt democratic and deliberative processes. For this reason it could not be said, *a priori*, that such a system would necessarily be undesirable. But in Eastern European nations with a history of ethnic and religious tensions, even a secession right modified in this way would pose significant risks to self-governance. A prolonged deliberative period over the question of continued ties to the nation could create all of the threats emphasized above. Probably the best result is not to create the right at all.

A final possibility would be to create a right to secede but to make it non-justiciable – that is, to make the right one that courts will not recognize or enforce. India's Constitution follows this strategy mainly with respect to certain 'positive' rights, including the right to subsistence.[70] Such rights are recognized in the sense that the constitution makes them binding on the legislature, but the courts are unable to protect them. The argument for entrenched but non-enforceable rights is that their entrenchment establishes norms that government is morally and politically obliged to respect, but whose judicial enforcement would create, in especially severe forms, the various difficulties produced when judges lacking policy-making competence or a good electoral pedigree are responsible for the vindication of constitutional rights.[71] The right to subsistence is a plausible candidate for this strategy because of the vagueness of the right and, more fundamentally, the obvious problems in its judicial definition and implementation. Perhaps the right to secede should be placed in this category.

The principal difficulty with this claim is that non-justiciable rights are usually those whose elaboration would strain judicial capacities. Here there is no such problem. To make the right to secession non-justiciable would reflect not a problem of definition or implementation, but instead ambivalence about the right itself. As distinguished from the right to subsistence, there is nothing vague about the right to secede. Moreover, as the recent experiences of constitutionalism in Eastern Europe and China reveal, judicially unenforceable constitutional rights are frequently not rights at all. By itself this consideration makes it important to ensure that constitutional rights are generally enforceable, lest the specification of unenforceable rights lead, in a system unaccustomed to such rights at all, to a process in which constitutional rights are generally not subject to real-world vindication.

If the case for a right to secede is persuasive, then the right should be both entrenched in the text and judicially enforce-

able. If the case is weak, then an unenforceable right is no
better than no right at all. In any case, the right to secede does
not have the characteristics that sometimes justify entrenched
but unenforceable rights.

CONCLUSION

Claims for recognition of a constitutional right to secede raise
large questions about the nature of constitutional protections
in the emerging Eastern European democracies. I have suggested that constitutional protections should often be understood as an effort to facilitate rather than merely to frustrate
democratic processes. Such efforts take many forms: the protection of rights central to self-government; the creation of
fixed and stable arrangements by which people may order their
affairs; the removal of especially charged or intractable questions from the public agenda; the creation of incentives to
compromise, deliberation, and agreement; and the solution of
difficulties posed by collective action problems, myopia, impulsiveness, and prisoners' dilemmas. Ideas of this sort provide a
helpful if partial foundation for considering possible provisions
in new constitutions. In any case, they suggest that a right to
secede does not belong in a founding document.

  In some cases, a right to secede will be fully justified as a
matter of political morality. Nothing I have said argues against
the view that sub-units sometimes have good reasons for seceding. On the contrary, I have attempted to catalogue the reasons
for secession and in the process to show that those reasons are
often powerful. But the existence of occasionally powerful
moral claims supplies insufficient reason for constitutional
recognition of the right to secede. A nation that recognizes this
right, and is prepared to respect it, may well find that it has
thereby endangered ordinary democratic processes. A decision
to allow a right of exit from the nation will divert attention from
matters at hand, allow minority vetoes on important issues,
encourage strategic and myopic behaviour, and generally compromise the system of self-government. For this reason, a waiver
of the right to secede should be seen as a natural part of
constitutionalism, which frequently amounts to a pre-commitment strategy directed against problems of precisely this sort.
People deciding on constitutional provisions often choose, in

advance, to waive seemingly important rights when the waiver would serve the general interest.

To say this is not, I emphasize, to deny that there are good reasons why a sub-unit might want to secede. In Eastern Europe, it is plausible to say that such reasons exist in several places. I have suggested that, even when this is so, there are generally more direct means of accomplishing the desired goals, such as local self-determination through federalism, firm protection of civil rights and civil liberties, and institutional and substantive guarantees against economic exploitation. It may be that the more direct means are in some circumstances inadequate. In such cases, however, the proper remedy is to reach a negotiated solution, to exercise the unwritten right to revolt, or to apply the pressure of domestic and international law, rather than to create a constitutional right to secede.

NOTES

I am grateful to Akhil Amar, Marcella David, Jon Elster, Larry Kramer, Bernard Manin, and Michael McConnell for helpful comments, and to Sean Donahue and Simon Steel for research assistance. This chapter was originally prepared for a conference sponsored by the Liberty Fund, Inc., at the University of Arizona in December 1990, and I am most grateful to the participants in that conference for valuable assistance. An earlier version of this chapter appeared in the *University of Chicago Law Review*, 58, 2, Spring 1991.

1 Constitution (Fundamental Law) of the Union of Soviet Socialist Republics, Art. 72: 'Each Union Republic shall retain the right freely to secede from the USSR.' The translation is reprinted in John N. Hazard, The Union of Soviet Socialist Republics 31, in Albert P. Blaustein and Gisbert H. Flanz, eds, 18 *Constitutions of the Countries of the World* (Oceana, 1990).
2 Dwight L. Dumond, *The Secession Movement, 1860–1861* 120–1 (Macmillan, 1931).
3 As a formal matter of constitutional interpretation, the issue has been settled since Texas *v.* White, 74 US 700, 724–6 (1869) (holding secession of Texas from the Union unconstitutional because the states' acceptance of the federal Constitution represented a waiver of the right to secede). See also Akhil Reed Amar, Some New World Lessons for the Old World, 58 *U. Chi. L.R.* 483, 501–2 and n. 68, (1991) (discussing secession).
4 Lincoln set out the basic Madisonian view: 'Perpetuity is implied, if not expressed, in the fundamental law of all national governments . . . . [N]o government proper ever had a provision in its organic law

for its own termination.' First Inaugural Address (4 March 1861), reprinted in T. Harry Williams, ed., *Selected Writings and Speeches of Abraham Lincoln* 117 (Hendricks, 1943) ('Lincoln Writings').

5 There are active secession movements elsewhere – in Canada and India, for example – and while I do not explore them here, this chapter bears on the issue of secession generally.

6 See Draft Constitution of the Slovak Republic, Arts 2, 7 (on file with *U. Chi. L.R.*).

7 It would follow that courts should not find such a right to be implicit in constitutions.

8 Lincoln made many of these arguments:

> Plainly, the central idea of secession is the essence of anarchy. A majority held in restraint by constitutional checks and limitations, and always changing easily with deliberate changes of popular opinions and sentiments, is the only true sovereign of a free people. Whoever rejects it does, of necessity, fly to anarchy or to despotism. Unanimity is impossible; the rule of a minority, as a permanent arrangement, is wholly inadmissable; so that, rejecting the majority principle, anarchy or despotism in some form is all that is left.

First Inaugural Address (4 March 1861), in Williams, ed., *Lincoln Writings* 117, 120 (cited in note 4).

9 My argument builds largely on the theory and practice of constitutionalism in the United States and, to a lesser extent, on more general Western political and constitutional theory. I do not mean to suggest that American and Western traditions and approaches provide the only basis for evaluating the constitutional implications of a right to secede. In view of the underlying issues, however, it would be surprising if other traditions and approaches did not reach similar conclusions.

10 Thomas Jefferson, Letter to Samuel Kercheval (12 July 1816), reprinted in Merrill D. Peterson, ed., *The Portable Thomas Jefferson* 558–61 (Viking, 1975).

11 For an extreme example, see Roberto Mangabeira Unger, *Politics: A Work in Constructive Social Theory* 454–7 (Cambridge, 1987).

12 James Madison, Letter to Thomas Jefferson (14 February 1790), reprinted in Marvin Meyers, ed., *The Mind of the Founder: Sources of the Political Thought of James Madison* 230–1 (Bobbs-Merrill, 1973).

13 By using the word 'entrenching' here and elsewhere, I refer to simple constitutionalization, not to a decision to immunize a constitutional provision from amendment. I assume throughout that constitutional provisions are much more difficult to change than ordinary statutes, but nonetheless amendable if there is a consensus that they should be.

14 For a valuable collection of essays on this topic, see Jon Elster and Rune Slagstad, eds, *Constitutionalism and Democracy* (Cambridge, 1988).

15 The right to property is an ambiguous case; it is a democratic right

as well as a private one. Private property provides security and independence from government, and these are preconditions for citizenship – a theme that played a large role in republican thought. See J.G.A. Pocock, ed., *The Political Works of James Harrington* 53–63, 67–8, 144–52 (Cambridge, 1977).

16 For an extended elaboration of this theme, see John Hart Ely, *Democracy and Distrust* (Harvard, 1980).

17 See Federalist 51 (Madison), in Clinton Rossiter, ed., *The Federalist Papers* 320–5 (New American Library, 1961).

18 See ibid at 323 (federalism and the separation of powers create a 'double security' for individual rights because '[t]he different governments will control each other, at the same time that each will be controlled by itself').

19 I borrow here from Stephen Holmes, Precommitment and the paradox of democracy, in Elster and Slagstad, eds, *Constitutionalism and Democracy* 195 (cited in note 14), and Stephen Holmes, Gag rules or the politics of omission, in ibid. at 19.

20 See Arthur S. Miller, An Inquiry into the Relevance of the Intentions of the Founding Fathers, with Special Emphasis upon the Doctrine of Separation of Powers, 27 *Ark. L. Rev.* 583, 588–9 (1973) (efficiency was a principal rationale for the separation of powers, in the view of influential framers such as John Adams, Thomas Jefferson, John Jay, and James Wilson).

21 See Federalist 70 (Hamilton), in Rossiter, ed., *The Federalist Papers* 423-31 (cited in note 17) (describing the need for a vigorous, unitary executive).

22 See Holmes, Gag rules, in Elster and Slagstad, eds, *Constitutionalism and Democracy* (cited in note 14).

23 See Meyers, ed., *The Mind of the Founder* 502–9 (cited in note 12). In fact, the failure of the framers to eliminate slavery in the original Constitution was attributable to ideas of this sort. The example reveals that the decision to take an issue off the political agenda is also a decision to resolve that issue one way rather than another. Such a decision may well be objectionable on democratic or other grounds.

24 See generally Jon Elster, *The Cement of Society* (Cambridge, 1989); Edna Ullmann-Margalit, *The Emergence of Norms* (Oxford, 1977).

25 Compare Jean Hampton, *Hobbes and the Social Contract Tradition* (Cambridge, 1986).

26 US Const., Art. IV, s. 1, cl. 1.

27 US Const., Art. I, s. 8, cl. 3.

28 See, for example, Gibbons *v.* Ogden, 22 US 1 (1824).

29 Though protectionism can be self-destructive as well, the mere perception of self-interest is sufficient for purposes of this argument.

30 For a standard treatment, see John Fiske, *The Critical Period of American History, 1783–89* 144–5 (Houghton Mifflin, 1916) ('[T]he different states, with their different tariff and tonnage acts, began to make commercial war upon one another'). For a revisionist view,

see Edmund W. Kitch, Regulation and the American Common Market, in A. Dan Tarlock, ed., *Regulation, Federalism, and Interstate Commerce* 9–19 (Oelgeschlager, Gunn and Hain, 1981) (states under Articles of Confederation actually co-operated to promote freedom of trade).

31 There is a close parallel here in the recent experience of the European Community with regard to the 1992 economic union. See, for example, Wayne Sandholtz and John Zysman, 1992: Recasting the European Bargain, 42 *World Pol.* 95 (1989).

32 See, for example, Hunt *v.* Washington State Apple Advertising Commission, 432 US 333 (1977) (North Carolina statute requiring only federal grades on all closed containers of apples shipped into state violated Commerce Clause because it burdened interstate sales of Washington apples and discriminated against such sales).

33 In the United States, judicial review is itself a product of reasoning based on constitutional structure rather than text. See Marbury *v.* Madison, 5 US 137 (1803). It would be far simpler, however, to make that power explicit.

34 This theme runs throughout The Federalist. See, for example, Federalist 10 (Madison), in Rossiter, ed., *The Federalist Papers* 77–84 (cited in note 17) (representative government, spread over a large and diverse electorate, can prevent factional passions from dominating public affairs); Federalist 78 (Hamilton), in ibid. at 464–9 (independent, life-tenured judiciary with authority to proclaim unconstitutional acts void is an important check on majority power).

35 See Federalist 78 (Hamilton), in ibid. at 464, 467 (judicial review of the constitutionality of laws maintains primacy of 'intention of the people' over 'intention of their agents').

36 See Federalist 51 (Madison), in ibid at 320, 324–5 ('multiplicity of interests, and . . . multiplicity of sects' can promote democratic government through a system of checks and balances).

37 The Soviet Constitution guarantees a panoply of individual rights that makes the US Bill of Rights pale by comparison, though neither the courts nor other branches of government have traditionally respected or enforced most of these rights. Article 39, for example, guarantees full 'social, economic, political and personal rights'; Art. 40 guarantees the right to work; Art. 41 recognizes a right to rest and leisure; Art. 49 guarantees a right to petition for redress of grievances; and Art. 50 guarantees freedom of speech, press, and assembly. See generally Chapter 7 of the Soviet Constitution, reprinted in Hazard, The Union of Soviet Socialist Republics 2–30, in Blaustein and Flanz, eds, *Constitutions of the World* (cited in note 1).

38 This was Lincoln's view:

If the minority will not acquiesce, the majority must, or the government must cease.

. . . If a minority in such case will secede rather than acquiesce, they make a precedent which in turn will divide and ruin them; for a minority of their own secede from them whenever a majority refuses to be controlled by such minority.

First Inaugural Address (4 March 1861), in Williams, ed., *Lincoln Writings* 114, 120 (cited in note 4).

39 See, for example, Clines, Ukrainians Declare Republic Sovereign, *NY Times* 17 July 1990 ('[T]he declarations of sovereignty thus far are laying out a kind of negotiating agenda for Mr. Gorbachev's promised attempt to redefine the union more favorably for the republics . . . .').

40 See, for example, Jon Elster, *Sour Grapes* (Cambridge, 1983) (discussing adaptive preferences). Family law also supplies a ready counter-argument: restrictions on divorce may increase the power of the stronger party by denying exit to the weaker. It may also, by adapting desires, produce one of the most pernicious forms of inequality, in which the disadvantaged accept their fate because there is no alternative. There are undoubtedly parallels here as well in the secession setting.

41 It may be responded that the presence of a secession right may actually tend to enable rather than disable politics; a sub-unit might be more inclined to accept impositions by the central government as long as it is assured that when the impositions become cumulatively intolerable it can leave. In a well-functioning democracy, however, there is no problem with sub-unit 'acceptance' of national decrees. Because the decrees are unlikely to be punitive, and because the sub-unit will participate in forming them, acceptance by sub-units is generally forthcoming. A secession right is therefore unnecessary to promote acceptable legislation.

42 See Bohlen, East Europe's Past, *NY Times* (16 December 1990), Gorbachev Explains Proposed Union Pact to Party, *NY Times* A11 (11 December 1990).

43 These considerations point out the asymmetry between two seemingly parallel rights, that of emigration and that of secession. The right to emigrate is an important check on tyranny – as, plausibly, is the right to secede. But the right to emigrate does not create the twin and related risks of strategic behaviour and inflamed ethnic or cultural conflict. The right to secede, unlike the right to emigrate, is exercised by sub-units rather than individuals, aggregates a number of citizens at once, and thus solves a collective action problem faced by individual people who seek to emigrate. This solution to the collective action problem poses the difficulties of strategic behaviour and inflamed conflict.

44 For a discussion of the economic difficulties facing these countries, see Steven Greenhouse, East Europe Finds Pain on Journey to Capitalism, *NY Times* A1 (10 November 1990).

45 See, for example, Wise, Czechs, Slovaks Reach Agreement on Federal, Regional Power-sharing Plan. *Washington Post* (14 November 1990), Gorbachev Explains Proposed Union Pact (cited in note 42).

46 US Const., Art. I, s. 10, cl. 1 (barring the states from passing 'any . . .

Law impairing the Obligation of Contracts'). See also Federalist 44 (Madison), in Rossiter, ed., *The Federalist Papers* 280, 282–3 (cited in note 17).

47 For an example from the American experience, see David M. Potter, *The Impending Crisis, 1848–1861* 209–11 (Harper and Row, 1976) (describing the breakdown of reasoned deliberation that occurred when Senator Charles Sumner, the prominent Massachusetts abolitionist, was beaten with a cane by South Carolina Representative Preston Brooks after Sumner had ridiculed the 'loose expectoration' in the speech of Brooks's relative, Senator Andrew Butler, a supporter of slavery).

48 See Bohlen, East Europe's Past (cited in note 42); Clines, Dizzying Disunion, *NY Times* (26 October 1990), Jonathan Kaufman, Tunnel at the End of the Light for Eastern Europe, *Boston Globe* 1 (21 October, 1990); Chuck Sudetic, Ethnic Rivalries Push Yugoslavia to Edge, *NY Times* A14 (14 October 1990) ('Ethnic Rivalries'); Simon Jenkins, Nationalism's Dark Cloud over the Democratic Battlefield of Europe, *Sunday Times* (London) C3 (7 January 1990).

49 See Clines, Byelorussia Joins Sovereignty Move, *NY Times* A4 (28 July 1990).

50 See Clines, Ukrainians Declare Republic Sovereign, *NY Times* A1 (17 July 1990)

51 See Ukrainians Rally Against Moscow, *NY Times* A10 (1 October 1990); Sudetic, Ethnic Rivalries (cited in note 48), Pellar, Czechs Fear for Federation *Reuters Library Report* (7 December 1990).

52 For an especially helpful discussion, overlapping with the argument here, see Allen Buchanan, Toward a Theory of Secession, 101 *Ethics* 322 (1991). The credibility of the moral case makes it especially troublesome to suggest that military force should be used to stop secession – a difficult problem that I cannot discuss in detail here. Sometimes military force will be justified because the ground for secession is itself weak or involves oppression, as in the case of the American Civil War. Sometimes such force will deter other secession movements, and this will justify force when the secession movements are not, all things considered, legitimate ones. But the consequences of the use of military force are generally unpredictable and often worse than first anticipated. In this light the question whether a nation should be kept together through official violence cannot be sensibly answered in the abstract. At any rate, one need not and should not extrapolate from the American experience the proposition that civil war is always preferable to secession.

53 By traditional liberal understandings, I mean to include rights to freedom of speech, freedom of religion, freedom from unreasonable searches and seizures, private property, and the rule of law. See Stephen Holmes, *Benjamin Constant and the Making of Modern Liberalism* 131–8 (Yale, 1984). I do not discuss here the more particular view that secession is necessary to prevent (what some consider to be) abuses of government in the form of redistri-

bution of resources, social and economic regulation, and taxation methods that are characteristic of Western industrialized democracies. This view, associated with the ideas about the state set out in different forms in Robert Nozick, *Anarchy, State, and Utopia* (Basic, 1974), and Richard A. Epstein, *Takings* (Harvard, 1985), might on certain assumptions argue powerfully in favour of a secession right as a means of disabling government. If one wants to disable government in this broad way, a secession right might be more easily justified – though even here alternative mechanisms might be preferable, and the cure might be worse than the disease.

Note also that a right to secede might be sought, not to disable modern government, but to establish a territorial right vindicated by history, or to ensure self-government by ethnic or other groups. See also pp. 30–1 (arguing that economic self-interest of a sub-unit is not a sufficient reason for a right to secede).

54 In America, judicial review – itself an extratextual practice – did not take root until fourteen years after the enactment of the written Constitution. Marbury *v.* Madison, 5 US 137 (1803).

55 Thomas Jefferson, Letter to W. Crawford (20 June 1816), quoted in Lee C. Buchheit, *Secession: The Legitimacy of Self-determination* 109 (Yale, 1978).

56 See, for example, Shapiro *v.* Thompson, 394 US 618 (1969) (holding unconstitutional a state statutory provision denying welfare to residents who have not resided in the jurisdiction for at least one year on grounds that personal liberty includes freedom to travel throughout country without unreasonable burdens or restrictions); Kramer *v.* Union Free School District, 395 US 621 (1969) (invalidating state statute limiting right to vote in school district elections to those who own or lease taxable real property in the district or who are parents of children enrolled in the schools).

57 US Const., Art. V.

58 The Iraqi annexation of Kuwait is a recent example, though here it was necessary to resort to force to bring about compliance with principles of international law.

59 This is the ambiguous and controversial right of self-determination. See Buchheit, *Secession* at 8–20 (cited in note 55). The principle of self-determination, recognized in the United Nations Charter and in numerous UN Declarations, came to have great importance in the era of decolonization, though the contours of the right – particularly with respect to armed intervention by third parties intent on furthering the right – remain unclear. See also United Nations Declaration on Principles of International Law Concerning Friendly Relations and Co-operation Among States in Accordance with the Charter of the United Nations, which proclaims 'The principle of equal rights and self-determination of peoples' ('[A]ll peoples have the right freely to determine, without external interference, their political status . . . and every State has the duty to respect this right in accordance with the provisions of the Charter'). UN Res. 2625 (24 October, 1970) in Dusan J. Djonovich, ed., 13

United Nations Resolutions, Series I (General Assembly Resolutions) 337, 339 (Oceana, 1976).

60 See, for example, Keller, Lithuania Agrees to Delay, *NY Times* A1 (30 June 1990); Celestine Bohlen, Gorbachev Bars Independence Bids of two Baltic Lands, *NY Times* A1 (15 May 1990); Bill Keller, Moscow Lays out Terms for Baltics, *NY Times* A18 (13 June 1990).

61 This term originated with Madison. See Federalist 48 (Madison), in Rossiter, ed., *The Federalist Papers* 308, 338 (cited in note 17).

62 For purposes of law and morality, it is both necessary and difficult to make temporal and other distinctions. Sub-units initially absorbed by aggression or other unjust means often become well integrated into a union over time and come to enjoy many benefits from membership in the union. (Hawaii is an example.) At least when a good deal of time has passed, it is hardly clear that injustices of several generations past by themselves justify secession.

63 The phrasing here is deliberately vague. A detailed discussion of when sub-units once annexed through aggression have a good moral justification for secession would take me far beyond the current discussion. For a valuable discussion of the crucial territorial dimension to secession claims, see Lea Brilmayer, Secession and Self-determination: A Territorial Interpretation, 16 *Yale J. Intl L.* 177 (1991).

64 The attempt at secession by the American South is an example. In such a case, secession would be unjustified even as a matter of political morality. A desire to oppress all or part of the citizenry is not a good basis for secession. The American Civil War was of course fought partly over these grounds.

65 This is, of course, the strategy followed by the United States Constitution. See US Const., Art. I.

66 If the argument emphasizes the injustice of the original entry, as in the case of the Baltic states, then it is not simply based on cultural integrity and should be analysed as on pp. 33–4.

67 US Const., Art. V.

68 Such a settlement might of course be blocked with a constitutional prohibition against secession, even of the voluntary kind. But it is unclear how such a prohibition could be beneficial.

69 The State of New York has created such a process for dealing with the secessionist demands of Staten Island, a sub-unit of the City of New York that may prefer to become an independent municipality. Staten Island residents must first approve secession in two referenda, with a period for hearings between the two votes; the state legislature would then have to pass legislation approving the secession. See City of New York *v.* State of New York, 557 NYS2d 914, 158 AD2d 169 (1990) (rejecting equal protection challenge to this scheme).

70 Part IV of the Indian Constitution includes 'Directive Principles of State Policy', which are non-justiciable. See Art. 37: 'The provisions contained in this Part shall not be enforceable by any court, but the principles therein laid down are nevertheless fundamental in the

governance of the country and it shall be the duty of the State to apply these principles in making laws.' These provisions include minimalization of inequalities in income and elimination of inequalities in status, facilities, and opportunities (Art. 38, cl. 2); 'equal pay for equal work for both men and women' (Art. 39(d)); free and compulsory elementary education (Art. 45); the securing of a 'living wage' for all workers (Art. 43). The right to subsistence is most directly stated in Art. 39, which provides: 'The State shall, in particular, direct its policy towards securing: (a) that the citizens, men and women equally, have the right to an adequate means of livelihood . . . .' Constitution of India (1949), reprinted in Albert P. Blaustein *et al.* India 62–4, in Blaustein and Flanz, eds, 7 *Constitutions of the Countries of the World* (cited in note 1).

71 See Lawrence Gene Sager, Fair Measure: The Legal Status of Underenforced Constitutional Norms, 91 *Harv. L. Rev.* 1212 (1978).

Chapter 3

Federalism and confederalism

Murray Forsyth

Federalism is currently 'in the air' in Europe. To be sure, it has suffered some dramatic reverses. The very modest reference to the 'federal goal' of European unification that was included in the draft treaty debated by the European Council at Maastricht in December 1991 roused fierce opposition from the British government and was finally deleted from the text. The fate of the Maastricht Treaty itself is, at the moment of writing, still in doubt. Meanwhile, at the other end of Europe, the Federation of the Soviet Union has finally collapsed after a life of sixty-nine years; it was formally wound up in the same month as the Maastricht meeting. In south-east Europe the Yugoslav Federation disintegrated amidst bloodshed in the course of 1991 and 1992 with the secession and international recognition of Croatia and Slovenia and civil war in Bosnia-Hercegovina. Only the federal rump of Serbia-Montenegro remains. In east Central Europe a third federal state, that of Czechoslovakia, is currently under severe strain, and may well fall apart in 1993.

These dramatic events might seem to indicate that federalism is on the retreat as a component element of European politics. This would be a superficial interpretation of the situation, however. It overlooks the fact that, from London to Moscow, the issue of federalism, or more precisely the question of the merits, demerits, and implications of federal and confederal systems of government, has moved gradually into the mainstream of political debate over the past five or so years, in a way that is unprecedented. From being a concept debated primarily by smallish groups of specialists, groups more or less ignored by the public eye, federalism has become a concept on which leading statesmen and women across the continent air their views, something to be confronted and examined, something about which it is necessary to have a view, even if it is a negative one. It has entered the common language of European political debate rather in the same way that the 'environment' did several years ago. In this sense federalism is now 'in the air' in Europe. Brugman's words, which seemed a little melodramatic in 1969, are today not wide of the mark: 'federalism is the spectre which is haunting Europe'.[1]

Moreover the actual extent of the current retreat from federalism – in terms of the dismantling of federal structures – needs to be measured with care. It has to be put into context. The retreat is by no means a general one, and the peculiar features of the failed communist federal systems deserve to be underlined. The aim of this chapter is to make an overall assessment of the existing position with regard to federal institutions in Europe, to look at the reasons for the recent expansion and contraction of federal structures, and to consider the prospects for the future.

FEDERALISM IN CENTRAL AND WESTERN EUROPE: THE PRESENT SITUATION

The ending of the Cold War has brought about a fundamental change in the political concept of 'Europe', a change that is best understood by looking back to the onset of this vast struggle. The demand for the unconditional surrender of Germany in the Second World War, the ensuing vacuum at the heart of Europe when the fighting ended, the filling of the vacuum by the two great flanking powers of the Soviet Union and the United States of America, the escalation of tension between these two powers, and the process of bloc-building that took place between 1947 and 1955, effectively eliminated the old political concept of 'Central Europe', and replaced it by that of 'Western' and 'Eastern' Europe, two separate entities, each under the aegis of its protective superpower, facing each other across a frontier that ran through Germany.

The two blocs or hegemonies were not precisely symmetrical in structure, and the differences between them go a long way towards explaining the different destiny of federalism in Eastern and Western Europe today. The Atlantic bloc was an almost classic hegemonic relationship, that is to say, a flexible, mutual relationship between a leading power and its less powerful followers, in which the leader actively encouraged its followers to unite under its aegis. The Soviet bloc was, from the start, far closer to an imperial relationship, with one major power dictating to its lesser neighbours. From Stalin's death onwards the Soviet Union would probably have preferred to change the system into a more voluntary and unforced relationship of allegiance, but it was never able to achieve this, periods of relaxation being followed by dictatorial intervention to reassert control. Plans by the smaller powers of Eastern Europe to form federal unions amongst themselves, which were actively canvassed in the immediate post-war period, were swept aside by the Soviet Union, and were never encouraged in later years. Thus when the empire in the east collapsed it did not leave behind a self-subsistent grouping of its former subordinates but a disunited aggregate of weak entities, a new vacuum, to be filled this time probably from the west.

At the same time the ending of the East–West confrontation, the evaporation of the Soviet bloc, the corresponding relaxation of the Atlantic bloc, and the erasure of the frontier between the two, leading to the reunification of Germany, has brought about the re-emergence, if in a modest and attenuated form, of 'Central Europe'. Here it is necessary to be clear about the terms being used. The phrase 'Central Europe' is an ambiguous one. Friedrich Naumann, in his celebrated book on *Mitteleuropa* published during the First World War, meant by it a union of the allied German and Austro-Hungarian empires. The term has also been taken to refer to the successor states of the Austro-Hungarian empire – in particular Austria, Czechoslovakia, and Hungary – which do not regard themselves culturally as forming part of 'Eastern' Europe – but as being a distinctive projection of 'Western' European civilization towards the east. 'Central Europe' in this sense can certainly be said to have re-emerged with the ending of the Cold War, and its revival has stirred a considerable debate about its 'special character'. The term is not, however, being used in either of these two senses here, but rather in the more straightforward one of the political powers that occupy the geographical centre of Europe – Germany above all, and Austria. Switzerland clearly also falls into this category, although its long adherence to neutrality tends to lead to it being seen as a special case.

The ending of the Cold War has permitted Central Europe in this third sense to re-emerge. The 'East' and the 'West' Europe so neatly separated by the long struggle are now gradually being transformed into categories relative to a single centre or core, rather than to two centres standing wholly or in large part outside Europe. The progressive winding up of the overseas empires of the powers on the western seaboard of Europe, that took place during the period of the Cold War, has served to make this new relativity of the different parts of Europe to one another even more pronounced than it might otherwise have been. The maritime powers of the eastern seaboard of Europe, whose destinies began to diverge from those of the central land mass from the sixteenth century onwards, are now 'back in the fold', though some of them – Great Britain in particular are finding the adjustment a difficult one. Put another way, Europe as a self-connected network of states is now with us once again.

In describing the present condition of federalism in Europe the first thing to be noted is that the re-emergent centre of the continent is a congeries of federal states. The most important of them, in terms of its size, present economic strength, and future potential, is clearly Germany. Austria, too, is a federal state and its neighbour, Switzerland, is the longest-lived federal union in the world. It should be remembered that the reunification of Germany in 1990 represented an extension of federalism. The German Democratic Republic had abolished its federal structure in 1952; its space was 'refederalized' with reunification. The integration of the five new economically weak Eastern *Länder* (and East Berlin) into the existing federal structure has threatened to disturb the balance of the latter, and this problem has been one of the main reasons why federalism has moved into the foreground of political debate in Germany.

The three federal systems of Central Europe have certain common characteristics that mark them off from the model of federalism represented by the United States of America. The differences relate in particular to the way powers are distributed between the federal government and the member states – the Central European model does not follow the principle of 'dual federalism' embraced in America – and to the ethos and organization of the judicial system. On the other hand, one must be careful not to draw the line of distinction between the 'Central European tradition' and the American one too absolutely, and must not suggest that the three Central European federations are identical. The Swiss system, for example, reflects the impact of the American example in certain important respects – notably the equality of representation of the cantons in the upper house of parliament – and the Austrian upper chamber is far weaker than its German counterpart. One must also remember that the German and Austrian federations are ethnically homogeneous while the Swiss is not. With these reservations it is possible to speak of a distinctively Central European type of federalism.

The area to the west and south-west of Central Europe is generally and traditionally regarded as the terrain of the large (by European standards) unitary states, where the imperatives of state-building and empire, and the presence of natural boundaries, have combined historically to contain and curtail the pressures for looser, federative structures based on ethnic or regional identity. The examples of France (so often used as the textbook example of the unitary state), the United Kingdom, and Spain spring to mind. What has to be stressed is that in this area, over the past twenty-five years, there has been a significant counter-movement away from unitarism. Belgium and Spain, even if they do not officially designate themselves as federal states, may now legitimately be referred to as such – though the process by which they have transformed themselves from unitarism to federalism is not yet at an end. Both, it should be noted, are post-imperial powers, and the loss of empire has meant the loss of an important 'safety valve' for internal differences – as it has in the United Kingdom. It is also probable that the very triumph overseas of the anti-imperial idea of national self-determination has lent strength in both countries to the idea of challenging ethnic 'imperialism' at home in the name of the same doctrine. The rolling back of external colonialism leads on by a natural progression to the idea of rolling back 'internal colonialism'.

The Belgian transformation has taken place through a succession of constitutional reforms, in 1970, 1980 and 1988–9 respectively. By these reforms, to quote a recent Belgian treatise on constitutional law, the country

> evolved from a unitary decentralized State, in which language had no particular significance in terms of the institu-

tional framework, into a federal State *sui generis*, which ensured the autonomy and (peaceful) coexistence of two different cultures, while safeguarding the rights of the linguistic and ideological minorities.[2]

The two different cultures are, of course, those of the Flemish-speaking and French-speaking population respectively. What makes the Belgian system peculiar and complex is that this small country is now simultaneously divided into three regions – Wallonia, Flanders and the capital city, Brussels – and into three communities – the French, the Flemish, and the Germanophone.

In Spain, since the death of General Franco in 1975, a similar process of transformation has taken place, although the modalities by which it has been achieved have been very different. The new Spanish Constitution of 1978 did not define the territorial or spatial structure of the Spanish state, but instead provided the framework and the procedures for the acquisition of autonomy by the country's nationalities and regions. As a result of the implementation of these mechanisms the Spanish state – the 'State of the Autonomies' as it is frequently called – is now made up of seventeen Autonomous Communities, each with its own Statute of Autonomy, its own legislative and executive powers, and its own material resources for the implementation of these powers. The process of 'autonomization' has created many problems, several of which remain to be solved, but there can be little doubt that it has taken Spain beyond the bounds of the unitary decentralized state and into the category of the federal state. To be sure, it is a federal state *sui generis*, like the Belgian state; but then, all federal states, like all unitary states, can be said to be *sui generis* – this does not, and should not, prevent us from making generalizations about them.

Pressures for regionalization or autonomization in the west and south of Europe are of course not confined to Spain and Belgium – they can be seen very clearly in Italy and the United Kingdom, for example. Only in the two former countries have they crystallized into recognizably federal structures, however, and so this account has been limited to them.

The European Community, by its very existence, has strengthened the tendencies towards regionalization in its member states, and is likely to strengthen them yet further in the future.

The impulsion acts in a variety of ways. The lessening of the importance of national boundaries provides a greater opportunity for regions to assert themselves as international actors. The Community's own regional policy acts as a stimulus to this. The presence of the Community enables nationalist movements within the member states (such as the Scottish, for example) to demand autonomy without laying themselves open to the accusation that their policies will result in the creation of tiny, closed, unviable units. There is also likely to be an increasing 'demonstration effect' as the Community develops. This is because the strongly organized regional units of the federal member states – for example, the German *Länder* – will press, and have pressed, for guarantees that their powers will not be eroded by the transference of competences to the European level. They have called for regional representation at the European level, and the 'Committee of the Regions' provided for in the Maastricht Treaty is one response to their demands. Although the proposed committee is only advisory, this kind of mechanism is likely to add to the status and ambitions of the other less well organized or powerful regions in the Community. The accession of other federal states (Austria, for example, which applied for membership in 1989) will strengthen this tendency.

The European Community itself must also be included in any survey of federal structures in Europe. There is a strong tendency amongst Europeans (outsiders such as Americans and Canadians seem to have fewer inhibitions) to avoid calling the Community a federal body, and to see it rather as something which may or may not evolve *into* a federal body. The original draft of the Maastricht Treaty itself suggested this. Commentators use a range of terms to try and indicate that the Community is something more than a 'normal' international organization while avoiding the word 'federal'. 'Supranational' is one, and 'regime' is another. Perhaps most popular of all is the phrase '*sui generis*'. As a way of avoiding or rejecting any attempt to classify the Community the phrase is patently inadequate. As we have already remarked, all unitary and all federal states are *sui generis*, but this does not prevent one from drawing a distinction between the two types and gaining insights from it. An apple may be different from a pear but they are both kinds of fruit.

The key feature which distinguishes the European Community from an international organisation and places it within the spectrum of federal bodies may be summed up as follows. The institutions of the Community have the right and power, accorded to them by a treaty concluded for an unlimited period, to make directly applicable law within a broad sphere of competence, law which takes precedence over the law of the member states. There are thus two levels of government, properly so called, in the Community, and this is the very heart of what makes a federal system. Hence, despite all the current rhetoric about the federal future of the Community, the real argument is about the deepening and extension of an existing federal structure, an argument that is not only about strengthening the powers at the centre, but also about the guarantee of the powers of the members. The British government has unfortunately confused matters by constantly equating federalism with 'centralization' and by claiming to combat federalism by insisting on the retention of powers at the national level – not grasping that federalism is as much to do with the preservation of powers at the regional level as it is with the establishment of powers at the union level.

The Community is best described as an economic confederation that is moving gradually into the field of defence and security, as well as attempting to round off its economic competences. It should not be mistaken, above all by the countries of Eastern Europe that are so interested in joining it, for an instrument of economic 'co-operation' or a body that leaves the sovereignty of its members intact. As a confederation it alters the constitutional status of its members.

This latter point is worth stressing because the concept of confederation is frequently defined, both in Europe and elsewhere, by reference to some simple, mechanical criterion – the possession of a right of secession by the members, the international recognition of the members as states, the absence of a direct legislative power, or of a direct taxing power, by the centre, and so on – which does not do justice to it. Often it is defined in such a way as to suggest that it is nothing more than a conventional international organisation that does not affect the sovereign statehood of its participants; the element of 'union' present in all federal bodies is overlooked. In which case, it may be argued, there is no reason for using the term 'confederation' at all, and it might as well be jettisoned to avoid confusion. If, however, as seems more accurate, 'confederation' is taken to denote a genuinely federal body, and not an international organisation, but nonetheless a federal body of the looser kind – 'looseness' here being measured not by one simple, mechanical criterion, but by reference to a whole range of factors – then the term remains a useful part of the federal vocabulary.

FEDERALISM IN EASTERN AND SOUTH-EAST EUROPE

If federalism in Western Europe has been expanding, the most important recent development, when we look eastwards, has been the collapse, or threatened collapse, of three of the federations that were established there under communist auspices: the Soviet Union, and the Yugoslav and Czecho-slovakian Federations. It is often asserted that this debacle demonstrates the incapacity of federal systems to hold together member units which are ethnically heterogeneous. Is this a fair deduction? More generally: What is the significance of the failure of these regimes for the student of European federalism?

We will focus on the Federation of the Soviet Union, as this was by far the most important of the three, and served as a model for the others. The Soviet Union was founded in 1922 on the pattern, and round the core, of the first formally constituted 'state' to be established by the Bolsheviks after the revolution of October 1917, namely the Russian Socialist Federated Soviet Republic (RSFSR). The latter, now renamed simply the Russian Federation, and led by Boris Yeltsin, is still with us, and has thus outlived its more inclusive descendant – though it is itself currently under threat from the selfsame forces that struck down the Union, and its leader will need all his skill to hold it together as a federation.

It has to be asked at the outset why the first great communist state was expressly federal in character. The answer would seem to be that the federal concept was adopted by the Bolsheviks first and foremost as an instrument for legitimizing their determination to keep the core of the various subject nation-alities of the Tsarist empire united behind the new regime and its revolutionary objectives. The Bolsheviks had no fondness for federalism as such; they had no fondness for national sentiments or national traditions as such. They were rationalist, universalist, and unitarist to the core. They believed in the emancipation of 'man' not merely from the constraints of 'class' but from the swaddling clothes of 'nationality' as well. But the Bolsheviks were sufficiently realistic to recognize that there was a 'nationality problem', even if it was only a 'transitional' one, and federalism, with its non-imperial emphasis on equality, was deemed by them to be the appropriate 'transitional mechanism' for meeting this transitional problem.

Communist federalism was thus geared, from the start, to the problem posed by 'nationalities'. Its sub-units were primarily designed, and often deliberately engineered, to correspond to ethnic and linguistic boundaries, and not to historical–political ones. (Though the compromises that were made in practice between these two principles have been at the root of many of the difficulties that have beset communist federal systems, not least that of Yugoslavia.) The stated aim was to treat such ethnic and linguistic groupings equally, and the powers or rights granted to the federal sub-units were largely cultural and linguistic ones.

This should not, however, lead us to mistake the extent or nature of the nationality-oriented federalism adopted by the communists. Hans Kohn, who was not wholly unsympathetic to what was being attempted in the Soviet Union, wrote the following perceptive passages on the subject of cultural autonomy there in 1933:

> The Communist state can grant entire lingual autonomy and liberty, but it cannot recognize cultural autonomy and liberty. The doctrinal content of Marxism must be given expression in every tongue, as it has to be carried to every people. The state thus sets out to develop and assist every tongue; all are equal in its view, as in its view all men, whatever their endowment, are equal. . . . [But its] purpose is to set the cultural life of all peoples on a new basis. Accordingly it destroys the bonds that unite the life of the people with the past . . . Only the popular elements of the existing national cultures, unassociated with traditional religion and close to the life of the masses, are to be retained and interwoven with the new uniform Socialist culture, the attainment of which is the purpose of all education in the Soviet Union.[3]

Kohn's words convey well the instrumental, centrally engineered and inauthentic quality of communist 'cultural' federalism. Despite the claim, made in the original Constitution of 1918, that the RFSFR was a 'free union of free peoples', it never rested on a federal pact between equal partners, and the people who were subsequently incorporated into the Federation were never consulted about their wishes. It was not until seventy-four years after its founding, in March 1992, that a Federation Treaty was finally put before the member republics for signature, and significantly two of them refused to sign. The fact is that from its foundation until the last few years the RFSFR has been a unitary state, with some regional decentralization, in which power has been concentrated in the Russian bureaucracy in Moscow.[4]

This unitary structure became in turn the core of the wider 'Union of Socialist Soviet Republics'. The latter originated in alliances between the new Bolshevik regime in the RFSFR and similar regimes that had seized power in the Ukraine, Belorussia and elsewhere, and force had frequently to be used to crush internal opposition to the movement towards unification. Unlike the RFSFR, the Union was founded upon a 'Declaration' and a 'Treaty', in December 1922, which led to a Constitution that was ratified two years later. It is significant, however, that neither the Declaration nor the Treaty was referred to in the subsequent Constitutions of the Union.[5]

Moscow, the capital of one facade federation, now became simultaneously the capital of another, closely modelled on the first. The motive for keeping to the federal formula was almost exactly the same in both cases. As Pearson writes, federalism represented

> a conciliatory line calculated to soothe those larger non-Russian nations (like the Armenians, Azerbaidzhanis, Belorussians, Georgians and Ukrainians) so recently reincorporated into the territorially *revanchist* Bolshevik state. Cheated of independence after a few short months and agitated at the prospect of a unitary Bolshevik authority prosecuting assimilationist russification, such nations might well be mollified and reconciled to Soviet authority with a federal face. Justifiable as an expedient half-way house on the road to socialism, federalism could operate as a compromise

device for reaping the benefits of empire without the opprobrium of tsarism.[6]

It has often been asserted the USSR was not so much a
socialist federation as a colonial empire, in which the largest
national group, the Russians, dominated and exploited the
other nationalities. This is too big an issue to explore here.
Clearly the sheer size of the Russian component, the fact that
the Russian capital was simultaneously the capital of the Union,
and the enforcement of Russian as the official language of the
Union, lend some credence to it. However, it must also be
recognized that Russian national traditions were also systematically trampled on by the communist leaders of the Union,
and that, at the end, the leader of the Russian Federation
showed no enthusiasm for the maintenance of the Union. The
words of the dissident Igor Shafarevich, written in 1974, are
worth recalling:

> the basic features of national life in the USSR are a direct
> result of the hegemony in our country of socialist ideology.
> This ideology is the enemy of every nation, just as it is hostile
> to individual human personality. It is able to exploit the
> aspirations of this or that people temporarily, for its own
> purposes, but its fundamental trend is towards the maximum
> destruction of all nations. The Russians no less than the
> others are its victims; indeed, they were the first to come
> under fire.[7]

The original USSR was made up of four republics, of which two
were themselves formally organized as federations – the RSFSR
and the Transcaucasian Federation (another forced union, that
was later dissolved) – and two were unitary states – the Ukraine
and Belorussia. Between 1924 and 1940 the number of member
republics gradually increased to sixteen; it stayed at this number
until 1956, when it fell to fifteen; then between 1989 and 1991
it fell back rapidly, as a result of secession, first to twelve, then to
eleven, to nine and finally to zero.[8]
Was this sudden dissolution a demonstration of the ineffectiveness of federalism when faced with multiple and deep
ethnic differences? It seems more accurate, for reasons that will
have already become evident, to see it as a resurgence of the
nationalities of the Soviet Union, big and small, Russian as well

as Baltic, against a unitary ideological regime that had systematically crushed the genuine expression of national traditions and loyalties, had conspicuously failed to bring about economic advance, and had also failed to harness the loyalties of the regions to the centre. Mikhail Gorbachev performed the first, vital step of breaking the ideological crust, by calling into question, through his reform programme, the right of the Communist Party to monopolise power. The federal system, bogus as it was, provided, paradoxically perhaps, the framework – in the form of the ethnically and linguistically delimited subunits – through and within which the nationalist resurgence against a crude and discredited ideological centralism could then express itself practically.

Gorbachev, as President of the Union, tried desperately to breathe genuine life into the federal system in order to contain the nationalist eruption. He tried to place the system on a new, more equal treaty basis; he held the first and only referendum in the USSR's history on the issue. But he was always one step behind the accelerating demands for national independence, and the conservative coup against the new Treaty of Union in August 1991 served to seal its fate, and his. The Commonwealth of Independent States (CIS) that has emerged out of the ruins of the Soviet Union is as yet a pale and shadowy thing, and it is too early to say whether it represents the starting point for the creation of a genuine economic and security confederation, or simply a committee for dividing up the assets of the old Union amongst the successor states.

The breakdown of the Yugoslav Federation, and the crisis into which the Czechoslovak Federation fell, are the product of a similar combination of forces to those that destroyed the Soviet Union. However, without going into the details, it must to be said that the policy of decentralization embarked upon by the Communist regime in Yugoslavia in the 1960s, and the subsequent rise to power of Slobodan Milosevic in Serbia, give the Yugoslavian story a different flavour. It is possible that, with a less inflexible leader in Serbia, and greater encouragement from outside, Yugoslavia could have transformed itself into a genuine confederation – as the Slovenes and Croats themselves proposed in 1991. In Czechoslovakia at the moment – where the ethnic situation is far less complex than in the other two cases – the Slovaks are currently pressing for the transformation of the state into a confederal union, while the Czechs are insisting on the retention of a federation, or, failing that, separation.

CONCLUSION

Federalism has registered significant advances in Central and Western Europe over the past twenty-five years, both at the level of the existing states, and at the interstate level. The break-up of the Soviet empire in Eastern Europe, the collapse of the Soviet Union, the shocks to the Russian Federation, and even the collapse of the Yugoslav Federation, while they may seem at first sight to involve a defeat for federalism, in reality have destroyed its bogus forms, and opened up the possibility of the further expansion of genuine, authentic federalism in Europe, whether through the accession of states in this area to the federal union developing in Western and Central Europe or through the formation of unions amongst themselves. Several of the countries of Eastern Europe have already expressed their wish to become full members of the European Community.

The factors that will impel, and, in some instances, already are impelling, the countries of this area in the direction of federal arrangements are broadly the same as those that have operated in the other half of the continent, namely the problem that small and medium-sized states face of securing their economic future in competition with great economic powers, and the problem they face of securing their political future within the interstices of the world balance of power. The long experience of the eastern countries with imperial or one-sided forms of union, and their desire to preserve their newly recovered cultural identity, are likely to strengthen the attraction of genuinely federal arrangements, based on mutuality and a guaranteed division of powers.

It would be naive, however, to suppose that the movement towards federal arrangements will be smooth or rapid. Even in the West the movement to strengthen and deepen the existing union, through the bundle of measures included in the Maastricht Treaty, has met with unexpected difficulties. In the East the nationalism that has helped to destroy the old structures of the East could harden into a profound antipathy towards any close arrangements with foreigners; it could produce, and examples of this are already apparent, an intensification of intolerance towards ethnic minorities within the newly liberated nations; it could lead to aggressive claims on the territories of neighbours in the name of national self-determination. The huge legacy of economic problems may produce a reversion to autocratic or dictatorial rule. Nor should the criticism that has been made here of the thesis that the collapse of the communist federations demonstrates the incapacity of federal systems to cope with ethnic heterogeneity be taken to suggest that the creation and maintenance of ethnically heterogeneous federal systems is a simple thing. No federal blueprint can resolve a situation of deep ethnic suspicion. Respect for the equal status of the 'other nationality' is essential if federal structures are to grow. Such things cannot be forced.

The future outlook may be illustrated by drawing a parallel. The idea of the liberal, representative state, based on the principle of the liberty and equality of individual citizens, burst upon the European scene with the French revolution of 1789 and the Constitution of 1791. That constitution did not last long, and the ideal it embodied suffered a constant series of setbacks, as well as provoking a vast barrage of ridicule, scorn and scepticism, throughout the nineteenth and through much of the twentieth century. Despite this, the ideal eventually won increasing acceptance, and is now firmly entrenched in the political systems of much of Europe, and is being eagerly embraced by most of the rest. Similarly the constitution that was proposed for the Austrian empire in the year 1849, in the Moravian town of Kremsier – the so-called Kremsier Constitutional Draft – was the first in Europe to apply the principles of liberty and equality to the national groupings within a large body politic. It too was short-lived, and its principles have also suffered continual setbacks and ridicule in the intervening period, as well as being distorted, as we have seen, to serve ideological ends totally at variance with them. Doubtless they will face further reverses in the future. But are they not as firmly grounded in right and reason as those of 1789? And are they not therefore likely to win through in the end, as those of 1789 have done?

NOTES

1 Henri Brugmans, *La Pensée politique du fédéralisme* (Leyden, Sijthoff, 1969), 21. The phrase is, of course, an adaptation of the claim by Marx and Engels in the *Communist Manifesto* that communism was the spectre haunting Europe.
2 André Alen, ed., *Treatise on Belgian Constitutional Law* (Deventer, Kluwer, 1992), 5.
3 Hans Kohn, *Nationalism in the Soviet Union* (London, Routledge, 1933), 99–101.
4 Anton Bebler, 'Das Schicksal des Kommunistischen Foederalismus', *Europa-Archiv*, series 13, 1992, 378.
5 Bebler, op. cit., 379.
6 Raymond Pearson, 'The historical background to Soviet federalism', in Alastair McAuley, ed., *Soviet Federalism* (Leicester, Leicester University Press, 1991), 24.
7 Igor Shafarevich, 'Separation or Reconciliation?', in Alexander Solzhenitsyn, *From under the Rubble* (London, Harvill, 1975), 97.
8 Bebler, op. cit., 379.

Part II

Cosmopolitan and communitarian perspectives

Chapter 4

Justice and boundaries

Onora O'Neill

BOUNDARIES IN POLITICAL PHILOSOPHY

Boundaries creep into political philosophy without us noticing. For example, within the liberal tradition of political discourse a theory of justice is typically deployed to give some account of universal rights and of the limits of legitimate state powers, yet before we know it we are talking about the powers not of the state but of *states*. As soon as we have states, we also, of course, have boundaries between states, yet these new arrivals are hardly noticeable until somebody raises a question about the just location of boundaries. At that point familiar discussions about notions of self-determination and about the status of a right to secession get going – without prior consideration of the nature or justice of boundaries. Yet it seems to me that it might be worth reflecting on the justice of boundaries before we start asking which boundaries there may or should justly be. My reflections on the matter are quite incomplete, but are guided by a couple of ideas, which it may be as well to state explicitly before I start out on what will otherwise certainly seem a meandering and wilful path – and may still seem wayward even with these signposts. The first idea is that traditional arguments about state and nation ought to be relevant, but that we must be very careful not to accept the terms of those traditional debates uncritically. The second idea is that there ought to be at least some link between discussions of the scope of ethical principles and the justification of boundaries.

If we look at current debates in political philosophy it may seem that the problem of justifying boundaries could arise only for those who advocate universal principles – many of them liberals of one sort or another – and would not even arise for communitarians, relativists and other historicists, who will always look at matters from some determinate location, hence from within and as legitimately limited by some set of boundaries. I think the supposed myopia of communitarian and kindred positions provides little insight. It is true that for communitarians boundaries are, so to speak, only visible from the inside. That is perhaps why some of them are drawn to the metaphor of horizon, rather than boundary: horizons are limits that we neither reach nor cross, as we do boundaries, but which we may enlarge or shrink. Where some actual boundary is taken to be the horizon of thought, what lies beyond that pale must be either incomprehensible to insiders, or no concern of theirs. In this case the legitimacy not merely of boundaries but of certain actual boundaries has been built into the very account of political discourse – or even of all discourse. An attempt to think away boundaries that are constitutive can only disorient all discourse. Yet any attempt to vindicate boundaries from 'within' cannot take seriously – indeed may not be able to acknowledge – either the predicaments of those who are excluded, or the alternatives for those who have been included. A ruthless relativism may suppress these concerns, at costs so high and implausible that I shall leave them unexplored.[1]

Today I want to leave aside the particular difficulties of taking any type of communitarian – or more broadly relativist – view of boundaries and to see how boundaries are overlooked within those sorts of political philosophy that argue for some version of moral cosmopolitanism yet largely reject forms of institutional cosmopolitanism.[2] What, for example, justifies Rawls's assumption that justice for a society 'conceived for the time being as a closed system isolated from other societies' can serve as the paradigm for all justice?[3] How convincingly does Nozick get from the assumption that individuals have rights, which will need enforcing, to the claim not merely that some minimal state is just, but that there may justly be a plurality of such minimal states, although this will curtail the rights of those outside their 'own' state?[4] More generally, how can those who argue for universal principles of justice, or for human rights, endorse structures that entail that the rights people actually have depend on where they are, or more precisely on which place recognizes them as citizen rather than as alien? Would not a consistent account of universal principles of justice reject as unjust the differentiated restrictions on rights that boundaries must entail? These themes seem to me as topical as they are murky: perhaps fittingly, the topic of boundaries has no very clear boundaries of its own. So I start by considering a jamboree of arguments, some of which have been around for some time, but many of which seem to me not to answer questions they have been intended to address. In the last part of the chapter I shall go on to a rather more systematic, but also rather general, account of the scope of justice and suggest a way of looking at borders which at least has definite implications, and may have advantages.

STATES, TERRITORIES AND IDENTITIES

It is often said that a plurality of political units, hence of states, is needed for justice, because world government would concentrate power too much, and so endanger the very consideration – e.g. order, freedom, other rights – that are thought to legitimate government. The division of powers on a global scale is then said to be just because it is needed to safeguard us from global tyranny, just as a domestic division of powers safeguards us from lesser tyrannies.

This argument takes us a certain distance, but it fails to show that the appropriate form of global division of powers is a division into territorially defined states, whose boundaries limit all government functions and all citizens' rights at a single spatial demarcation. After all, the division of powers that people have in mind as important when they put forward the same argument for the constitutions of particular states is not a division into distinct territories. Moreover, it does not look as if a system of territorially defined sovereign states is a particularly good way of avoiding tyranny – even if it does avoid global tyranny. Sovereign states often abuse their citizens, and there are dangerously few restraints on the methods they use to settle their disputes with other sovereign states. The arguments that were brought against absolutist, undivided conceptions of 'internal' sovereignty during the Enlightenment, above all in the many criticisms of Hobbes, may be matched by contemporary criticism of exaggerated 'realist' insistence on the need for absolute 'external' sovereignty. Excess concentration of power within states is dangerous; so is excess independence of states from one another. The vast effort that goes into the construction of regional and international structures and organizations testifies that a division into terrorially defined sovereign states has long been seen as a risky and imperfect way of avoiding the tyranny of world government.

A modified argument in favour of a plurality of territorially defined states might be this. Although a territorially demarcated division of powers is not by itself a safeguard against tyranny, it is a component of any set of institutions which provides an adequate safeguard.[5] At least some powers of government have to be exercised across contiguous and spatially limited territories. We may think of police powers and public services. We may think that we do not want a world police force or a world sewage system. Neither would be alert to local needs, both would concentrate excess powers. However, this argument also can be turned in two other ways. In the first place, there are a lot of territorially based functions of government that we have reason to want globally co-ordinated. We do want global regulation of air waves, air traffic, drug traffic and environmental standards. So we have reason to hope that even police forces and waste disposal policies are co-ordinated across state boundaries. Secondly, even when we do think that some government functions, or at least some aspects of those functions, are best exercised within territorial demarcations, still we would need an argument to show why all demarcations should coincide for a vast range of distinct functions – for it is only by superimposing the demarcations for many intrinsically distinguishable matters that we arrive at a world of bounded states. A diversity of territorial limitations would not otherwise add up to a system of state boundaries. The evident link between territoriality and some tasks of government does not then provide clear reasons for establishing or maintaining a plurality of sovereign states, which will circumscribe all the functions of government at a single set of territorial boundaries. Would it not make more sense to start with functional rather than territorial divisions of the tasks of government? And if we did so, would not the optimal territorial arrangements probably differ for different types of governmental function? It seems unlikely that any straightforwardly functional or instrumental argument would lead from an account of the ends of government or of just government (e.g. order, freedom, other rights) to a vindication of a system of territorially defined sovereign states. Of course, there may be other ways in which such an argument might be constructed.[6]

At this point some of the less radical arguments deployed by the communitarians and their predecessors are tempting. For it may be said that territory isn't really the basic issue. What makes it just to limit all government powers at the boundaries of territorial states is a deeper argument, that starts from claims about nations, peoples or communities, that is, from what are now called identities. It is because groups of people recognize one another as members of one community, and recognize certain others as outsiders, that they can legitimately aim to establish states, which are divided from other states, hence from other nations and communities, by boundaries. Within those boundaries they can then do things in their own way and preserve and develop their own traditions; beyond those boundaries they make either no claim or claims of a different and more questionable sort – e.g. irredentist or imperialist claims. Such arguments are typically strengthened by pointing out that a feeling of affiliation to nations or communities is not a mere matter of preference, but the basis of the very sense of self and identity of the persons so linked. Hence the romance of the nation-state, and more everyday stories of community life.

There are some difficulties in linking this romance with the banalities of boundaries and territories. The most fundamental of these is that membership of communities is usually neither inclusive nor exclusive within any given territory. That is to say, a given community will often share a territory with others whom it does not regard, or who do not regard themselves, as members, and that many who are regarded as members by themselves and by others will also be regarded as members of other communities both by themselves and by others. Both problems are recalcitrant.

Consider first the case of those who are not regarded as (full) members, but live in the same territory as some well defined nation or community. There may, of course, be ways of forcing on such people some outsider status – they may be physically displaced (e.g. expelled, 'resettled', pushed on to reservations) or socially marginalised (e.g. ghettoized or assigned a more or less uncomfortable minority status). Alternatively there may be ways of subjecting outsiders to policies of cultural, social and religious assimilation and incorporation which would destroy or damage not them but their differing sense of identity. However, if the basic argument in favour of the justice of boundaries and a plurality of states appeals to the importance of nationality or community for a sense of identity, it can hardly be just either to displace or to marginalize or to assimilate those whose sense of identity is other: if identities matter, minority identities matter.

Secondly, there are many members of most communities who sense themselves to be simultaneously members of other communities. Sometimes a dual identity is assumed to be obviously coherent and unproblematic – at least by most people. This is often the case with dual identities of which one is thought to fall within the other – for example, provincial and national, national and regional identities. Many people today take it that there is now no problem in being Breton and French, or Scots and British, or Irish and European – although there are still people who see a problem in each of these dual identities. Yet in our century certain other intrinsically no less plausible combinations of senses of identity have become problematic. Notoriously to remain German and Jewish became impossible. In other cases it is a matter of pressure and context. To be Irish and British is unproblematic in Britain but has become problematic in Ireland. (In the United States I was even once told that it was a contradiction to be Irish and Protestant, and by implication that nobody could have the identity which I had lifelong taken myself to have.) If membership of a community is essential to somebody's sense of identity it is clearly a grave injury if they are required to give up either all or part of what they are, or if what they are is not recognized by others.

Arguments about these matters are sometimes well muddied by adding the vocabularies of nation or community on to those of state and citizenship. For if we take it that to be a citizen is *ipso facto* to be a member of 'the community', then the problem of non-members living within the same territory can ostensibly be made invisible, once citizenship is available to all inhabitants. Notoriously minorities are often unconvinced by this failure to recognize what they are. By the same magic, the problem of membership of multiple communities can also be made to vanish, by treating citizenship (which is seldom multiple) as settling who is a member of the community. In this way questions of identity can be and have been obscured in much public debate.[7]

However, there are good reasons to keep the legal and political notions of state and citizenship and the social and cultural categories of community membership or national affiliation or identity quite separate. If we hope to use notions of community or nation or people as a basis for arguing for a plurality of states – nation-states – divided by boundaries, then we cannot define these notions themselves in terms of the state-based notions of citizenship, on pain of undercutting the hoped-for justification.

Another, and more robust, way of handling the problems of outsiders and dual membership can be read out of Rousseau, who writes that he would wish to be a member of a state whose antique origins are lost in 'the darkness of time',[8] and whose citizens see themselves as a single community with a common good. He looked more to the traditional world of Swiss peasant life than to the conflict-ridden realities of the Geneva he purportedly admired to assure himself that such communities were possible, and knew well enough that his wish was not satisfied by any actual community. There are few if any communities so homogeneous that all their members identify with a single conception of the common good, hence few for which any General Will can be defined. Rousseau's General Will is the will not of the actual inhabitants of any historical state, some of whom may lack full allegiance to any given conception of that community and its good, while others have multiple allegiances or identities, but the will of 'corrected' citizens who have been 'forced to be free', and who now correctly identify with the community – or, putting the matter bluntly, identify with the corrected community. This is why Rousseau's Sovereign, the embodiment of the General Will 'merely by virtue of what it is, is always what is should be'.[9]

REALIGNING TERRITORIES AND IDENTITIES

Since such wished-for homogeneous communities do not exist, Rousseau, followed by many others, considers how they may be created by a combination of nostalgic and utopian strategies. Nostalgic looking back to an archaic earlier time of supposed homogeneous community – Swiss peasants wisely settling affairs of state under an oak – allegedly legitimates a certain view of who now counts as a community member, and who as an outsider, as alien, as non-member. Utopian looking forward points to a future in which a process of nation-building will have reformed everybody within certain boundaries, by imposing a single form of identity, a single national allegiance in which all will the common good. Later nationalists often follow Rousseau in combining nostalgic and utopian elements: a mythical past is to be one of the tools for forging a united future, which is then (mis)conceived of as a 'return to roots'. In this way people who live within actual state boundaries, who are seldom homogeneous, and nearly always include some who do not share the majority identity and others who have multiple identities, are to be forced to be free.

Some results of implementing such strategies can be seen in at least partly benign forms in the constitution of a previously missing sense of national identity in some actual states (rather obviously the United States; less obviously Ireland), and in largely malign form in the totalitarian versions inculcated in Nazi Germany and in rather different ways in Eastern Europe under formerly existing socialism.[10] The weight placed on mythical past and on desired future may vary greatly. Historicist conceptions of nationality stress origins more, Rousseauian and Kantian discussions of civil religion and ethical commonwealth and contemporary discussions of 'constitutional patriotism' view community and identity as task rather than either as origin or as fate.[11]

However, once we begin to think of national or community identity as something to be constituted rather than as a given reality, appeals to (national) identity to vindicate state boundaries look a great deal less impressive. Any given appeal may be countered by pointing out other possible conceptions of (national) identity. If the elements and scope of a (national or community) sense of identity are not given but constructed, then it is always an open question whether they should not have been, or should now be, differently constructed, and whether those who do not like the *status quo* should not be urged – or, if we follow Rousseau, forced – to change their sense of identity rather than to challenge existing boundaries. A nationalism that appeals to processes of identity formation in order to create a homogeneous nation has no simple answer to those who urge assimilation into other identities. Looked at in this way, nationalism and assimilationism, secession and imperialism, historicism and civil religion, are just different programmes for identity formation, that urge people to construct or fasten on differing accounts of shared origins or on differing visions of shared destinies, which could then be used to 'justify' differing boundaries.

The flimsiness of all such appeals to national or other identity as justification for maintaining or changing territorial demarcations and boundaries is often obscured by relying once again on hybrid concepts such as the 'nation-state' or 'community of citizens' whose proper use tacitly presupposes the very alignment of identity and territory that is in question. If the social conceptions of nation, tribe, community or people are to do the work of justifying the territorial boundaries between political units, they must not be redefined in terms that presuppose these boundaries. Such definitional strategies undercut the aim of vindicating territorial boundaries or changes in boundaries by appeals to national and other identities.

Another approach to the disparities between territorial realities and actual conceptions of (national) identity accepts that a single sense of identity is rarely found in all who share a given territory, and aims to align the two by permitting or requiring those with the 'wrong' sense of identity to change not their share of identity but their location. As a strategy this has a lot to be said against it, because it is always unjust and often impossible. Policies of forced relocation are hugely unjust; policies of supposedly 'voluntary' transfer are often driven by fear. Moreover, any proposed alignment of identity to territory by relocation is not merely unjust but impossible when sense of identity itself is bound to territory, so that the two are not detachable. The same territories may be integral to the actual sense of identity of groups with differing, even antagonistic, conceptions of their own identity – witness the Palestinian/Israeli problem and many of the struggles in former Yugoslavia. To give up the homeland may amount to giving up a sense of identity.

A yet more general reason for doubting any strategy for justifying territorial boundaries by appeal either to the present or to some revised pattern of senses of identity or allegiance is this. The concepts by which people define who they are – in which they articulate their sense of identity – are all of them concepts without sharp borders, and hence cannot provide a basis for sharp demarcations such as political boundaries between states. Most concepts do not merely permit borderline cases but are strictly boundaryless, in that their sense is given by a pair of a larger number of contrasts, rather than by the existence of a well defined set of items of which the concept is true.[12] Although we have clear ideas of what it means to be red as opposed to yellow, or a child as opposed to an adult, or Irish as opposed to British, this is not because anybody can form the sets that contain all and only those items that are red, or are children or are Irish. Our understanding of national and community identity is always framed in terms of boundaryless concepts – so cannot provide an adequate basis for fixing sharp boundaries. These considerations also suggest why our under-standing of national identity is so often given in terms of certain contrasts – we identify who counts as a fellow countryman only in so far as we identify others as foreigners or even as enemies. When furthest from home we greet as compatriots others with whom we have tenuous links; when closest to home we may see those from the next valley as foreign.

This scattering of arguments has looked back in an un-systematic way over various chapters of political philosophy, in which appeals to national identity have been thought to have some justifying role in explaining why there must or may justly be a plurality of territorially bounded states. I think that the arguments are not individually impressive. An adequate ap-proach to these issues would reject both the fiction that all government functions for some group have to be confined within common territorial limits, and the myth that the world does or ought to be made to consist of homogeneous nations lodged in mutually exclusive territories with well defined boundaries.

LEGITIMATE BOUNDARIES WITHOUT MYTHS

I want now to try to say something a bit more positive, if rather modest, by sketching some arguments for the legitimacy of a plurality of political units, hence of boundaries, without invok-ing these particular myths and fictions. Before I do this I would

like to head off one misunderstanding. It is not part of my
argument to suggest that a sense of national (or tribal, religious, cultural or community) identity is a myth or illegitimate
or unimportant. All too clearly these matters are not mythical,
surely they are important, and presumably they can be appro-
priately appealed to for some purposes. The failure of the
arguments just surveyed suggests only that the various types of
identity that are or could become important to people don't
provide promising starting points for justifying a system of
arranging political power by division into mutually excluding
nation-states that jointly exhaust all territories. Nationality and
other sorts of community may be very important even if they
have little to do with the legitimacy of political boundaries. I
also think it clear that securing a national state may sometimes
be *instrumentally* important in securing justice for some – we
have only to think of the predicament of the Kurds. But equally
securing a national state for some can be instrumental in
bringing injustice to others – we have only to think of the
nationalities problems of the former USSR.

The question of the legitimacy of boundaries can hardly be
raised unless we take some view of the scope of principles of
justice. Questions of scope are not settled by showing that
principles of justice are universal principles: for a principle to
be universal is only for it to hold for all cases in some domain. It
is the definition of that domain which would settle issues of
scope. A universal principle might, for example, hold for
all inhabitants of a certain area, or for all human beings, or for
all members of a certain class, or for all adult males. In many
contemporary debates the issue of the scope of principles of
justice – and more generally of morality – is treated as the
question of establishing the moral status or standing of those
entitled to just treatment. Most of these debates take it for
granted that all adult, normal human beings have this standing
– they count, for example, as persons or as holders of rights –
and then move on to ask who and what else have moral
standing. Debates have raged about the moral standing and
claims of foetuses, of children, of the terminally ill, of animals
and of numerous other cases. These debates are familiar and
extraordinarily repetitive. One reason why they are so repetitive
may be that most of the protagonists are looking for an
essentialist answer: they hope to identify some essential property

or set of properties which confers personhood or moral standing. Yet they are often wholly unwilling to argue for any of those metaphysical positions which could establish essentialist claims. This is particularly clear in the endlessly rehearsed abortion debates. The so-called 'right to life' groups may not have found any metaphysical arguments that convince their opponents of their essentialist claims, but they have lured those opponents onto essentialist terrain, which those who defend no metaphysical essentialism find both slippery and sloping.

For reasons that I will not go into here, I doubt whether we can show that any property or set of properties is either necessary or sufficient for moral standing. Yet if we cannot, it seems that we will have no clear view of the scope of principles of justice, or of other moral principles, so will hardly be in a position to start thinking about how this might be relevant to the status of political boundaries. Unless *both* the scope and the content of justice are fixed, it may remain obscure whether boundaries obstruct justice, or whether they are indispensable elements of its institutional embodiment. If we do not know the scope of justice, how can we either vindicate or criticise the practice of differentiating rights on a territorial basis? Indeed, how could we even come to any view of the relativist and communitarian strategies of interpreting the boundaries of actual communities as the boundaries of justice?[13]

An alternative way of approaching the question of the scope of justice might be to take it as a practical rather than a theoretical question. That is to say, we could give up the search for a theoretical demarcation of the sphere of justice that requires essentialist claims or sharp demarcations where none is available, and note that we need an account of the scope of justice in contexts of action where there is a potential for conflict. A practical account of the scope of justice can perhaps be premised not on the metaphysics of the person, but on the assumptions to which agents are already committed whenever they act in circumstances where justice can be an issue. To see that a practical approach to the scope of justice might be very different from a general, theoretical approach we need only consider the practically unimportant case of justice to previous generations. Since we cannot affect any but surviving predecessors, there is no practical need to identify a limit to the scope of justice to predecessors. It does not matter from a practical point of view at what point our remotest predecessors acquired moral standing (we do not need to know whether Neanderthal men and women were right holders). Yet if there were a comprehensive, 'perspectiveless' account of the scope of justice we could expect it to distinguish predecessors who had moral standing from those who did not. From a practical point of view nothing need be said or assumed about such cases. Seen from such a theoretical perspective, a practical account of moral standing might be judged to have gaps: yet these notional gaps may be wholly irrelevant to action.

However, a practical approach to questions of scope will be no advantage if it too needs some account of the metaphysics of the person to provide the criterion of moral standing. This demand may perhaps be avoided by working not from any view of the nature of persons, but from an account of the circumstances of action, or more narrowly from the circumstances of justice.

Hume formulates the classical version[14] of these circumstances when he identifies moderate scarcity and confined generosity as the key elements of the circumstances of justice. Rawls has offered[15] a rather more extensive account that combines the objective and the subjective circumstances of justice. Hume and Rawls use these premises as part of an account of the content as well as the scope of principles of justice. For present purposes our concern is only with their scope.[16] For this purpose it may in fact be sufficient to take a weaker view of the circumstances of justice than either Hume or Rawls proposes, and to view them simply as the circumstances that hold when a plurality of finite agents share a world. Each of these elements of the circumstances of justice needs brief comment and vindication.

To be part of a plurality of agents who share a world is a significant circumstance of justice because it excludes the case of pseudo-pluralities, among whom conflict would be impossible, hence justice without a task. Circumstances of justice are missing among bodily distinct beings who are so co-ordinated, whether by instinct or by pre-established harmony, that conflict, and so also the mediation of conflict by principles of justice, are pre-empted. The circumstances of justice are always also circumstances of possible injustice. The classical formulation of this thought is Aristotle's criticism of Plato: '. . . if unification advances beyond a certain point, the city will not be a city at all'[17] – and hence the political virtue, justice, will be without point. Circumstances of justice are circumstances in which conflict between agents is possible – and may be avoidable, or at least regulatable, by institutions of justice. This view does not assume any strong form of individualism, but only that conflict and the mediation of conflict by whatever means have a place only among pluralities of at least partially distinct agents.

Finitude is a distinct element of any circumstances of justice. Taken strictly, plurality already entails some sorts of finitude: there cannot be pluralities all of whose members enjoy un-limited dimensions, possessions or powers. However, finitude forms a distinct element of the circumstances of justice because it is important not to introduce false assumptions about the powers of the agents who compose a given plurality. Fictions of idealized self-sufficiency or rationality or of idealized cognitive or physical powers, that might in principle be found in some pluralities of finite agents, but to which the members of human pluralities do not measure up, are often used but seldom if ever justified in the construction of theories of justice. Human action, and thereby also human justice, as they can actually exist, are predicated not on mere plurality, but on a plurality of mutually vulnerable beings who never achieve more than quite limited and specific forms of rationality, independence and self-sufficiency.

Finitude and plurality are necessary conditions for questions of justice to arise, but they are not sufficient. A plurality of finite agents who were not also connected to one another could not come into conflict. Their action would never be predicated on the agency or collaboration of those unknown others. For example, the inhabitants of Viking Dublin and their con-temporaries in Peru neither knew of nor affected one another's lives. Their actions were in no way predicated on one another's capacity to act. It would be absurd to ask whether they dealt with one another either justly or unjustly. Although a set consisting of a plurality of finite agents can be formed by taking Dubliners and Peruvians of that time, circumstances of justice would not obtain between members of the conjoined sub-sets because they did not share a world. By 'sharing a world' I do not mean to invoke any presumption of close community, let alone Hannah Arendt's particularly strong understanding of this phrase, but

only the relation that holds when agents premise action –
whether co-operative or hostile or neither – on the competent
agency either of nearby or of distant others.

Where all three elements of the circumstances of justice –
plurality, finitude and sharing a world – obtain, injustice can
occur, and issues of justice can always be raised. It is clear that
today these circumstances are not confined within the boundaries of states, or within the more uncertain boundaries of
nations or of communities. Although the most familiar case of
a world shared by a plurality of finite agents is that of a
community whose members interact a great deal, interaction
now hardly ever stops at political or at other boundaries. Action-
at-a-social-distance is a commonplace on which we constantly
rely in the modern world. In saying that we rely on it we are
saying only that we presuppose its possibility, in that we predicate our plans, policies and individual acts on such interaction. We trade, we broadcast, we travel, we negotiate. For
practical purposes we are already committed to viewing both
nearby and distant and unknown others as agents like ourselves.
Hence if we think that there are ethical principles – principles
of justice – whose scope includes all with whom we interact, we
cannot exclude distant others. Although the notions of 'global
community' or 'global society' may be no more than a sentimental rhetoric of cosmopolitanism, the weaker relation of
sharing a world with distant others is one that agents today
cannot consistently deny.

And yet these realities are often denied. 'Idealized' conceptions of sovereignty and self-sufficiency, or on the other
hand of community and unity, are used as strategies by which
the scope of justice can be surreptitiously set in preferred ways.
By idealizing sovereignty and independence we obscure our
connectedness to certain others and the fact that we share a world
with them; by idealising community and unity we obscure the
distinctness of others and overlook plurality. In either case,
claims of justice are ruled out of order. Between them these
strategies can be and have been used both to exclude some
('enemies', 'foreigners') from all moral concern, and to deny
the separateness of others ('our own', 'dependants') and so
play down the full demands of justice between insiders.

In the circumstances of action that we actually find and rely
on in the late twentieth century, neither sort of idealization is

either attained or approximated. Foreigners and other 'outsiders' are not others with whom we do not, let alone cannot, interact and share a world. Compatriots, intimates and kin, with whom we may share much, do not form an 'ideal' united community that pre-empts plurality and the need for justice. In all these cases we have to do with a plurality of finite beings who assume they share a world with others, and who cannot then define the limits of justice to exclude those others of whom they make these assumptions. Others cannot consistently be discounted, once they are already relied upon as distinct yet connected agents.

Given our present actual commitments and involvements in acting, we cannot then coherently argue that moral concern, and least of all that justice, stops either at boundaries of states, or at social boundaries of other sorts. Anyone who makes such moves in *our* world evidently shifts ground illegitimately. If we assume that 'foreigners' are people with whom it is possible to trade, translate and negotiate, who can be expected to carry complex and intelligent roles, we cannot rescind the imputations of agency, rationality, competence and so on, to which we are committed, midway in the argument. If in other cases we take these to be legitimate bases of moral concern, we must do the same in these cases. Hence even a minimal conception of the circumstances of justice as those of an agent who lives among a plurality of finite others who are taken to share the same world has strong and expansive implications for the scope of justice in the contemporary world, and in particular strong implications for nearly all contemporaries because our plans and practices are in fact predicated on sharing a world with so many others.

JUSTICE ACROSS BORDERS

The practical implication of these thoughts for the justice of state boundaries is not, however, that only a world without state boundaries could be a just world. Such a world – a world state – might concentrate so much power that it risked or instituted much injustice. The common reasons given for fearing world government and its colossal concentration of powers seem to me serious reasons. The reasons for thinking that justice is helped by bonds of sentiment between citizens, and can be destroyed by lack of all such bonds, are also strong. The evidence that those bonds are easier to forge when a sense of identity is shared is also considerable.

However, while boundaries may be necessary for justice, actual boundaries are often impediments to justice. In saying this I do not mean that they are drawn at the wrong places. It is not in itself unjust that some nations find themselves divided by state boundaries (e.g. post-war Germany), or that others find themselves sharing a state with people they come not to regard as part of their own nation (Serbs and Croats). Given the non-coincidence of national and other identities with territory, such outcomes are unavoidable, and in themselves no injustice. There cannot be rights to live in homogeneous, territorially bounded nation-states, and those who imagine that a right to self-determination can or must be interpreted in this way embark on dangerous self-deception. The way in which boundaries can be unjust is rather that they can be used to discount the claims to justice of those on the far side of some boundary either in whole or in part. (They can also become part of an institutional framework for inflicting injustice on insiders – witness the case of East Germany, but since this case is uncontroversial it can be left to one side.)

The more interesting case is that of boundaries which systematically inflict injustices on outsiders. The case can be sketched by contrasting two hypothetical states, for which we need make no assumptions about the presence or absence of a homogeneous national identity. If the boundaries are just, the two states will acknowledge that those beyond their boundaries too have claims to just treatment, and in so far as their action affects those beyond the boundaries they will seek to do them no injustice. If the boundaries are unjust, the policies and practices of at least one state will impinge on those who live in the other, in ways that do the other injustice. Typically this will be justified – it will not be seen as injustice – under the heading of not interfering in the internal affairs of another sovereign state, or of having no responsibilities towards non-citizens. However, once the legitimacy of treating actual state boundaries as limits of justice has been called into question, an appeal to sovereignty or to assumed lack of responsibilities to non-citizens cannot automatically outweigh an appeal to justice. For in this context the appeal to sovereignty or to lack of responsibilities is simply the appeal to use state borders to limit the scope of justice, even when there are other considerations to show that the scope of justice ought not to be restricted in this way. This is not to say justice demands the complete abrogation of sovereignty or the abolition of states – but it does demand an interpretation of sovereignty that does not constitute an arbitrary limit to the scope of justice.

If these consideration are convincing, they may have very significant and complex implications for justifiable intervention in the case of human rights violations beyond state boundaries, for the justice of legislation that selectively restricts boundary crossing, whether for asylum, travel, migration, abode, work, settlement or to take up citizenship,[18] and for the justice of an economic order predicated on transnational economic interaction which lacks both transnational powers of taxation and transnational institutions to relieve poverty. An account of just borders which takes account of these issues need not deny the importance of nations and of national identity: but it must deny that they create claims to bounded states which exercise absolute internal or external sovereignty. The legitimate claims of nations cannot be to impermeable boundaries, which limit justice to those beyond them, but at most to a political order within which nations and other communities of identity can secure, celebrate and hand on their specific ways of life and senses of identity.[19]

NOTES

1 Wittgensteinians and communitarians both treat boundaries as constitutive of ethical discourse. Sophisticated examples of the two approaches are provided by Peter Winch, *Ethics and Action* (Routledge and Kegan Paul, London, 1972), and Michael Walzer, *Spheres of Justice: A Defence of Pluralism and Equality* (Martin Robertson, Oxford, 1983). For further references and for criticisms of the two ways of limiting the reach of ethical discourse see Onora O'Neill, 'The Power of Example' in *Constructions of Reason: Explorations of Kant's Practical Philosophy* (Cambridge University Press, Cambridge 1989), pp. 165–86, as well as 'Ethical Reasoning and Ideological Pluralism', *Ethics* 98 (1988), 705–22.

2 For this distinction see Charles Beitz, 'Cosmopolitan Liberalism and the States System', this volume; Beitz's discussion of Rawls's handling of boundaries and international justice in *Political Theory and International Relations* (Princeton University Press, 1979) is also

instructive on this theme. Many recent writers, especially those with Hegelian tendencies, and particularly since the gentle revolutions of 1989, but by no means only they, have mounted explicit attacks on institutional cosmopolitanism, and provided arguments for the indispensability of concepts of nation and national identity in political philosophy. See, for example, D.N. McCormick, 'Nation and Nationalism' in his *Legal Right and Social Democracy* (Clarendon, Oxford, 1982, chapter 13) and more recently 'Is Nationalism Philosophically Credible?' in *Issues of Self-determination,* ed. William Twining (Aberdeen University Press, 1990); Alasdair MacIntyre, *Is Patriotism a Virtue?* (Philosophy Department, University of Kansas, 1984). However, very little of this writing addresses the tangled connection between (national) identity and territoriality which is the theme of this chapter.

3 John Rawls, *A Theory of Justice* (Harvard University Press, Cambridge, Mass, 1971), 8. For Rawls's account of international justice see pp. 378–82, and for comments the works by Beitz cited above, and Thomas Pogge, *Realizing Rawls* (Columbia University Press, New York, 1990).

4 Robert Nozick, *Anarchy State and Utopia* (Blackwell, Oxford, 1974).

5 Even here there are exceptions: former Pakistan; island states.

6 See Thomas Baldwin, 'Territoriality' in *Jurisprudence: Cambridge Essays,* ed. Hyman Gross and Ross Harrison (Cambridge University Press, Cambridge, 1992, pp. 207–30) for a stimulating exploration of the links – and the surprising missing links – between statehood and territoriality.

7 This move is not confined to liberal writers – see for example Walzer, *op. cit.*

8 Jean-Jacques Rousseau, *A Discourse on Inequality,* trans. Maurice Cranston (Penguin Books, Harmondsworth, 1984), Dedication, 59.

9 Jean-Jacques Rousseau, *The Social Contract,* trans G.D.H. Cole, (Dent, London, 1913), Book I, chapter vii.

10 For these examples see Oliver MacDonagh, *States of Mind: A Study of Anglo-Irish 1780–1980* (Allen and Unwin, London, 1982), and Vaclav Havel's essay 'The Power of the Powerless' in *Living in Truth,* ed. Jan Vadislav (Faber and Faber, London, 1986). MacDonagh's work will surprise those who imagine that Irish nationalism, the model for many later nationalist movements, is of great antiquity; Havel's essay captures the daily face of the attempted reformation of sense of identity under really existing socialism.

11 On civil religion, see both *The Social Contract* and Immanuel Kant, *Religion Within the Limits of Reason Alone,* trans. Theodore M. Green and Hoyt H. Hudson (Harper and Row, New York, 1960); on constitutional patriotism and related themes see Jürgen Habermas, 'Ist der Herzschlag der Revolution zum Stillstand gekommen?' in *Die Ideen von 1798 in der deutschen Rezeption,* ed. Forum für Philosophie, Bad Homburg (Suhrkamp, Frankfurt-am-Main, 1989); and also Ulrich K. Preuss, *Revolution, Fortschritt und Verfassung: zu einem neuen Verfassungsverständnis,* (Wagenbach, Berlin, 1990).

12 Mark Sainsbury, *Concepts without Boundaries*, Inaugural Lecture (Philosophy Department, King's College London, 1990).
13 See the references in note 1.
14 David Hume, *A Treatise of Human Nature*, ed. L.A. Selby Bigge, revised 1958 (Routledge and Kegan Paul, London), pp. 494–5.
15 *A Theory of Justice*, pp. 126–30.
16 I believe that a non-metaphysical approach can provide the basis of an account of the content of principles of justice, but will leave this large claim dangling in mid-air: here I assume only that we can establish some universal principles of justice, but leave it open which ones we can establish.
17 Aristotle, *Politics*, 1261a.
18 On some of these issues see Brian Barry and Robert E. Goodin, eds, *Free Movement: Ethical Issues in the Transnational Migration of People and of Money* (Harvester Wheatsheaf, Hemel Hempstead, 1992).
19 See the works by D.N. McCormick, cited above, and Iso Camartin, *Von Sils-Maria aus Betrachtet: Ein Blick von dem Dach Europas* (Suhrkamp, Frankfurt, 1991). Securing national and other identities through policies that respect minorities and their cultures is neither a soft nor a minimal option, especially where national identity has been inflated into aspiration to sovereignty over territory that others share; but it is a political goal which is compatible with the realities of intermingled nations.

Chapter 5

Cosmopolitanism and sovereignty

Thomas W. Pogge

The human future suddenly seems open. This is an inspiration; we can step back and think more freely. Instead of containment or détente, political scientists are discussing grand pictures: the end of history, or the inevitable proliferation and mutual pacifism of capitalist democracies. And politicians are speaking of a new world order. My inspiration is a little more concrete. After developing a rough, cosmopolitan specification of our task to promote moral progress, I offer an idea for gradual global institutional reform. Dispersing political authority over nested territorial units would decrease the intensity of the struggle for power and wealth within and among states, thereby reducing the incidence of war, poverty, and oppression. In such a multi-layered scheme, borders could be redrawn more easily to accord with the aspirations of peoples and communities.

INSTITUTIONAL COSMOPOLITANISM BASED ON HUMAN RIGHTS

Three elements are shared by all cosmopolitan positions. First, *individualism*: the ultimate units of concern are *human beings*, or *persons*[1] – rather than, say, family lines, tribes, ethnic, cultural, or religious communities, nations, or states. The latter may be units of concern only indirectly, in virtue of their individual members or citizens. Second, *universality*: the status of ultimate unit of concern attaches to *every* living human being *equally*[2] – not merely to some sub-set, such as men, aristocrats, Aryans, whites, or Muslims. Third, *generality*: this special status has global force. Persons are ultimate units of concern for *everyone* – not only for their compatriots, fellow religionists, or such like.

Let me separate three cosmopolitan approaches by introducing two distinctions. The first is that between legal and moral cosmopolitanism. *Legal* cosmopolitanism is committed to a concrete political ideal of a global order under which all persons have equivalent legal rights and duties – are fellow citizens of a universal republic.[3] *Moral* cosmopolitanism holds that all persons stand in certain moral relations to one another: we are required to respect one another's status as ultimate units of moral concern – a requirement that imposes limits upon our conduct and, in particular, upon our efforts to construct institutional schemes. This view is more abstract, and in this sense weaker, than legal cosmopolitanism: though compatible with the latter, it is also compatible with other patterns of human interaction – e.g. with a system of autonomous states and even with a plurality of self-contained communities. Here I present a variant of moral cosmopolitanism, though below I also discuss whether this position mandates efforts to move from our global *status quo* in the direction of a more cosmopolitan world order (in the sense of legal cosmopolitanism).

The central idea of moral cosmopolitanism is that every human being has a global stature as an ultimate unit of moral concern. Such moral concern can be fleshed out in countless ways. One may focus on subjective goods and ills (human happiness, desire fulfilment, preference satisfaction, or pain avoidance) or on more objective ones (such as human need fulfilment, capabilities, opportunities, or resources). Also, one might relativize these measures, e.g. by defining the key ill as *being worse off than anyone need be*, or as *falling below the mean* – which is equivalent to replacing straightforward aggregation (sum-ranking or averaging) by a version of maximin or egalitarianism, respectively. In order to get to my topic quickly, I do not discuss these matters, but simply opt for a variant of moral cosmopolitanism that is formulated in terms of *human rights* (with straightforward aggregation).[4] In doing so, I capture what most other variants likewise consider essential. And my further reflections can, in any case, easily be generalized to other variants of moral cosmopolitanism.

My second distinction lies *within* the domain of the moral. It concerns the nature of the moral constraints to be imposed. An *institutional* conception postulates certain fundamental principles of *justice*. These apply to institutional schemes and are thus second-order principles: standards for assessing the ground rules and practices that regulate human interactions. An *interactional* conception, by contrast, postulates certain fundamental principles of *ethics*. These principles, like institutional ground rules, are first-order in that they apply directly to the conduct of persons and groups.[5]

Interactional cosmopolitanism assigns direct responsibility for the fulfilment of human rights to other (individual and collective) agents, whereas institutional cosmopolitanism assigns such responsibility to institutional schemes. On the latter view, the responsibility of persons is then indirect – a shared responsibility for the justice of any practices one supports: one ought not to participate in an unjust institutional scheme (one that violates human rights) without making reasonable efforts to aid its victims and to promote institutional reform.

Institutional and interactional conceptions are again compatible and thus may be combined.[6] Here I focus, however, on a variant of institutional cosmopolitanism while leaving open the question of its supplementation by a variant of interactional cosmopolitanism. I hope to show that making the institutional view primary leads to a much stronger and more plausible overall morality. Let us begin by examining how our two approaches would yield different accounts of human rights and human rights violations.

On the interactional view, human rights impose constraints on conduct, while on the institutional view they impose constraints upon shared practices. The latter approach has two straightforward limitations. First, its applicability is contingent, in that human rights are activated only through the emergence of social institutions. Where such institutions are lacking, human rights are merely latent and human rights violations cannot exist at all. Thus, if we accept a purely institutional conception of human rights, then we need some additional moral conception if we wish to deny that all is permitted in a very disorganized state of nature.

Second, the cosmopolitanism of the institutional approach is contingent as well, in that the *global* moral force of human rights is activated only through the emergence of a *global* scheme of social institutions, which triggers obligations to promote any feasible reforms of this scheme that would enhance the fulfilment of human rights. So long as there is a plurality of self-contained cultures, the responsibility for such violations does not extend beyond their boundaries.[7] It is only because all human beings are now participants in a single, global institutional scheme – involving such institutions as the territorial state, a system of international law and diplomacy as well as a world market for capital, goods, and services – that all human rights violations have come to be, at least potentially, everyone's concern.[8]

These two limitations do not violate generality. I have a duty towards *every* other person not to co-operate in imposing an unjust institutional scheme upon her – even while this duty triggers human-rights-based obligations only to fellow participants in the same institutional scheme. This is analogous to how the duty to keep one's promises is general even while it triggers obligations only *vis-à-vis* persons to whom one has actually made a promise.

We see here how the institutional approach makes available an appealing intermediate position between two interactional extremes: it goes beyond simple libertarianism, according to which we may ignore harms that we do not directly bring about, without falling into a utilitarianism of rights *à la* Shue, which commands us to take account of all relevant harms whatsoever, regardless of our causal relation to these harms.[9]

Consider a human right not to be enslaved. On an interactional view, this right would constrain persons, who must not enslave one another. On an institutional view, the right would constrain legal and economic institutions: slavery must not be permitted or enforced. This leads to an important difference regarding the moral role of those who are neither slaves nor slaveholders. On the interactional view, such third parties have no responsibility *vis-à-vis* existing slaves, unless the human right in question involved, besides the negative duty not to enslave, also a positive duty to protect or rescue others from enslavement. Such positive duties have been notoriously controversial. On the institutional view, by contrast, some third parties may be implicated far more directly in the human rights violation. If they are not making reasonable efforts towards institutional reform, the more privileged participants in an institutional scheme in which slavery is permitted or even enforced – even those who own no slaves themselves – are here seen as co-operating in the enslavement, in violation of a *negative* duty.

The institutional view thus broadens the circle of those who share responsibility for certain deprivations and abuses beyond what a simple libertarianism would justify, and it does so without having to affirm positive duties.

To be sure: working for institutional reform is doing something (positive). But, in the context of practices, this – as even libertarians recognize – does not entail that the duty in question is therefore a positive one: the negative duty not to abuse just practices may also generate positive obligations, as when one must act to keep a promise or contract one has made. Once one is a participant in social practices, it may no longer be true that one's negative duties require merely forbearance.

The move from an interactional to an institutional approach thus blocks one way in which the rich and mighty in today's developed countries like to see themselves as morally disconnected from the fate of the less fortunate denizens of the Third World. It overcomes the claim that one need only refrain from violating human rights directly, that one cannot reasonably be required to become a soldier in the global struggle against human rights violators and a comforter of their victims worldwide. This claim is not refuted but shown to be irrelevant. We are asked to be concerned about human rights violations not simply in so far as they exist at all, but only in so far as they are produced by social institutions in which we are significant participants. Our negative duty not to co-operate in the imposition of unjust practices, together with our continuing participation in an unjust institutional scheme, triggers obligations to promote feasible reforms of this scheme that would enhance the fulfilment of human rights.

One may think that a shared responsibility for the justice of the social institutions in which we participate cannot plausibly extend beyond our national institutional scheme, in which we participate as citizens, and which we can most immediately affect. But such a limitation is untenable because it treats as natural or God-given the existing global institutional framework, which is in fact imposed by human beings who are collectively quite capable of changing it. Therefore at least we – privileged citizens of powerful and approximately democratic countries – share a collective responsibility for the justice of the existing global order and hence also for any contribution it may make to the incidence of human rights violations.[10]

The practical importance of this conclusion evidently hinges on the extent to which our global institutional scheme is causally responsible for current deprivations. Consider this challenge: 'Human rights violations and their distribution have local explanations. In some countries torture is rampant, while it is virtually non-existent in others. Some regions are embroiled in frequent wars, while others are not. In some countries democratic institutions thrive, while others bring forth a succession of autocrats. And again, some poor countries have developed rapidly, while others are getting poorer year by year. Therefore our global institutional scheme has very little to do with the deplorable state of human rights fulfilment on earth.'

This challenge appeals to true premises but draws an invalid inference. Our global institutional scheme can obviously not figure in the explanation of *local* human rights violations, but only in the *macro*explanation of their *global* incidence. This parallels how Japanese culture may figure in the explanation of the Japanese suicide rate or how the laxity of US handgun legislation may figure in the explanation of the North American homicide rate, without thereby explaining particular suicides/homicides or even intercity differentials in rates. In these parallel cases the need for a macro-explanation is obvious from the fact that there are other societies whose suicide/homicide rates are significantly lower. In the case of *global* institutions, the need for a macro-explanation of the overall incidence of human rights violations is less obvious because – apart from some rather inconclusive historical comparisons – the contrast with observable alternative global institutional schemes is lacking. Still, it is highly likely that there are feasible (i.e. practicable and accessible) alternative global regimes that would tend to engender lower rates of deprivation. This is clear, for example, in regard to economic institutions, where the centrifugal tendencies of certain free-market schemes are well understood from our experience with various national and regional schemes. This supports a generalization to the global plane, to the conjecture that the current constitution of the world market must figure prominently in the explanation of the fact that our world is one of vast and increasing international inequalities in income and wealth (with consequent huge differentials in national rates of infant mortality, life expectancy, disease, and malnutrition). Such a macro-explanation does not pre-empt micro-explanations of why one poor country is developing rapidly and why another is not. It would explain why so few are while so many are not.

Consider this further challenge to the practical moral importance of our shared responsibility for the justice of our global institutional scheme: 'An institutional scheme can be held responsible for only those deprivations it *establishes*, i.e. (at least implicitly) *calls for.* Thus, we cannot count against the current global regime the fact that it tends to engender a high incidence of war, torture, and starvation because nothing in the existing (written or unwritten) international ground rules calls for such deprivations – they actually forbid both torture and the waging of aggressive war. The prevalence of such deprivations therefore indicates no flaw in our global order and, *a fortiori*, no global duties on our part (though we do of course have some local duties to see to it that *our* government does not bring about torture, starvation, or an unjust war).'

This position is implausible. First, it would be irrational to assess social institutions without regard to the effects they predictably engender. For an institutional change (e.g. in economic ground rules) might benefit everyone (e.g. by increasing compliance, or through incentive effects). Second, social institutions are human artefacts (produced and abolished, perpetuated and revised by human beings) and it would be unprecedented not to take account of the predictable effects of human artefacts. (We choose between two engineering designs by considering not merely their suitability for their particular purpose but also their incidental effects, e.g. on pollution and the like, in so far as these are predictable.) Third, we consistently take incidental effects into account in debates about the design of *domestic* institutions (incentive effects of penal and tax codes, etc.).[11]

These arguments reaffirm my broadly consequentialist assessment of social institutions, which leads us to aim for the feasible global institutional scheme that produces the best pattern of human rights fulfilment, irrespective of the extent to which this pattern is established or engendered. We thus consider the existing global institutional scheme unjust in so far as the pattern of human rights fulfilment it tends to produce is inferior to the pattern that its best feasible alternatives would tend to produce. This broadly consequentialist variant of institutional cosmopolitanism accords with how the concern for human rights is understood within the Universal Declaration of Human Rights. Section 28 reads: 'Everyone is entitled to a social *and international* order in which the rights and freedoms set forth in this Declaration can be fully realised' (my emphasis).[12]

This result suggests a further difference between the interactional and institutional approaches, concerning the way each counts violations of certain human rights. It cannot reasonably be required of an institutional scheme, for example, that it reduce the incidence of physical assaults to zero. This would be impossible; and approximating such an ideal as closely as possible would require a police state. The institutional approach thus counts a person's human right to physical integrity as fully satisfied if her physical integrity is *reasonably* secure.[13] This entails that – even in the presence of a shared institutional scheme – some of what count as human rights violations on the interactional view (e.g. certain assaults) do not count as human rights violations on the institutional view (because the persons whose physical integrity was violated were reasonably well protected). Conversely, some of what count as human rights violations on the institutional view (e.g. inadequate protection against assaults) may not register on the interactional view (as when insufficiently protected persons are not actually assaulted).

Let me close the more abstract part of my discussion with a sketch of how this institutional view relates to social and economic human rights and the notion of distributive justice. A man sympathetic to the moral claims of the poor, Michael Walzer, has written: 'the idea of distributive justice presupposes a bounded world, a community, within which distributions take place, a group of people committed to dividing, exchanging, and sharing, first of all among themselves'.[14] This is precisely the picture of distributive justice that Robert Nozick (among others) has so vigorously attacked. To the notion of dividing he objects that 'there is no *central* distribution, no person or group entitled to control all the resources, jointly deciding how they are to be doled out'.[15] And as for the rest, he would allow persons to do all the exchanging and sharing they like, but strongly reject any enforced sharing implemented by some redistribution bureaucracy.

The institutional approach involves a conception of distributive justice that differs sharply from the one Walzer supports and Nozick attacks. Here the issue of distributive justice is not how to distribute a given pool of resources or how to improve upon a given distribution but, rather, how to choose or design the economic ground rules, which regulate property, co-operation, and exchange and thereby condition production and distribution. (On the particular view I have defended, for example, we should aim for a set of economic ground rules under which each participant would be able to meet her basic social and economic needs.) These economic ground rules – the object of distributive justice on the institutional approach – are prior to both production and distribution and therefore involve neither the idea of an already existing pool of stuff to be doled out nor the idea of already owned resources to be *re*distributed.

The institutional conception of distributive justice also does not presuppose the existence of a community of persons committed first of all to share with one another. Rather, it has a far more minimal rationale: we face a choice of economic ground rules that is partly open – not determined by causal necessity, nor pre-empted by some God-given or natural or neutral scheme that we must choose irrespective of its effects. This choice has a tremendous impact on human lives, an impact from which persons cannot be insulated and cannot insulate themselves. Our present global economic regime produces a stable pattern of widespread malnutrition and starvation among the poor (with some 20 million persons dying every year from hunger and trivial diseases), and there are likely to be feasible alternative regimes that would not produce similarly severe deprivations. In such a case of avoidable deprivations, we are confronted not by persons who are merely poor and starving but by victims of an institutional scheme – impoverished and starved. There is an injustice in this economic scheme, which it would be wrong for its more affluent participants to perpetuate. And that is so quite independently of whether we and the starving are united by a communal bond or committed to sharing resources with one another – just as murdering a person is wrong irrespective of such considerations. This is what the assertion of social and economic human rights comes to within the proposed institutional cosmopolitanism.

This institutional cosmopolitanism does not, as such, entail crisp practical conclusions. One reason for this is that I have not – apart from allusions to Rawls and the Universal Declaration – given a full list of precisely defined human rights together with relative weights or priority rules. Another reason is that this institutional cosmopolitanism bears upon the burning issues of the day only in an indirect way, mediated by empirical regularities and correlations. This is so chiefly because of its broadly consequentialist character, i.e. its commitment to take the engendered consequences of an institutional scheme as seriously, morally, as its established consequences. Whether an institutional scheme *establishes* avoidable deprivations or inequalities (such as slavery or male suffrage) can be read off from the (written or unwritten) ground rules characterizing this scheme. With regard to *engendered* deprivations and inequalities, however, we face far more complex empirical questions about how the existing institutional scheme, compared with feasible modifications thereof, tends to affect the incidence of human rights violations – such as rates of infant mortality, child abuse, crime, war, malnutrition, poverty, personal dependence, and exclusion from education or health care.

The intervention of such empirical matters, and the openness of the notion of human rights, do not mean that no conclusions can be drawn about the burning issues – only that what we can conclude is less precise and less definite than one might have hoped.

THE IDEA OF STATE SOVEREIGNTY

Before discussing how we should think about sovereignty in light of the proposed institutional cosmopolitanism, let me define this term, in a somewhat unusual way, as a two-place relation: A is *sovereign* over B if and only if

1 A is a governmental body or officer ('agency'), and
2 B are persons, and
3 A has unsupervised and irrevocable authority over B

   (a) to lay down rules constraining their conduct, or
   (b) to judge their compliance with rules, or
   (c) to enforce rules against them through pre-emption, prevention, or punishments, or
   (d) to act on their behalf *vis-à-vis* other agencies (ones that do

or do not have authority over them) or persons (ones whom A is sovereign over, or not).

A has *absolute sovereignty* over B if and only if

1 A is sovereign over B, and
2 No other agency has any authority over A or over B which is not supervised and revocable by A.

Any A having (absolute) sovereignty over some B can then be said to be an (absolute) sovereign (the one-place predicate).[16]

Central to contemporary political thought and reality is the idea of the autonomous territorial state as the pre-eminent mode of political organization. In the vertical dimension, sovereignty is very heavily concentrated at a single level – it is states and only states that merit separate colours on a political map of our world. For nearly every human being, and for almost every piece of territory, there is exactly one government with pre-eminent authority over, and primary responsibility for, this person or territory. And each person is thought to owe primary political allegiance and loyalty to this government with pre-eminent authority over him or her. National governments dominate and control the decision-making of smaller political units as well as supranational decisions, which tend to be made through intergovernmental bargaining.[17]

From the standpoint of a cosmopolitan morality – which centres around the fundamental needs and interests of individual human beings, and of *all* human beings – this concentration of sovereignty at one level is no longer defensible. What I am proposing instead is not the idea of a world state, which is really a variant of the pre-eminent state idea. Rather, the proposal is that governmental authority – or sovereignty – be widely dispersed in the vertical dimension. What we need is *both* centralization *and* decentralization – a kind of second-order decentralization away from the now dominant level of the state. Thus, persons should be citizens of, and govern themselves through, a number of political units of various sizes, without any one political unit being dominant and thus occupying the traditional role of the state. And their political allegiance and loyalties[18] should be widely dispersed over these units: neighbourhood, town, county, province, state, region, and world at large. People should be politically at home in all of them, without converging upon any one of them as the lodestar of their political identity.[19]

Before defending and developing this proposal by reference to my institutional cosmopolitanism, let me address two types of objection to any vertical division of sovereignty.

Objections of type 1 dispute that sovereignty can be divided at all. The traditional form of this objection rests on the belief that a *juridical state* (as distinct from a lawless state of nature) presupposes an absolute sovereign. This dogma of absolute sovereignty arises (e.g. in Hobbes and Kant) roughly as follows. A juridical state, by definition, involves a recognized decision mechanism that uniquely resolves any dispute. This mechanism requires some agency because a mere written or unwritten code (constitution, holy scripture) cannot settle disputes about its own interpretation. But so long as this agency is limited or divided – whether horizontally (i.e. by territory or by governmental function) or vertically (as in my proposal) – a juridical state has not been achieved because there is no recognized way in which conflicts over the precise location of the limit or division can be authoritatively resolved. A genuine state of peace requires then an agency of last resort – ultimate, supreme, and unconstrained. Such an agency may still be limited by (codified or uncodified) obligations. But these can obligate merely *in foro interno* because to authorize subjects, or some second agency, to determine whether the first agency was overstepping its bounds would enable conflicts about this question for which there would be no legal path of resolution.[20]

This argument, which – strictly construed – would require an absolute world sovereign, has been overtaken by the historical facts of the last two hundred years or so, which show conclusively that what cannot work in theory works quite well in practice. Law-governed coexistence is possible without a supreme and unconstrained agency. There is, it is true, the possibility of *ultimate* conflicts: of disputes in regard to which even the legally correct method of resolution is contested. To see this, one need only imagine how a constitutional democracy's three branches of government might engage in an all-out power struggle, each going to the very brink of what, on its understanding, it was constitutionally authorized to do. From a theoretical point of view, this possibility shows that we are not insured against, and thus live in permanent danger of, constitutional crises. But this no longer undermines our confidence in a genuine division of powers: we have learned that such crises need not be frequent or irresolvable. From a practical point of view, we know that constitutional democracies can endure and can ensure a robust juridical state.

This same point applies in the vertical dimension as well. Just as it is nonsense to suppose that (in a juridical state) sovereignty *must* rest with one of the branches of government, it is similarly nonsensical to think that in a multi-layered scheme sovereignty *must* be concentrated on one level exclusively. As the history of federalist regimes clearly shows, a vertical division of sovereignty can work quite well in practice, even while it leaves some conflicts over the constitutional allocation of powers without a legal path of authoritative resolution.

Objections of type 2 oppose, more specifically, a *vertical* dispersal of sovereignty: there are certain vertically indivisible governmental functions that form the core of sovereignty. Any political unit exercising these core functions must be dominant – free to determine the extent to which smaller units within it may engage in their own local political decision-making, even while its own political process is immune to regulation and review by more inclusive units. Vertical distributions of sovereignty, if they are to exist at all, must therefore be lopsided (as in current federal regimes).

To be assessable, such a claim stands in need of two clarifications, which are rarely supplied. First, when one thinks about it more carefully, it turns out to be surprisingly difficult to come up with examples of indivisible governmental functions. Eminent domain, economic policy, foreign policy, judicial review; the control of raw materials, security forces, education, health care, and income support; the regulation and taxation of resource extraction and pollution, of work and consumption can all be handled at various levels and indeed *are* so handled in existing federal regimes and confederations. So what are the governmental functions that supposedly are vertically indivisible? Second, is their indivisibility supposed to be derived from a conceptual insight, from empirical exigencies, or from moral desiderata? And which ones?

Since I cannot here discuss all possible type 2 objections, let me concentrate on one paradigm case: Walzer's claim that the authority to fix membership, to admit and exclude, is at least part of an indivisible core of sovereignty: 'At some level of political organization something like the sovereign state must take shape and claim the authority to make its own admissions policy, to control and sometimes to restrain the flow of immigrants.'[21] Walzer's 'must' does not reflect a conceptual or empirical necessity, for in those senses the authority in question quite obviously *can* be divided – e.g. by allowing political units on all levels to veto immigration. It is on moral grounds that Walzer rejects such an authority for provinces, towns, and neighbourhoods: it would 'create a thousand petty fortresses'.[22] But if smaller units are to be precluded from controlling the influx of new members, then immigration must be controlled at the state level: 'Only if the state makes a selection among would-be members and guarantees the loyalty, security, and welfare of the individuals it selects, can local communities take shape as "indifferent" associations, determined only by personal preference and market capacity.'[23] The asserted connection is again a moral one: it is certainly factually possible for local communities to exist as indifferent associations even while no control is exercised over migration at all; as Walzer says, 'the fortresses too could be torn down, of course'.[24] Walzer's point is, then, that the insistence on openness (to avoid a thousand petty fortresses) is asking too much of neighbourhoods, unless the state has control over immigration: 'The distinctiveness of cultures and groups depends upon closure. . . . If this distinctiveness is a value, . . . then closure must be permitted somewhere.'[25]

But is the conventional model really supported by the rationale Walzer provides? To be sure, Walzer is right to claim that the value of protecting cohesive neighbourhood cultures is better served by national immigration control than by no control at all.[26] But it would be much better served still if the state were constrained to admit only immigrants who were planning to move into a neighbourhood that was willing to accept them. Moreover, since a neighbourhood culture can be as effectively destroyed by an influx of fellow nationals as by an influx of immigrants, neighbourhoods would do even better if they had some authority to select from among prospective domestic newcomers or to limit their number.

Finally, neighbourhoods may often want to bring in new members from abroad – persons to whom they have special ethnic, religious, or cultural ties – and they would therefore benefit from a role in the national immigration control process that would allow them to facilitate the admission of such persons. Thus there are at least three reasons for believing that Walzer's rationale – cohesive neighbourhood cultures ought to be protected without becoming petty fortresses – is actually *better* served by a division of the authority to admit and exclude than by the conventional concentration of this authority at the level of the state.

SOME MAIN REASONS FOR A VERTICAL DISPERSAL OF SOVEREIGNTY

Having dealt with some preliminary obstacles, let me now sketch four main reasons favouring, over the *status quo*, a world in which sovereignty is widely distributed vertically.

1. *Peace/security.* Under the current regime, interstate rivalries are settled ultimately through military competition, including the threat and use of military force. Moreover, within their own territories, national governments are free to do virtually anything they like. Such governments therefore have very powerful incentives and very broad opportunities to develop their military might. This is bound to lead to the further proliferation of nuclear, biological, chemical, and conventional weapons of mass destruction. And in a world in which dozens of competing national governments control such weapons, the outbreak of devastating wars is only a matter of time. It is not feasible to reduce and eliminate national control over weapons of mass destruction through a programme that depends upon the voluntary co-operation of each and every national government. What is needed, therefore, is the centrally enforced reduction and elimination of such weapons – in violation of the prevalent idea of state sovereignty. Such a programme, if implemented soon, would be much less dangerous than continuing the *status quo.* It could gain the support of most peoples and governments, if it increased the security of all on fair terms that were effectively adjudicated and enforced.

2. *Reducing oppression.* Under the current global regime, national governments are effectively free to control 'their' populations in whatever way they see fit. Many make extensive use of this freedom by torturing and murdering their domestic

opponents, censoring information, suppressing and subverting democratic procedures, prohibiting emigration, and so forth. This problem could be reduced through a vertical dispersal of sovereignty over various layers of political units that would check and balance one another as well as publicize one another's abuses.

3. *Global economic justice.* The magnitude and extent of current economic deprivation – over 20 million persons die every year from poverty-related causes – calls for some modification in the prevailing scheme of economic co-operation. One plausible reform would involve a global levy on the use of natural resources to support the economic development of the poorest areas.[27] Such a levy would tend to equalize *per capita* endowments and also encourage conservation. Reforms for the sake of economic justice would again involve some centralization – though without requiring anything like a global welfare bureaucracy.

Global economic justice is an end in its own right, which requires, and therefore supports, a reallocation of political authority. But it is also important as a means towards the first two purposes. War and oppression result from the contest for power within and among political units, which tends to be the more intense the higher the stakes. In fights to govern states, or to redraw their borders, far too much is now at stake by way of control of people and resources. We can best lower the stakes by dispersing political authority over several levels *and* institutionally securing economic justice at the global level.

This important point suggests why my first three considerations – though each supports some centralization – do not on balance support a world state. While a world state could lead to significant progress in terms of peace and economic justice, it also poses significant risks of oppression. Here the kind of multi-layered scheme I propose has the great advantages of affording plenty of checks and balances and of assuring that, even when some political units turn tyrannical and oppressive, there will always be other, *already fully organized* political units (above, below, or on the same level) which can render aid and protection to the oppressed, publicize the abuses, and, if necessary, fight the oppressors.

There are two further important reasons against a world state. Cultural and social diversity are likely to be much better protected when the interests of cultural communities at all levels are represented (externally) and supported (internally) by co-ordinated political units. And the scheme I propose could be gradually reached from where we are now (through what I have called second-order decentralization), while a world state – involving, as it does, the annihilation of existing states – would seem reachable only through revolution or in the wake of some global catastrophe.

4. *Ecology.* Modern processes of production and consumption are liable to generate significant negative externalities that, to a large and increasing extent, transcend national borders. In a world of competing autonomous states, the internalization of such externalities is generally quite imperfect because of familiar isolation, assurance, and co-ordination problems. Treaties among a large number of very differently situated actors require difficult and time-consuming bargaining and negotiations, which often lead to only very slight progress, if any. And even when treaties are achieved, doubts about the full compliance of other parties tend to erode each party's own commitment to make good-faith efforts towards compliance.

Now one might think that this fourth reason goes beyond my institutional cosmopolitanism, because there is no recognized human right to a clean environment. Why should people not be free to live in a degraded natural environment if they so choose? In response: perhaps they should be, but for now they won't have had a choice. The degradation of our natural environment ineluctably affects us all. And yet most people are effectively excluded from any say about this issue which, in the current state-centric model, is regulated by national governments unilaterally or through intergovernmental bargaining heavily influenced by huge differentials in economic and military might.

This response suggests replacing *Ecology* with a deeper and more general fourth reason, which might be labelled *Democracy*: persons have a right to an institutional order under which those significantly and legitimately[28] affected by a political decision have a roughly equal opportunity to influence the making of this decision – directly or through elected delegates or representatives.[29] Such a human right to political participation also supports greater local autonomy in matters of purely local concern than exists in most current states or would exist in a world state, however democratic. In fact, it supports just the kind of multi-layered institutional scheme I have proposed. Before developing this idea further, let me consider an objection. One might say, against a human right to political participation, that what matters about political decisions is that they be correct, not that they be made democratically by those concerned. But this objection applies, first of all, only to political choices that are morally closed and thus *can* be decided correctly or incorrectly. I believe that we should reject a view on which almost all political choices are viewed as morally closed (with the correct decision determined, perhaps, through utility differentials), but I have no space here to defend this belief. Second, even when political choices *are* morally closed, the primary and ultimate responsibility for their being made correctly should lie with the persons concerned. Of course, some other decision procedure – such as a group of experts – may be more reliable for this or that kind of decision, and such procedures (judges, parliaments, cabinets, etc.) should then be put in place. This should be done, however, by *the people* delegating, or abstaining from, such decisions. It is ultimately up to them, and not to self-appointed experts, to recognize the greater reliability of, and to institutionalize, alternative decision-making procedures.

Given the postulated human right to political participation, the proper vertical distribution of sovereignty is determined by three sets of considerations. The first favour decentralization, the second centralization, while the third may correct the resulting balance in either direction.

First, decision-making should be decentralized as far as possible. This is desirable in part, of course, in order to minimize the decision-making burdens upon individuals. But there are more important reasons as well. In so far as decisions are morally closed, outsiders are more likely to lack the knowledge and sensitivities to make responsible judgments – and the only practicable and morally acceptable way of delimiting those who are capable of such judgments is by rough geographical criteria. In so far as decisions are morally open, the end must be to maximize each person's opportunity to influence the social conditions that shape her life – which should not be diluted for the sake of enhancing persons' opportunities to influence decisions of merely local significance elsewhere. At least persons should be left free to decide for themselves to what extent to engage in such exchanges. The first consideration does not then rule out *voluntary* creation of central decision-making mechanisms (even though their structure – dependent upon unanimous consent – would tend to reflect the participants' bargaining power). Such centralization may be rational, for example, in cases of conflict between local and global rationality (tragedy-of-the-commons cases: fishing, grazing, pollution) and also in regard to desired projects that require many contributors because they involve co-ordination problems or economies of scale, for example, or because they are simply too expensive (construction and maintenance of transport and communication systems, research and technology, space programmes, and so forth).

The second consideration favours centralization in so far as this is necessary to avoid excluding persons from the making of decisions that significantly (and legitimately) affect them. Such decisions are of two – possibly three – kinds. Inhabiting the same natural environment and being significantly affected by what others do to it, we have a right to participate in regulating how it may be used. And since the lives each of us can lead are very significantly shaped by prevailing institutions – such as marriage, reproduction and birth control, property, money, markets, and forms of political organization – we have a right to participate in their choice and design. These two kinds of decision arise directly from Kant's point that human beings cannot avoid influencing one another: through direct contact and through their impact upon the natural world in which they coexist. A right to participate in decisions of the third kind is more controversial. There are contexts, one might say, in which we act as a species and thus should decide together how to act. Examples might be our conduct towards other biological species (extinction, genetic engineering, cruelty), ventures into outer space, and the preservation of our human heritage (ancient skeletons and artefacts, great works of art and architecture, places of exceptional natural beauty). In all these cases it would seem wrong for one person or group to take irremediable steps unilaterally.

The significance of the second consideration depends heavily upon empirical matters, though it does so in a rather straightforward and accessible way. It is obvious upon minimal reflection that the developments of the past few centuries have greatly increased the significance of this consideration in favour of centralization. This is so partly because of rising population density, but much more importantly because of our vastly more powerful technologies and the tremendously increased level of global interdependence. Concerning technologies, the fact that what a population does within its own national borders – stockpiling weapons of mass destruction, depleting non-renewable resources, cutting down vegetation essential for the reproduction of oxygen, emitting pollutants that are destroying the ozone layer and cause global warming – now often imposes very significant harms and risks upon outsiders brings into play the political human rights of these outsiders, thereby morally undermining the conventional insistence on absolute state autonomy. Global interdependence is best illustrated by the emergence of truly global capital and commodity markets (as dramatically illustrated by the stock market crash of October 1987): a change in Japanese interest rates, or a speculative frenzy of short-selling on the Chicago Futures Exchange, can literally make the difference between life and death for large numbers of people half a world away – in Africa, for example, where many countries depend upon foreign borrowing and cash crop exports. Such interdependence is not bad as such (it can hardly be scaled back in any case), but it does require democratic centralization of decision-making: as more and more persons are significantly affected by certain institutions, more and more persons have a right to a political role in shaping them. The possibility of free bargaining over the design of such institutions does not satisfy the equal-opportunity principle, as is illustrated in the case of commodity markets by the fact that African populations simply lack the bargaining power that would allow them significantly to affect how such markets are organized. (This argument withstands the communitarian claim that we must reject supranational democratic processes for the sake of the value of national autonomy. Such rejection does indeed enhance the national autonomy of the advantaged First World populations. But their gain is purchased at the expense of poorer populations, who, despite fictional or *de jure* state sovereignty, have virtually no control over the most basic parameters that shape their lives – a problem heightened by the fact that even their own rather impotent governments face strong incentives to cater to foreign interests rather than to those of their constituents.)

The first two considerations by themselves yield the result that the authority to make decisions of some particular kind should rest with the democratic political process of a unit that (1) is as small as possible but still (2) includes as equals all persons significantly and legitimately affected by decisions of this kind. In practice, some trading-off is required between these two considerations because there cannot always be an established political process that includes as equals all and only those significantly affected. A matter affecting the populations of two provinces, for example, might be referred to the national parliament or might be left to bargaining between the two provincial governments. The former solution caters to (2) at the expense of (1): involving many persons who are not legitimately affected. The latter solution caters to (1) at the expense of (2): giving the persons legitimately affected not an equal opportunity to influence the matter but one that depends on the relative bargaining power of the two provincial governments.

The first two considerations would suffice on the ideal-theory assumption that any decisions made satisfy all moral constraints with regard to both procedure (the equal-opportunity requirement) and output (this and other human rights). This assumption, however, could hardly be strictly true in practice. And so a third consideration must come into play: what would emerge as the proper vertical distribution of sovereignty from a balancing of the first two considerations alone should be modified – in either direction – if such modification significantly increases the democratic nature of decision-making or its reliability (as measured in terms of human rights fulfilment). Let me briefly discuss how this third consideration might make a difference.

On the one hand, one must ask whether it would be a gain for human rights fulfilment on balance to transfer decision-making authority 'upward' to larger units – or (perhaps more plausibly) to make the political process of smaller units subject to regulation and/or review by the political process of more inclusive units. Such authority would allow the larger unit, on human rights grounds,[30] to require revisions in the structure of the political process of the smaller one and/or to nullify its political decisions, and perhaps also to enforce such revisions and nullifications.

Even when such interventions really do protect human rights, this regulation and review authority has some costs in terms of the political human rights of the members of the smaller unit. But then, of course, the larger unit's regulation and review process may itself be unreliable and thus may produce human rights violations either by overturning unobjectionable structures or decisions (at even greater cost to the political human rights of members of the smaller unit) or by forcing the smaller unit to adopt structures and decisions that directly violate human rights.

On the other hand, there is also the inverse question: whether the third consideration might support a move in the direction of *de*centralization. Thus one must ask to what extent the political process of a larger unit is undemocratic or unreliable, and whether it might be a gain for human rights fulfilment on balance to transfer decision-making authority 'downward' to smaller units – or to invest the political process of such sub-units with review authority. Such an authority might, for example, allow provincial governments, on human rights grounds, to block the application of national laws in their province. This authority is justified if and only if its benefits (laws passed in an undemocratic manner or violating human rights are not applied) outweigh its costs (unobjectionable laws are blocked in violation of the political rights of members of the larger unit).

How such matters should be weighed is a highly complex question, which I cannot here address with any precision. Let me make two points nevertheless. First, a good deal of weight should be given to the actual views of those who suffer abridgements of their human rights and for whose benefit a regulation and/or review authority might thus be called for. If most blacks in some state would rather suffer discrimination than see their state government constrained by the federal government, then the presumption against such an authority should be much weightier than if the opposition came only from the whites. This is not to deny that victims of injustice may be brainwashed or may suffer from false consciousness of various sorts. It may still be possible to make the case for a regulation and/or review authority. But it should be significantly more difficult to do so.

Second, commonalities of language, religion, ethnicity, or history are strictly irrelevant. Such commonalities do not give people a claim to be part of one another's political lives, nor does the lack of such commonalities argue against restraints. The presence or absence of such commonalities may still be empirically significant, however. Thus suppose that the members of some smaller unit share religious or ethnic characteristics that in the larger unit are in the minority (e.g. a Muslim province within a predominantly Hindu state). Our historical experience with such cases may well support the view that a regulation and review authority by the larger unit would probably be frequently abused or that a review authority by the smaller unit would tend to enhance human rights fulfilment overall. The relevance of such information brings out that the required weighings do not depend on value judgments alone. They also depend on reasonable expectations about how alternative arrangements would actually work in one or another concrete context.

The third consideration must also play a central role in a special case: the question of where decisions about the proper allocation of decision-making should be made. For example: should a dispute between a provincial parliament and a national legislature over which of them is properly in charge of a particular decision be referred to the provincial or to the national supreme court? Here again one must present arguments to the effect that the preferred locus of decision-making is likely to be more reliable than its alternative.

Nothing definite can be said about the ideal number of levels or the exact distribution of legislative, executive, and judicial functions over them. These matters might vary in space and time, depending on the prevailing empirical facts to be accommodated by my second and third considerations (externalities, interdependence; unreliabilities) and on persons' preferences as shaped by the historical, cultural, linguistic, or religious ties among them. The human right to political participation also leaves room for a wide variety, hence regional diversity, of decision-making procedures – direct or representative, with or without political parties, and so on. Democracy may take many forms.

THE SHAPING AND RESHAPING OF POLITICAL UNITS

One great advantage of the proposed multi-layered scheme is, I have said, that it can be reached gradually from where we are now. This requires moderate centralizing and decentralizing moves involving the strengthening of political units above and below the level of the state. In some cases, such units will have to be created, and so we need some idea about how the geographical shape of new political units is to be determined. Or, seeing that there is considerable dissatisfaction about even the geographical shape of existing political units, we should ask more broadly: what principles ought to govern the geographical separation of political units on any level?

Guided again by the cosmopolitan ideal of democracy, I suggest these two procedural principles as a first approximation:

1. The inhabitants of any contiguous territory of reasonable shape may decide – through some majoritarian or supermajoritarian procedure – to join an existing political unit whose territory is contiguous with theirs and whose population is willing – as assessed through some majoritarian or supermajoritarian procedure – to accept them as members.[31] This liberty is conditional upon the political unit or units that are truncated through such a move either remaining viable (with a contiguous territory of reasonable shape and sufficient population) or being willingly incorporated, pursuant to the first clause, into another political unit or other political units.

2. The inhabitants of any contiguous territory of reasonable shape, if sufficiently numerous, may decide – through some majoritarian or supermajoritarian procedure – to form themselves into a political unit of a level commensurate with their number. This liberty is subject to three constraints. There may be sub-groups whose members, pursuant to their liberty under (1), are free to reject membership in the unit to be formed in favour of membership in another political unit. There may be sub-groups whose members, pursuant to their liberty under (2), are free to reject membership in the unit to be formed in favour of forming their own political unit on the same level.[32] And the political unit or units truncated through the requested move must either remain viable (with a contiguous territory of reasonable shape and sufficient population) or be willingly incor-

porated, pursuant to the first clause of (1), into another political unit or other political units.

It will be said that acceptance of such principles would trigger an avalanche of applications. It is surely true that a large number of existing groups are unhappy with their current membership status; there is a significant backlog, so to speak, that might pose a serious short-term problem. Once this backlog has been worked down, however, there may not be much redrawing activity, as people will then be content with their political memberships, and most borders will be supported by stable majorities.

Moreover, as the advocated vertical dispersal of sovereignty is implemented, conflicts over borders will lose much of their intensity. In our world, many such conflicts are motivated by morally inappropriate considerations – especially the following two. There is competition over valuable or strategically important territories and groups because their possession affects the distribution of international bargaining power (economic and military potential) for the indefinite future. And there are attempts by the more affluent to interpose borders between themselves and the poor in order to circumvent widely recognized duties of distributive justice among compatriots.[33] Under the proposed multi-layered scheme – in which the political authority currently exercised by national governments is both constrained and dispersed over several layers, and in which economic justice is institutionalized at the global level and thus inescapable – territorial disputes on any level would be only slightly more intense than disputes about provincial or county lines are now. It is quite possible that my two principles are not suitable for defining a right to secession in our present world of excessively sovereign states.[34] But their plausibility will increase as the proposed second-order decentralization progresses.[35]

Finally, the incidence of applications can be reduced through two reasonable amendments. First, the burden of proof, in appealing to either of the two principles, should rest with the advocates of change, who must map out an appropriate territory, organize its population, and so forth. This burden would tend to discourage frivolous claims. Second, it might be best to require some supermajoritarian process (e.g. proponents must outnumber opponents plus non-voters in three consecutive referenda over a two-year period). Some such provision would especially help prevent areas changing back and forth repeatedly (with outside supporters moving in, perhaps, in order to tip the scales). Let me briefly illustrate how the two principles would work in the case of nested political units. Suppose the Kashmiris agree that they want to belong together as one province but are divided on whether this should be a province of India or of Pakistan. The majority West Kashmiris favour affiliation with Pakistan, the East Kashmiris favour affiliation with India. There are four plausible outcomes: a united Kashmiri province of Pakistan (P), a united Kashmiri province of India (I), a separate state of Kashmir (S), and a divided Kashmir belonging partly to Pakistan and partly to India (D). Since the East Kashmiris can, by principle (2), unilaterally insist on D over P, they enjoy some protection against the West Kashmiri majority. They can use this protection for bargaining, which may result in outcome S (if this is the second preference on both sides) or even in outcome I (if that is the second preference of the West Kashmiris while the East Kashmiris prefer D or S over P).[36]

The conventional alternatives to my cosmopolitan view on settling the borders of political units reserve a special role either for historical states and their members (compatriots) or for nations and their members (fellow nationals). The former version is inherently conservative, the latter potentially revisionist (by including, e.g., the Arab, Kurdish, and Armenian nations and by excluding multinational states like the Soviet Union or the Sudan). The two key claims of such a position are: (1) Only (encompassing) groups of compatriots/fellow nationals have a right to self-government. (2) Such government may be exercised even over unwilling geographical sub-groups of compatriots/fellow nationals (who at most have a liberty of individual emigration).[37] Those who hold such a conventional position are liable to reject my cosmopolitan view as excessively individualist, contractarian, or voluntaristic. Examples of this sentiment are easy to find: 'the more important human groupings need to be based on shared history, and on criteria of non-voluntaristic (or at least not wholly contractarian) membership, to have the value that they have'.[38] In so far as this is an empirical claim – about the preconditions of authentic solidarity and mutual trust, perhaps – I need not disagree with it.[39] If indeed a political unit is far more valuable for its members when they share a common descent and upbringing (language, culture, religion), then people will recognize this fact and will themselves seek to form political units along these lines. I don't doubt that groups seeking to change their political status under the two principles would for the most part be groups characterized by such unchosen commonalities.

But would I not give any other group, too, the right to change its political status, even if this meant exchanging a more valuable for a less valuable membership? Margalit and Raz ridicule this idea through their examples of 'the Tottenham Football Club supporters', 'the fiction-reading public', and 'the group of all the people whose surnames begin with a "g" and end with an "e"'.[40] Yet these examples – apart from being extremely far fetched – are ruled out by the contiguity requirement, which a 'voluntarist' can and, I believe, should accept in light of the key function of government: to support shared rules among persons who cannot avoid influencing one another through direct interaction and through their impact upon their common environment. A more plausible example would then be that of the inhabitants of a culturally and linguistically Italian border village who prefer an (*ex hypothesi*) less valuable membership in France over a more valuable membership in Italy. Here I ask: do they not, France willing, have a right to err? Or should they be forced to remain in, or be turned over to, a superordinate political unit against their will?

This example brings out the underlying philosophical value conflict. My cosmopolitanism is committed to the freedom of individual persons and therefore envisions a pluralist global institutional scheme. Such a scheme is compatible with political units whose membership is homogeneous with respect to some partly unchosen criteria (nationality, ethnicity, native language, history, religion, etc.), and it would certainly engender such units. But it would do so only because persons *chose* to share their political life with others who were like themselves in such respects – not because persons are entitled to be part of one another's political lives if and only if they share certain unchosen features.

One way of supporting the conventional alternative involves rejecting the individualist premiss that only human beings are ultimate units of moral concern.[41] One could then say that, once the moral claims of states/nations were taken into account alongside those of persons, one might well find that, all things considered, justice required institutional arrangements that were inferior, in human rights terms, to feasible alternatives – institutional arrangements, for example, under which the interest of Italy in its border village would prevail over the expressed interest of the villagers.

This justificatory strategy faces two main problems. It is unclear how states/nations can have interests or moral claims that are not reducible to interests and moral claims of their members (which can be accommodated within a conception of human rights). This idea smacks of bad metaphysics,[42] and also is dangerously subject to political/ideological manipulation (as exemplified by Charles de Gaulle, who was fond of adducing the interests of *la nation* against those of his French compatriots). Moreover, it is unclear why this idea should work here, but not in the case of other kinds of (sub- and supranational) political units, nor in that of religious, cultural, and athletic entities. Why need we not also take into account the moral claims of Catholicism, art, or baseball?

These problems suggest the other justificatory strategy, which accepts the individualist premiss but then formulates the political rights of persons with essential reference to the state/ nation whose members they are. This strategy has been defended, most prominently, by Michael Walzer, albeit in a treatise that focuses on international ethics (interactions) rather than international justice (institutions). Walzer approvingly quotes Westlake: 'The duties and rights of states are nothing more than the duties and rights of the men who compose them,' adding, 'the rights ... [to] territorial integrity and political sovereignty ... belong to states, but they derive ultimately from the rights of individuals, and from them they take their force. ... States are neither organic wholes nor mystical unions.'[43]

The key question is, of course, how such a derivation is supposed to work. There are two possibilities. The direct route would be to postulate either a human right to be governed by one's compatriots/fellow nationals[44] or a human right to participate in the exercise of sovereignty over one's compatriots/ fellow nationals. The former of these rights is implausibly demanding upon others (the Bavarians could insist on being part of Germany, even if all the other Germans wanted nothing to do with them) and would still fail to establish (B), unless it were also unwaivable – a duty, really. The latter right is implausibly demanding upon those obligated to continue to abide by the common will merely because they have once (however violently) been incorporated into a state or merely because they have once shared solidarity and sacrifices.

The indirect, instrumental route would involve the empirical claim that human rights (on a non-eccentric definition) are more likely to be satisfied, or are satisfied to a greater extent, if there is, for each person, one political unit that decisively shapes her life and is dominated by her compatriots/fellow nationals. This route remains open on my cosmopolitan conception (via the third consideration), though the relevant empirical claim would not seem to be sustainable on the historical record. Supposing that this sort of argument fails on empirical grounds, this institutional cosmopolitanism would favour a global order in which sovereignty was widely distributed vertically, while the geographical shape of political units was determined by the autonomous preferences of situated individuals in accordance with principles (1) and (2).

NOTES

This chapter has benefited from various incisive comments and suggestions by Andreas Follesdal, Bonnie Kent, Ling Tong, and my fellow participants at the 'Ethikon East/West Dialogue Conference on the Restructuring of Political and Economic Systems' (Berlin, January 1991). The chapter has previously appeared in *Ethics* 103 (1992).

1 The differences between the notions of a person and a human being are not essential to the present discussion.
2 There is some debate about the extent to which we should give weight to the interests of future persons and also to those of past ones (whose deaths are still recent). I leave this issue aside because it is at right angles to the debate between cosmopolitanism and its alternatives.
3 One recent argument for a world state is advanced in Kai Nielson: 'World Government, Security, and Global Justice' in Steven Luper-Foy, ed., *Problems of International Justice* (Boulder, Westview Press, 1988).
4 I have in mind here a rather minimal conception of human rights, one that rules out truly severe abuses, deprivations, and inequalities while still being compatible with a wide range of political, moral, and religious cultures. The recent development of, and

progress within, both governmental and non-governmental international organizations supports the hope, I believe, that such a conception might, in our world, become the object of a worldwide overlapping consensus. Cf. Thomas W. Pogge, *Realizing Rawls* (Ithaca, Cornell University Press, 1989), chapter 5.

5 Interactional cosmopolitanism has been defended in numerous works. A paradigm example is Henry Shue, *Basic Rights* (Princeton, Princeton University Press, 1980). Luban, another advocate of this position, puts the point as follows: 'A human right, then, will be a right whose beneficiaries are all humans and whose obligors are all humans in a position to effect the right' (David Luban, 'Just War and Human Rights' in Charles Beitz, M. Cohen, T. Scanlon, and A.J. Simmons, eds, *International Ethics* (Princeton, Princeton University Press, 1985), p. 209). Robert Nozick's *Anarchy, State, and Utopia* (New York, Basic Books, 1974) – however surprising the rights he singles out as fundamental – is also an instance of interactional cosmopolitanism. For institutional cosmopolitanism, see Charles Beitz, *Political Theory and International Relations* (Princeton, Princeton University Press, 1979), part 3; Charles Beitz: 'Cosmopolitan Ideals and National Sentiment'. *Journal of Philosophy* 80 (1983), 591–600; and Pogge, chapter 6.

6 This is done, for example, by John Rawls, who asserts (i) a natural duty to uphold and promote just institutions and also (ii) various other natural duties that do not presuppose shared institutions, such as duties to avoid injury and cruelty, duties to render mutual aid, and a duty to bring about just institutions where none at present exists. Cf. John Rawls, *A Theory of Justice* (Cambridge, Mass., Harvard University Press, 1971), pp. 114f and 334.

7 On the interactional approach, by contrast, any *positive* human rights would impose duties on persons anywhere to give all possible aid and protection in specified cases of need.

8 These two limitations are compatible with the belief that we have a duty to *create* a comprehensive institutional scheme. Thus Kant believed that any persons and groups who cannot avoid influencing one another ought to enter into a juridical state. Cf. Hans Reiss, ed., *Kant's Political Writings* (Cambridge, Cambridge University Press, 1970), p. 73.

9 The second extreme I am here alluding to is consequentialism *in ethics*, i.e. any consequentialist view that applies directly to agents – be it of the ideal or real, of the act, rule, or motive variety. There are also non-interactional variants of consequentialism, such as Bentham's utilitarianism, which applies to institutions.

10 Talk of such a contribution makes implicit reference to alternative feasible global regimes.

11 The supposed moral significance of the distinction between the established and the engendered effects of social institutions is extensively discussed in Pogge, §§ 2–4.

12 Similarly also Rawls's first principle of justice: 'Every person has the same indefeasible claim to a fully adequate scheme of equal basic

liberties, which scheme is compatible with the same scheme of liberties for all' (latest version, unpublished). In both cases the postulated entitlement or claim is clearly second-order.

13 This notion is defined in probabilistic terms, perhaps by taking account of various personal characteristics. Thus it is quite possible that the human right to physical integrity is today fulfilled in the United States for middle-aged whites or suburbanites but not for black youths or inner-city residents.

14 Michael Walzer 'The Distribution of Membership' in Peter Brown and Henry Shue, eds, *Boundaries* (Totowa, Rowman and Littlefield, 1981), p. 1. Cf. the largely identical chapter 2 of Michael Walzer, *Spheres of Justice* (New York, Basic Books, 1983), p. 31.

15 Nozick, *Anarchy*, p. 149.

16 It is quite possible, and not without historical justification, to define sovereignty the way I have defined absolute sovereignty. In that case the expression 'distribution of sovereignty' would be an oxymoron.

17 One promising exception to this is the European Parliament.

18 This includes the sentiments of patriotism, if such there must be. Beitz points out two respects in which patriotic allegiance to political units may be desirable. It supports a sense of shared loyalty ('Cosmopolitan Ideals'. p. 599). And it allows one to see oneself as a significant contributor to a common cultural project: 'Just as we can see ourselves as striving to realize in our own lives various forms of individual perfection, so we can see our countries as striving for various forms of social and communal perfection' ('Cosmopolitan Ideals', p. 600). Neither of these considerations entails that, say, Britain must be the sole object of your patriotic allegiance, rather than some combination of Glasgow, Scotland, Britain, Europe, humankind, and perhaps even such geographically dispersed units as the Anglican Church, the World Trade Union Movement, PEN, or Amnesty International.

19 Many individuals might, of course, identify more with one of their citizenships than with the others. But in a multi-layered scheme such prominent identifications would be less frequent and, most important, would not converge: even if some residents of Glasgow would see themselves as primarily British, others would identify more with Europe, with Scotland, with Glasgow, or with humankind at large.

20 This dogma – prefigured in Aquinas, Dante, Marsilius, and Bodin – is most fully stated in chapters 14, 26 and 29 of Thomas Hobbes, *Leviathan* (Harmondsworth, Penguin, 1981), who also introduces the idea of obligations *in foro interno*. For Kant's statements of it, see Reiss, pp. 75, 81 and 144f. The dogma maintained its hold well into the twentieth century, when it declined together with the Austinian conception of jurisprudence. Cf. Geoffrey Marshall: *Parliamentary Sovereignty and the Commonwealth* (London, Oxford University Press, 1957), part 1; S.I. Benn and R.S. Peters *Social Principles and the Democratic State* (London, Allen and Unwin, 1959), chapters 3 and

12; and Herbert L.A. Hart, *The Concept of Law* (London, Oxford University Press, 1961).
21 Walzer, 'Distribution', p. 10.
22 Ibid., p. 9.
23 Ibid., p. 9.
24 Ibid., p. 9.
25 Ibid., pp. 9–10.
26 Ibid., p. 9.
27 For further discussion of such a reform – backed perhaps by the idea that the world's resources should be owned or controlled by all its inhabitants as equals – see Beitz *Political Theory*, pp. 136–43, and Pogge, pp. 250–2 and 263–5.
28 The qualification 'legitimately' is necessary to rule out claims such as this: 'I should be allowed a vote on the permissibility of homosexuality, in all parts of the world, because the knowledge that homosexual acts are performed anywhere causes me great distress.' I cannot enter a discussion of this proviso here, except to say that the arguments relevant to its specification are by and large analogous to the standard arguments relevant to the specification of Mill's no-harm principle.
29 I understand *opportunity* as being impaired only by (social) *disadvantages* – not by (natural) *handicaps*. This is plausible only on a narrow construal of 'handicap'. Although being black and being female are natural features, they reduce a person's chances to affect political decisions only in certain social settings (in a racist/sexist culture). Such reductions should therefore count as disadvantages. By contrast, those whose lesser ability to participate in public debate is due to their low intelligence are not disadvantaged but handicapped. They do not count as having a less-than-equal opportunity.
   The postulated human right is not a group right. Of course, the inhabitants of a town may appeal to this right to show that it was wrong for the national government, say, to impose some political decision that affects them only. In such a case, the townspeople form a group of those having a grievance. But they do not have a grievance *as a group*. Rather, *each* of them has such a grievance of not having been given her due political weight – just the grievance she would have had, had the decision been made by other townspeople with her excluded.
30 Though not in defence of other procedural or substantive constraints to which the smaller unit may have chosen to commit itself. Compare here the situation in the United States, where federal courts may review whether laws and decisions at the state level accord with superordinate federal requirements, but not whether they accord with superordinate requirements of that state itself.
31 I won't try to be precise about 'reasonable shape'. The idea is to rule out areas with extremely long borders, or borders that divide towns, integrated networks of economic activity, or the like. Perhaps the inhabitants in question should have to be minimally

numerous; but I think the threshold could be quite low. If a tiny border village wants to belong to the neighbouring province, why should it not be allowed to switch?

The contiguity condition needs some relaxing to allow territories consisting of a small number of internally contiguous areas whose access to one another is not controlled by other political units. The United States would satisfy this relaxed condition through secure access among Puerto Rico, Alaska, Hawaii, and the remaining forty-eight contiguous states.

32 What if minority sub-groups are geographically dispersed (like the Serbs in Croatia)? In such cases, there is no attractive way of accommodating those opposed to the formation of the new political unit. My second principle would let the preference of the majority within the relevant territory prevail nevertheless. This is defensible, I think, so long as we can bracket any concern for human rights violations. Where justice is not at stake, it seems reasonable, if legitimate preferences are opposed and some must be frustrated, to let the majority prevail.

33 See Alan Buchanan *Secession* (Boulder, Westview Press, 1991), 114–25, and Thomas W. Pogge, 'Loopholes in Moralities', *Journal of Philosophy* 89 (1992), 79–98, at 88–90.

34 *That* topic is extensively discussed by Buchanan. While he takes the current states system for granted and adjusts his theory of secession accordingly, I am arguing that a more appealing theory of secession would be plausible in the context of a somewhat different global order. I thereby offer one more reason in favour of the latter.

35 For example: as European states will increasingly become subject to global and regional constraints – regarding military might, pollution, exploitation of resources, treatment of citizens, etc. – the importance of whether there is one state (Czechoslovakia) or two states (one Czech, one Slovak) would tend to decline: for the Slovaks, for the Czechs, and for any third parties in the vicinity.

36 Obviously, this story is not meant to reflect the actual situation on the Indian subcontinent.

37 While the precise definition of 'nation' and 'nationality' is not essential to my discussion, I do assume that nationality is not defined entirely in voluntaristic terms (e.g. 'a nation is a group of persons all of whom desire to constitute one political unit of which they are the only members'), in which case the two claims would become trivial. The definition may still contain significant voluntaristic elements, as in Renan's proposal: 'A nation is a grand solidarity constituted by the sentiment of sacrifices which one has made and those one is disposed to make again. It supposes a past . . .' (quoted in Brian Barry, 'Self-government Revisited', in David Miller and Larry Siedentop, eds, *The Nature of Political Theory* (Oxford, Clarendon Press, 1983), p. 136). So long as some non-voluntaristic element is present, at least one of the two claims can get off the ground: those who want to belong together as one

political unit may be prevented from doing so when they lack an appropriate history of solidarity and sacrifices.

38 Avishai Margalit and Joseph Raz, 'National Self-determination', *Journal of Philosophy* 57 (1990), 439–61, at 456.

39 Though one should ask how this claim squares with the history of the United States, in the nineteenth century, say. Those who enjoyed the rights of citizenship were highly heterogeneous in descent and upbringing, and they came as immigrants, through sheer choice. I do not believe these facts significantly reduced the level of solidarity and mutual trust they enjoyed, compared with the levels enjoyed in the major European states of that period. A careful study of this case might well show that people *can* be bound together by a common decision to follow the call of a certain constitution and ideology as well as the promise of opportunities and adventure. If so, this would suggest that what matters for solidarity and mutual trust is the *will* to make a political life together and that such will is possible without unchosen commonalities. This result would hardly be surprising, seeing how easily the closest friendships we form transcend such commonalities of facial features, native language, cultural background, and religious convictions.

40 Margalit and Raz, pp. 443 and 456.

41 For an example, see Brian Barry, 'Do Countries Have Moral Obligations?' in S.M. McMurrin, ed., *The Tanner Lectures on Human Value* II (Salt Lake City: University of Utah Press, 1981), pp. 27–44.

42 Rawls makes this point: 'we want to account for the social values, for the intrinsic good of institutional, community, and associative activities, by a conception of justice that in its theoretical basis is individualistic. For reasons of clarity among others, we do not want to ... suppose that society is an organic whole with a life of its own distinct from and superior to that of all its members in their relations with one another' (*Theory*, p. 264).

43 Michael Walzer *Just and Unjust Wars* (New York Basic Books, 1977), p. 53. Cf. Michael Walzer: 'The Moral Standing of States' in Beitz *et al.*, *International Ethics*, p. 219.

44 Walzer suggests this tack: 'citizens of a sovereign state have a right, in so far as they are to be ravaged and coerced at all, to suffer only at one another's hand' (*Wars*, p. 86).

Chapter 6

Cosmopolitan liberalism and the states system

Charles R. Beitz

The passing of the Cold War has released forces for change in world politics that are quite different from those that animated the Cold War period itself. A resurgence of national and ethnic separatism points towards the dismemberment of states which have survived intact since the settlements of 1945, and in some cases since those of 1919. Simultaneously, we are witnessing the emergence of forms of international collaboration, particularly in the economic realm, in which states surrender to supra-national institutions aspects of authority which have been regarded as ineliminable aspects of sovereignty.

These pressures – for disaggregation, on the one hand, and for consolidation, on the other – are distinct and in some ways contradictory. Yet both are revolutionary in the sense that they represent challenges to structural principles of the inter-national order that characterized most of the twentieth century. My assignment in this chapter is to report on the meaning of cosmopolitan morality as it relates to both of these challenges to the states system as we have known it – those arising from pressures for disaggregation of existing states, and those arising from movements towards confederation.

THE MEANING OF COSMOPOLITANISM

As it comes to us, the notion of *cosmos* refers to the universe or the macrocosm; it is everything there is. A cosmopolitan view-point would presumably be a point of view that corresponded with the cosmos, or, perhaps, one from which everything there is could be seen. The most natural contrast is with the local, the sectional, or the particularistic.

Two essential elements define a point of view as cosmopolitan: it is *inclusive* and *non-perspectival*. By 'inclusive', I mean that a cosmopolitan view encompasses all local points of view. It seeks to see the whole of which these are the parts. By 'non-perspectival', I mean that a cosmopolitan view seeks to see each part of the whole in its true relative size. There is no foreground and background; the proportions of things are accurately represented so that they can be faithfully compared. If local viewpoints can be said to be partial, then a cosmopolitan viewpoint is impartial.

The protean idea of the cosmopolitan occurs in international thought in more than one way. Here, as elsewhere, a cosmopolitan view aspires to see things whole – to regard the world in some sense as one entity. But this is vague, and in trying to be more precise we must distinguish between various different conceptions of the cosmopolitan.

The first and possibly the most familiar conception pertains to the way political institutions should be set up – to the political constitution of the world, so to speak. It holds that the world's political structure should be reshaped so that states and other political units are brought under the authority of supranational agencies of some kind – a 'world government', for example, or perhaps a network of loosely associated regional bodies. Although the details may vary, the distinctive common feature is some ideal of world political organization in which states and state-like units have significantly diminished authority in comparison with the *status quo* and supranational institutions have more.[1] I will call this *institutional* cosmopolitanism.[2]

A second kind of cosmopolitanism concerns itself, not with institutions themselves, but with the basis on which institutions, practices, or courses of action should be justified or criticized.[3] Its crux is the idea that each person is equally a subject of moral concern, or alternatively, that in the justification of choices one must take the prospects of everyone affected equally into account. This kind of cosmopolitanism is the natural offspring of the sort of individualist moral egalitarianism often associated with the Enlightenment: it applies to the whole world the maxim that answers to questions about what we should do, or what institutions we should establish, should be based on an impartial consideration of the claims of each person who would be affected by our choices. This is *moral* (or *ethical*) cosmopolitanism.

This idea has been expressed in more than one ethical tradition in the West, the most prominent being the natural law tradition and the forms of utilitarianism that rose to prominence in the eighteenth and nineteenth centuries. Today, it is a common element in virtually all forms of Western liberalism as well as in most of the plausible ethical doctrines associated with conservatism and social democracy. We are (almost) all cosmopolitans now. This is true even though the implications of moral cosmopolitanism for political institutions beyond the nation-state, and for the nation-state itself, are controversial.

Once again, the inclusive and non-perspectival character of the view are essential. The most important practical reflection of these features is scepticism that the boundaries between separate political entities have any deep moral significance. Moral cosmopolitanism is also sceptical about the intrinsic significance of inter-ethnic, inter-religious, and inter-racial boundaries. This does not mean that boundaries do not matter at all. What moral cosmopolitanism requires is that whatever moral or ethical importance we attribute to them must be explained in terms of the human values they advance as compared with the human values they deny or threaten, for all persons affected. In this respect, as in others, moral cosmopolitanism is best thought of as a kind of sceptical humanism.

Of the institutional and moral forms of the view, moral cosmopolitanism is the more basic. This is true, first of all, in a normative sense: moral cosmopolitanism supplies the most natural foundation for arguments on behalf of cosmopolitan institutions. It is also true in a historical sense: most of those who have advocated world government and similar reforms have been motivated by the more or less clearly articulated notion that global political institutions are the best (or perhaps the only) way to implement global moral concerns.

In spite of these connections, there is no necessary link between moral and institutional cosmopolitanism. Someone who adopts the point of view of moral cosmopolitanism is not necessarily committed to the belief that the world should be reorganized as a unitary or stateless political and legal order. Indeed, it might be argued that a state-based world order is more likely to be justifiable from a point of view that includes everyone – at least under contemporary conditions. (Similarly, one need not adopt the point of view of moral cosmopolitanism to adopt a cosmopolitan view about world political institutions – though it is hard to think of anyone who has defended institutional cosmopolitanism on other than cosmopolitan moral grounds.) Two points follow from this. First, the widely alleged undesirability of world government is not a good reason to reject the ethical aspiration it represents. If advocacy of world government is a mistake, this is more likely because it exhibits political naivety than philosophical error. More importantly, what moral cosmopolitanism requires of political institutions is a complex question – more complex than both the friends and the opponents of cosmopolitan views have sometimes appreciated. As I shall try to illustrate, although there are philosophical dilemmas in the notion of cosmopolitan political ethics, it is the political questions – for example, about the aims and conduct of global political reform – that are more difficult.

HUMAN RIGHTS

Moral cosmopolitanism is not so much the name of a definite moral doctrine as it is a label for a family of such doctrines that share a common view about justification. To move towards a position with definite normative content, some further questions need to be answered about the impartial egalitarianism that defines the cosmopolitan standpoint. The most important of these involve the interpretation of the notion of equality of treatment at its core and the valuation and comparison of alternative outcomes as they impinge on individual circumstances. These are difficult questions in moral theory and, while I cannot avoid presupposing answers to them, I cannot discuss them here.

All plausible versions of cosmopolitanism would probably agree on some key points. The most important is that everyone is entitled to political institutions that satisfy minimum standards of humanity and justice. The meanings of these terms may be contested, but there is a consensus on the central elements: for example, that minimally acceptable institutions should avoid torture, respect personal liberties, and strive to alleviate starvation and other forms of debilitating material deprivation. This is the spirit of the international doctrine of human rights, even though one must agree, as that doctrine has been articulated in the Universal Declaration and the various covenants, that it has grown beyond the idea of a basic minimum.[4]

The doctrine of universal human rights is cosmopolitan in its foundations without being cosmopolitan in its institutional requirements, and in this sense it illustrates the importance of distinguishing between moral and institutional cosmopolitanism. That is, the most natural foundation of human rights doctrine lies in the related cosmopolitan ideas that conceptions of individual well-being are not fundamentally relative to culture or geographical location and that, in the assignment of responsibility for satisfying basic individual needs, national (or cultural or ethnic) boundaries do not necessarily play a limiting role. At the same time, however, human rights doctrine does not prescribe any particular institutions (or set of institutions) for the world as a whole. Instead, it specifies minimum conditions that any institutions should satisfy. Accordingly, human rights doctrine does not rule out the possibility – indeed, it trades on the hope – that its institutional requirements can be satisfied within a political structure containing nation-states more or less as we know them today.

COSMOPOLITAN LIBERALISM AND THE SOVEREIGN STATE

For much of the modern age, sovereignty has been regarded as an essential element of statehood. Without labouring the subject here,[5] it is worth noting that the idea of sovereignty has two faces. Looking inward, it connotes the final authority of the state's institutions over the state's own people; institutions are sovereign if there is no appeal from their decisions. (This conception derives from, but is not the same as, the classical notion of sovereignty as ultimate authority lodged in a single set of hands – the view associated with Bodin and Hobbes, and later, Austin.) Looking outward, it signals the independence of the state from other agencies, whether they are imperial or international in character, within a given sphere. The clearest expression of external sovereignty in international law is found in the principle that a state has the right to exercise exclusive authority or jurisdiction over its territory and population.[6]

Today, it is a commonplace that political developments within and beyond the state have rendered the idea of sovereignty less and less illuminating in characterizing the state's relations with its own people and with other states. Just as the spread of constitutionalism and federalism has compromised the idea that there must be one institutional location at which ultimate legal authority is exercised, so the development of international law has limited and qualified the notion of exclusive domestic jurisdiction. As Stanley Hoffmann wrote many years ago, 'Sovereignty, rather than being a reservoir that is either full or empty, is a divisible nexus of power of which some may be kept, some limited, some lost.'[7] The traditional theory of sovereignty needs to be recognized for what it is (or was): an effort to represent as a timeless truth an important but historically specific feature of the development of the Western nation-state.

Sovereignty, of course, functions not only as a descriptive notion but also as the linchpin of a political ideal of international order. Indeed, there is no inconsistency in admitting that the sovereign state as traditionally conceived is something of an anachronism while holding that its revival – or, more properly, the revival of an international system composed of truly sovereign states – would be a desirable thing. The latter, of course, is an extreme and unusual view, but more moderate versions are common in contemporary international thought. Thus, even though one must recognize the limits of sovereignty as a descriptive concept, the idea may retain its normative force.

Movements for both confederation and disaggregation represent challenges to sovereignty in this normative sense. As background for a closer look at the ethical dimensions of these movements, it may be worthwhile to consider how the value of sovereignty, if any, might be accounted for from a cosmopolitan point of view. What is the special value of sovereignty? Or, to put the operative question more precisely, what is the value of preserving a large area of autonomous domestic jurisdiction for the national state?

A simple answer is that there is no special value.[8] And indeed, this may seem to be the only answer consistent with cosmopolitan morality. Sovereignty might appear to be a particularistic concern – something to care about only because it belongs to one's own country, or because it is a necessary condition of having a country one could care about at all. But a cosmopolitan morality, because it is inclusive and non-perspectival, seems to have no room for such values.

This is superficial. One reason is that unambiguously cosmopolitan values such as international peace may be best served in a system in which there is a convention of respect for the autonomous domestic jurisdiction of states. A familiar argument for a strong prohibition of intervention has this form. People differ about its persuasiveness, both because they differ about the weight of international peace, as compared with other values with which it may compete, and because they differ about the causal question of whether respect for state autonomy generally promotes more than it impedes the quest for peace. I do not want to go into this argument here.[9] I only mean to recall that there is nothing obvious in the idea that cosmopolitan moral commitments are antithetical to a world order based on 'sovereign' (or at least relatively autonomous) states.

There is another reason why the simple answer is superficial, which for our purposes deserves more emphasis. Cosmopolitanism need not be indifferent to particularistic values such as the loyalties and affiliative sentiments characteristic of membership in cultural or national groups. If it is a fact (as normally it is) that membership in a distinct political community has value for the members of that community, then, on a cosmopolitan view, this fact should matter for practical reasoning. The important question is not whether it should matter, but how.

Communitarian values may play two kinds of roles in practical judgment. First, they can lend extra weight to considerations about a community's own welfare relative to those about the welfare of outsiders; at the limit, they can block consideration of the interests of non-members altogether.[10] The effect on practical reasoning is analogous to that of pure time preference. The common notion that compatriots should take priority in foreign policy decision-making is often an instance of this mode of influence.[11]

Alternatively, communitarian values can be treated as inputs to an impartial deliberative process – as values to be weighed and balanced against all the other values at stake in a choice. For example, the fact that an institution like sovereignty might be a necessary condition of a group's having a meaningful common life would be a consideration in evaluating measures that would affect it. This fact would count because we assume that participation in a common life is a legitimate interest of members of the group. But it would not necessarily be determining, because the effect of these measures on the interests of non-members (and on the other interests of members) would also have to be brought into the balance before an overall assessment could be reached.

The inclusive and non-persepectival character of cosmopolitanism pretty clearly rules out the first mode of influence of communitarian values. On a cosmopolitan view, normative reasoning is incomplete if it fails to take account of the interests of everyone affected; and it is distorted if it privileges proximity in space or time for its own sake. However, the second mode of influence, in which communitarian values are treated simply as one set of inputs to the process of moral reasoning, is entirely consistent with a cosmopolitan approach to ethics. In fact, if membership in a flourishing community of a certain kind is a value for people, cosmopolitanism requires us to bring it into account.

Doing so in judgments about the importance of sovereignty may not be easy. First, there is the practical, though hardly insignificant, problem that communal values do not argue for sovereignty in the abstract, but for statehood for certain kinds of groups. Our world may be composed of sovereign states, but one would be badly misled if one regarded most of them, literally, as '*national* states', or as embodiments of coherent political communities. Some states embrace multiple communities and some include parts of communities that are divided among several states. Because political boundaries do not always follow communal boundaries, a legitimate concern for the integrity of communities will not always translate into sympathy for existing political divisions of the world, which means that communitarian concerns may come into conflict with other values that incline people to defend a state-based conception of world order. In other words, communitarianism in international politics need not be a conservative position. The decomposition of what was Yugoslavia, now well advanced, illustrates this all too sharply.

Even if there were no such practical problems about the communitarian account of the value of sovereignty, there would be the following difficulty of principle. A morally plausible communitarianism must always hedge its endorsement of sovereignty. What follows for politics from recognizing that communal attachments can be important for people is that certain kinds of groups may be entitled to political arrangements in which they can regard themselves as substantially self-governing. A more precise formulation of this idea would need to be hedged because any group's entitlement to statehood must, on a cosmopolitan view, be conditional. I turn to the conditions in a moment. For the present, we should simply observe that there is a structural reason why this should be so: since a cosmopolitan view strives to be inclusive, it will never be sufficient to consider only the desires and identifications of a limited group of people. The circumstances of everyone affected must be taken into account. We would be justified in recognizing an entitlement to statehood for a communal group only if doing so was not only best from the point of view of the group but also best overall. As we shall see, this significantly qualifies the responsiveness of cosmopolitanism to communitarian values.

CONFEDERATION AND DISAGGREGATION

In Europe today we witness pressures for both confederation and disaggregation – for combinations of states (and parts of states) and for dismemberment of states. What is the implication of cosmopolitanism for these pressures?

In answering this question, let me take the problem of self-determination as a paradigm. This problem arises when a group within a state moves to secede in order to form a separate and smaller state of its own. The secessionist group claims a right to determine its own political arrangements. The essential question is why, and under what conditions, a group would be entitled to a change in the political organization of the world so that it could govern itself.

The general form of a cosmopolitan account of self-determination would be instrumental. It would hold that a group is entitled to determine its own political arrangements when the prospective gain in respect for the important interests of its members outweighs the cost in respect for the important interests of others.[12] As I have indicated, one important interest is served by membership in a certain kind of group – roughly, one which has a pervasive, common culture and whose members tend to identify themselves with the group. Membership in such a group is usually a source of individual self-respect and identity, and a channel to the aspects of fulfilment that depend on access to cultural opportunities. An account of self-determination based on the interest in membership in a cultural group would be instrumental because it would turn on the hypothesis that the group could not prosper without political independence.[13]

But the interest in membership is not the only value that could be the basis of an instrumental case for self-determination. People's fortunes might be linked to the political independence of their group in other ways than through the flourishing of the group *per se*. For example, members of a group may be subjected to persecution or persistent economic injustice within a larger political framework, and achieving independence may be the only durable means of self-protection. Although a cosmopolitan argument for self-determination will always be instrumental, it may appeal to a variety of values.

A cosmopolitan argument for self-determination will also be conditional; in fact, it will be conditional in two different ways. First, it is enough to show that self-determination would enable members of a group to avoid harm to certain important interests. Because cosmopolitanism is committed to considering the interests of everyone affected, it is essential also to take into account the effects on non-members of a group's exercise of self-determination. Hence, a successful argument depends on showing that self-determination would not impose excessive, unavoidable costs on others – for example, by depriving them of a disproportionate share of natural resources and physical capital.

Second, the consequences of self-determination for members of the group itself need to be considered. It is too often assumed, and particularly by those with cosmopolitan or liberal sympathies, that self-determination is unproblematically a benefit for the communities that achieve it. The history of self-determination in the twentieth century suggests otherwise: it has more often served to legitimate local tyrannies than to foster democratic self-government. There are exceptions and they are important; and, of course, it would be a mistake in any event to think that the future must be like the past. But the unhappy consequences of so many successful movements for self-determination in recent history should at least caution against a too easy acceptance of the view that self-determination is always an unmitigated good for the individual members of the groups that succeed in separating from larger political structures.

I have suggested that, from a cosmopolitan perspective, the case for self-determination must be instrumental and therefore will always be conditional. There is a powerful temptation to take a different view – that the right to self-determination is unconditional rather than conditional because the value of self-government is intrinsic rather than instrumental. In its most extreme, voluntaristic, form this view holds that any set of individuals who identify themselves as a group are entitled to whatever political changes are required to enable them to establish an independent state.

There are many reasons to resist the temptation to take such a view. One is that the consequences for individual security and well-being of accepting and acting on the voluntaristic principle would most likely be very undesirable. A more basic reason for resisting is that the foundations of the view are obscure and, on the most straightforward construction, implausible. Most often, the idea that the value of self-government is intrinsic arises from conceptions of individual liberty by means of a kind of generalization – the right of a group to determine its own political conditions is seen as the expression on the large scale of the right of an individual to determine the course of his or her own life. This, however, invites confusion, both because it encourages an unwarranted enlargement of the scope of the individual liberties that underlie the supposed group right and because it leads one to overlook features peculiar to the large scale that bear on the rights of groups (eg., considerations related to territoriality and the distribution of resources).[14]

Self-determination is the paradigm case of a rearrangement of jurisdictional lines to coincide with ethnic, racial, or other kinds of group boundaries. Most cases of disaggregation (and some of confederation) follow the same pattern: a group presses demands for political rearrangements, basing its demands on the claim that political boundaries should follow the boundaries between social groups. Hence, I believe that the cosmopolitan approach to self-determination provides a good template for imagining a cosmopolitan approach to these other problems involving political rearrangement.

If this is right, then a cosmopolitan argument in favour of disaggregation, and by extension for confederation, would also be instrumental in form. It would hold that political rearrangement is a necessary means of achieving some further goods, and that these goods should weigh more heavily than the harms that the rearrangement would unavoidably bring about. As with self-determination, the fact that a group with a pervasive, common culture cannot flourish in an existing state should be a significant consideration in a cosmopolitan assessment of the value of political rearrangement, but it need not be determining.

Accordingly, a cosmopolitan analysis of confederation or disaggregation will depend heavily on the facts of each case. There are two sets of issues. First, because the case for rearrangement is instrumental, it needs to be shown that the change in question really would help to achieve certain important goods. For example, it will not always be true – and it is certainly not *necessarily* true – that the communal interests of members of a group would be enhanced if the group were separated off from other groups and provided with greater communal autonomy. Second, as with self-determination, it is essential to consider the impact of political rearrangement on everyone involved – not only the groups whose interests recommend it, but also anyone else who would be affected. Neither set of issues can be resolved in the abstract; both require attention to the facts of individual cases.

It is worth emphasizing the second set of issues. When a group separates from a larger entity to form a state of its own, its action has implications not only for members of the secessionist group but also for those left behind. The division of control over territory that normally accompanies the separation of peoples can mean depriving one group of access to natural and social wealth on which its way of life depends. When the deprivation is severe, or when its result is to reduce a group's standard of living to an unacceptable level, there is plainly cause for concern. The point is not that the prospect of deprivation should trump the pressure for self-rule; only that this prospect should matter in any plausible account of the moral issues associated with disaggregation. As with self-determination, so with forms of political reorganization designed to establish political autonomy for inclusive groups: a cosmopolitan cannot help being cautious and wanting to know more.

These comments have been relatively abstract, and a reader would be justified in wondering if there is any practical consequence. I noted earlier that moral cosmopolitanism and institutional cosmopolitanism are conceptually independent. They may, however, be contingently connected; and I believe that the questions of self-determination and disaggregation may illustrate one respect in which this is true. As we have seen, on a cosmopolitan view, whether a group is entitled to separate from a larger entity to form its own state, and if so on what terms, is a complicated question that is not easily resolved by resort to simple principles. It is, instead, a classic case for informed political judgment, and for some form of creative mediation as well. The likelihood of continuing pressures for political realignment makes it all the more urgent that we invent international institutions with the capacity and legitimacy to play constructive roles in accommodating these pressures.

To conclude, I noted earlier that it is best to think of moral cosmopolitanism as a kind of sceptical humanism. It aims to be a basis for criticism of the *status quo* and for evaluation of alternatives. It is not committed to any definite view about the ideally best structure of world order. For this reason, its indeterminacy about confederation, self-determination, and disaggregation should not come as a surprise. The skeletal version of moral cosmopolitanism that I have been presupposing insists that political arrangements and rearrangements be evaluated impartially in terms of their impact on the basic human rights and interests of all those affected. It does not prejudge the outcome of this evaluation.

NOTES

An earlier version of this chapter was prepared for the Ethikon Institute Conference on 'The Restructuring of Political and Economic Systems', Berlin, 4–6 January, 1991. I am grateful to the participants, and particularly to Chris Brown and Terry Nardin, for comments.

1 Perhaps the most familiar modern version of this kind of cosmopolitanism is the form of world federalism proposed by Grenville Clark and Louis Sohn in *World Peace Through World Law*, 3rd ed. (Cambridge, Harvard University Press, 1966).
2 We lack a comprehensive history of cosmopolitan thought about world institutions. See Walter Schiffer, *The Legal Community of Mankind* (New York, Columbia University Press, 1954).

3 In Chapter 5 above, Thomas Pogge distinguishes two varieties of what I call moral cosmopolitanism: one that applies to interpersonal transactions and one that applies to institutions and practices. The distinction is important, and I agree that a plausible cosmopolitanism should take institutions, not interpersonal transactions, as its primary subjects. I do not believe, however, that the distinction affects the basic structure of the view, which is my concern here.

4 For important discussions of the idea of a moral minimum, see Henry Shue, *Basic Rights: Subsistence, Affluence, and American Foreign Policy* (Princeton, Princeton University Press, 1980), and Amartya Sen, 'The Standard of Living', *The Tanner Lectures on Human Values* vol.7 (Cambridge, Cambridge University Press, 1987).

5 I have laboured it elsewhere. See my chapter, 'Sovereignty and Morality in International Affairs', in *Political Theory Today*, ed. David Held (Cambridge, Polity Press, 1991). See also F.H. Hinsley, *Sovereignty*, 2nd ed. (Cambridge, Cambridge University Press, 1986).

6 Ian Brownlie, *Principles of Public International Law*, 3rd, ed. (Oxford, Clarendon Press, 1979), 287–93.

7 Stanley Hoffman, *The State of War* (New York, Praeger, 1965), 120.

8 This and the following paragraphs are based on my chapter, 'Sovereignty and Morality in International Affairs'.

9 I criticized it at some length in *Political Theory and International Relations* (Princeton, Princeton University Press, 1979), part 2.

10 See Andrew Oldenquist, 'Loyalties', *Journal of Philosophy* 79, 4 (April 1982), 174–7.

11 The phrase is from Shue, *Basic Rights*, 132.

12 I took a view of this general form in *Political Theory and International Relations*, part 2.

13 My earlier account was insufficiently attentive to the role of communal goods in the argument for self-determination. More satisfactory in this respect is Avishai Margalit and Joseph Raz, 'Self-determination', *Journal of Philosophy* 87, 9 (September 1990), 448, 450–1.

14 As Raz and Margalit suggest, a more careful construction of this position carries us back to an instrumental argument like that discussed earlier. Ibid., 452–3.

Chapter 7

The nation-state: a modest defence

David Miller

In this chapter I shall attempt to set out the case that can be made on behalf of the nation-state, by which I mean a political institution exercising most of the powers and rights that we traditionally associate with 'sovereignty' over a group of people who share a common national identity. I describe the defence as a modest one partly in order to distance myself from bellicose forms of nationalism, but partly also because I do not believe that such an institution is always and everywhere a possibility. Even in the modern world there are circumstances in which the creation or maintenance of a nation-state is not a realistic possibility. But one may concede that, and also believe that in the majority of cases the nation-state represents the best form of government for contemporary societies and should be supported on those grounds.

Such a belief is so widely shared by ordinary citizens and politicians that it might seem scarcely worth defending. But theorists have been more sceptical, and among political philosophers especially there is a reluctance to see in the nation-state much more than a tiresome impediment to an ethically ordered world. Nation-states appear to be arbitrary sub divisions of the human race; once formed they breed a moral insularity which subverts the obligations of justice and humanity owed to one another by men and women simply *qua* members of the human species; and of course their rivalries and power struggles are immensely destructive. Ethical approaches to this phenomenon proceed along one or other of two tracks.[1] The more idealistic approach advocates replacing the nation-state with a world government capable of dispensing global justice. The more realistic concedes that the nation-state is likely to be with us for the foreseeable future and looks for ways of placing moral limits on its behaviour, through various schemes of international co-operation. Neither approach concedes that the nation-state may itself be an institution that can be defended on ethical grounds.

My defence of the nation-state proceeds in four parts. First I shall say something about what distinguishes nationality and national identity from other kinds of affiliations and allegiances, because failure to do this often results in puzzlement as to why *nations* should have any sort of priority in the setting of political boundaries. Second I shall set out the positive case for national self-determination, for giving nations the right through political institutions to decide their own destinies. Third I shall examine the limits to national self-determination, asking in particular whether self-determination must amount to full-blown sovereignty and to what extent the obligations owed to other political communities restrict the rights of any one community to determine its future. Finally I shall look at cases where nation and state do not at present coincide and ask what the principles laid out in the first three parts of the chapter imply for the issue of secession.

I

Let us begin, then, by looking more closely at national identities themselves, and in particular ask what differentiates them from other identities – individual or communal – that people may have. What does it mean to think of oneself as belonging to a national community? [2]

The first point to note, and it has been noted by most of those who have thought seriously about the subject, is that national communities are constituted by belief: a nationality exists when its members believe that it does. It is not a question of a group of people sharing some common attribute such as race or language. These features do not of themselves make nations, and only become important in so far as a particular nationality takes as one of its defining features that its members speak French or have black skins. This becomes clear as soon as one looks at the candidates that have been put forward as objective criteria of nationhood, as Ernest Renan did in his famous lecture on the subject:[3] to every criterion that has been pro-

posed there are clear empirical counter-examples. The conclusion one quickly reaches is that a nation is in Renan's
memorable phrase 'a daily plebiscite'; its existence depends on
a shared belief that its members belong together, and a shared
wish to continue their life in common. So in asserting a national
identity, I assume that my beliefs and commitments are mirrored
by those who I take to share that identity, and of course I may be
wrong about this. In itself this does not distinguish nationality
from other kinds of human relationship that depend on
reciprocal belief.

The second feature of nationality is that it is an identity that
embodies historical continuity. Nations stretch backwards into
the past, and indeed in most cases their origins are conveniently
lost in the mists of time. In the course of this history various
significant events have occurred, and we can identify with the
actual people who acted at those moments, reappropriating
their deeds as our own. Often these events involve military
victories and defeats. Renan thinks that the latter matter more
than the former: I am uncertain whether this is really so, but the
point he connects to it is a good one: 'sorrows have greater
value than victories; for they impose duties and demand
common effort'. The historic national community is a community of obligation. Because our forebears have toiled and
spilt their blood to build and defend the nation, we who are
born into it inherit an obligation to continue their work, which
we discharge partly towards our contemporaries and partly
towards our descendants. The historical community stretches
forward into the future too. This then means that when we
speak of the nation as an ethical community we have in mind
not merely the kind of community that exists between a group
of contemporaries who practise mutual aid among themselves
and which would dissolve at the point at which that practice
ceased; but a community which, because it stretches back and
forward across the generations, is not one that the present
generation can renounce. Here we begin to see something of
the depth of national communities which may not be shared by
other more immediate forms of association.

The third distinguishing aspect of national identity is that it is
an active identity. Nations are communities that do things
together, take decisions, achieve results, and so forth. Of course
this cannot be literally so: we rely on proxies who are seen as

embodying the national will: statesmen, soldiers, sportsmen, etc. But this means that the link between past and future that I noted a moment ago is not merely a causal link. The nation becomes what it does by the decisions that it takes – some of which we may now regard as thoroughly bad, a cause of national shame. Whether this active identity is a valuable aspect of nationality, or whether as some critics would allege merely a damaging fantasy, it clearly does mark out nations from other kinds of grouping, for instance churches or religious sects whose identity is essentially a passive one in so far as the church is seen as responding to the promptings of God. The group's purpose is not to do or decide things, but to interpret as best it can the messages and commands of an external source.

The fourth aspect of a national identity is that it connects a group of people with a particular geographical place, and here again there is a clear contrast with most other group identities that people affirm, such as ethnic or religious identities. These often have sacred sites or places of origin, but it is not an essential part of having the identity that you should permanently occupy that place. If you are a good Muslim you should make a pilgrimage to Mecca at least once, but you need not set up house there. A nation, in contrast, must have a homeland. This may of course be a source of great difficulties, a point I shall return to later, but it also helps to explain why a national community must be (in aspiration if not yet in fact) a political community. We have seen already that nations are groups that act; we see now that their actions must include that of controlling a chunk of the earth's surface. This leads us directly forward to the argument of the next section.

Finally, it is essential to national identity that the people who compose the nation are believed to share certain traits that mark them off from other peoples. It is incompatible with nationality to think of the members of the nation as people who merely happen to have been thrown together in one place and forced to share a common fate, in the way that the occupants of a lifeboat, say, have been accidentally thrown together. National divisions must be conceived as natural ones; they must correspond to what are taken to be real differences between peoples. This need not, fortunately, imply racism or the idea that the group is constituted by biological descent. The common traits can be cultural in character: they can consist in shared values, shared tastes or sensibilities. So immigration need not pose problems, provided only that the immigrants take on the essential elements of national character. Indeed it has proved possible in some instances to regard immigration as itself a formative experience, calling forth qualities of resourcefulness and mutual aid that then define the national character – I am thinking of the settler cultures of the New World such as the American and the Australian.

These five elements together – a community constituted by mutual belief, extended in history, active in character, connected with a particular territory, and thought to be marked off from other communities by its members' distinct traits – serve to distinguish nationality from other collective sources of personal identity. They are also a source of difficulty: it seems unavoidable that national identities will involve interpretations of both past and present that are to a greater or lesser extent imaginary or mythical. I have argued elsewhere that this imaginary element in national identity need not be a fatal weakness; indeed it may be a source of strength, since it allows national identities to be reworked to meet new political challenges.[4] I shall not repeat these arguments here, but take it for granted in what follows that nationality is inherently no less defensible than other shared forms of identity. My next task is to assess the case for building political institutions on this foundation.

II

It is possible to look at the relationship between nation and state in two different ways. On the one hand, the state may be more viable as an institution – it may be less prone to disruption, less obliged to govern its subject by brute force – if the society it regulates is a national community. On the other hand, nations may be more successful as communities if they are self-governing; they may be better able to satisfy the collective aspirations of their members. Both perspectives are necessary if we are to feel the full force of the argument for national self-determination. Let us consider them in turn.

From the first perspective, the key element is recognition of the role played by trust in a viable political community.[5] Much state activity involves the furthering of goals which cannot be achieved without the voluntary co-operation of citizens. For this activity to be successful, the citizens must trust the state, and they must trust one another to comply with what the state demands of them. Let me give a couple of examples. One concerns the provision of public goods such as a clean and healthy environment. The state can do certain things directly – it can fine polluters, for instance – but to achieve real results it must also very often rely on education and exhortation. Since adhering to the rules the state proposes will usually have costs, each person must be confident that the others will generally comply – and this involves mutual trust.[6] For another example, consider state grants or concessions to particular groups within the population, say financial support to an industry hard hit by changes in the terms of trade, or special funding for local authorities with inner-city problems. These dispensations are made on the understanding that other sections of the community would qualify for similar favourable treatment in the event that they too faced new and unforeseen difficulties. Such a practice cannot evolve if each sectional group jealously guards its own interests and insists that each dispensation should be strictly egalitarian. Again what is needed is mutual confidence which allows you to sanction aid to group G on this occasion with the assurance that group G would give you its reciprocal support when it was your turn to ask for help in the future.

Now a state might attempt to diminish its reliance on mutual trust by restricting its role to that of a nightwatchman, merely presiding over a market economy in which outcomes depended on separate individuals pursuing their own interests. Yet, quite apart from the question whether this is a viable possibility for a state in the late twentieth century, certain kinds of trust are still required to support the ground rules of a market: individuals must have confidence in one another to deal fairly, to keep contracts, and to refrain from using their industrial or financial muscle to oblige the state to intervene in the market on their behalf.[7]

I take it as virtually self-evident that ties of community are an important source of such trust between individuals who are not personally known to one another and who are in no position directly to monitor one another's behaviour. A shared identity carries with it a shared loyalty, and this increases confidence that others will reciprocate one's own co-operative behaviour. So far this does not discriminate between the various com-

munities that a person may belong to. The importance of
national communities here is simply that they are encompassing
communities which aspire to draw in everyone who inhabits a
particular territory. This aspiration is not always achievable, and
this gives rise to the problems we shall consider in section IV.
But in contrast, say, to religious communities, which tend to
define themselves exclusively, requiring adherence to a particular creed, nationality becomes a self-defeating idea if it is
not accommodating. If we wish to be a self-determining nation,
and if we share our territory with people who are like us in
respects A, B and C but unlike us in respect D, it would be
perverse to insist on D as a condition of membership. In real
cases groups may choose the perverse option; but where a
common national identity already exists, it can always potentially at least be extended to embrace all those who inhabit a
geographical area. Where this comes about it provides the basis
for mutual trust. Again, to say this is not to say that an adequate
degree of trust will in fact materialize – this is a perennial
problem in modern states – but at least the basis is there. In
states lacking a common national identity – say, states which are
little more than umbrella organizations holding together two or
three national or ethnic groups – politics at best takes the form
of group bargaining and compromise and at worst degenerate
into a struggle for domination. Trust may exist within the
groups, but not across them.[8]

I should make it clear that the argument I have sketched – a
viable political community requires mutual trust, trust depends
on communal ties, and nationality is uniquely appropriate here
as a form of common identity – could not serve as a reason for
adopting a national identity. A national identity depends upon
a pre-reflective sense that one belongs within a certain historic
group, and it would be absurd to propose to the subjects of state
X that, because things would go better for them if they adopted
a shared national identity, they should therefore conjure one
up. The purpose of the argument is primarily to show that state
boundaries should as far as possible coincide with national
boundaries, and secondarily to advocate the reshaping of
national identities – not wholesale, but bit by bit – so that
previously excluded groups are included. It is absurd to say,
'Fellow citizens, we are all subjects of the same state, so let us
forge a common national identity'; but it is not absurd to say,

'Fellow citizens, we share a common identity by virtue of A, B, and C, but D (religion, say) divides us. Let us work together to form a new identity within which D no longer matters.' Given that national identities are always in flux, and are consciously reshaped to some degree through public discussion, it is by no means untoward to take account of political realities when engaged in that reshaping.

So far we have been examining the link between nation and state from the first perspective. Now let us ask why it is valuable from a national point of view for the nation to be politically self-determining. The answer is implicit in the characterization of nationality given in section I. The demand for political self-determination flows directly from the other aspects of national identity, so directly that it is common to build such a demand into the very definition of a nation. Partly this has to do with protecting the common culture that the nation embodies.[9] Each person has an interest in preserving this culture, and to the extent that this requires political support – say, through education, through subsidies for the forms of expression that are central to the culture, and so forth – also has an interest in national self-determination. Although a foreign power might act in a tolerant spirit and allow the local culture to continue, the only secure way of protecting it is to have representatives of the national community making the decisions.

Partly also national self-determination is valuable because it corresponds to the idea of nations as active communities. As I argued earlier, nations cannot 'act' in the most literal sense. Their actions are the actions of their representatives, and, although these actions need not be confined to the political sphere, it is that sphere which provides the main instances. What matters is that the people who make political decisions should be seen as acting on behalf of the national community, embodying its principles and aspirations. The most obvious way to ensure this is to have an elected government, and this explains the often observed connection between nationalist and democratic ideas, but unelected leaders may also on occasion be able to stand symbolically for the nation, provided they have the appropriate background, affirm the right beliefs, etc.[10] So the argument here does not presuppose that everyone wants to be an active participant in politics. It is possible to have a sense that you are part of a self-determining community vicariously, provided you can identify yourself with the people who are actually making the political decisions.

So we have two powerful arguments for making the boundaries of nations and states coincide: the state is likely to be better able to achieve its goals where its subjects form an encompassing community, and conversely national communities are better able to preserve their culture and fulfil their aspirations where they have control of the political machinery in the relevant area. Although we cannot yet say that these arguments are decisive, since we have yet to examine possible counter-claims, they do seem to amount to a strong *prima facie* case on behalf of the nation-state.

III

I turn now to the question whether national self-determination requires a state with unlimited rights of sovereignty, and the related question of the obligations owed by one state to another, since if such obligations exist, they must immediately set bounds to what any one state can legitimately do in pursuit of its national interests. I take it for granted here that a defensible form of nationalism must include the requirement that each nation in asserting its claim for self-determination must respect the equal claims of others who may be affected by its actions. But before we come to the external limits to sovereignty that this requirement may impose, let us ask whether national self-determination demands full rights of sovereignty in the first place.

This question is difficult to answer in the abstract because the idea of national self-determination is somewhat indeterminate. First, nothing very substantial has been or can be said about the components of nationality itself. The set of characteristics which members of any particular nation see as setting themselves off from others will vary from case to case – in some instances language will play a key role, in others religion, and so forth. So we cannot say, for example, that the state must retain its sovereignty over questions of language but not over other cultural issues. Second, we cannot tell in advance which particular features of the social landscape will come to assume importance as markers of national identity. To take a current example, there is at present some debate in Britain (paralleled elsewhere in Europe) about the conditions under which it would be acceptable for a European currency to replace British currency. Some of those involved would wish to argue that the British people have a right not to have the European currency imposed on them without their consent (the implication would be that a referendum would be needed to legitimize the replacement of the pound by the ecu). Now we might think this was an absurd argument; no one could claim a constitutive attachment to a particular currency. But I do not believe that one can rule out *a priori* the possibility that having one's own currency could come to symbolise national self-determination. In this area, a collective belief that something is essential to national identity comes very close to making it so. Of course, the fact that national sentiments can depend in this way on beliefs which from some outside vantage point may seem patently absurd is part of what many political philosophers find distasteful about the whole idea. But once you combine the principle of national self-determination with the proposition that what counts for the purposes of national identity is what the nation in question takes to be essential to that identity, it follows that no prior limits can be set to claims for national sovereignty.

It does *not* follow, on the other hand, that nation-states must retain complete sovereignty over their internal affairs; there may be good reasons for transferring powers of decision upwards to confederal bodies, for instance. But such transfers must in the last resort be regarded as provisional, in the sense that nations have a residual claim to reappropriate rights of decision where they believe that vital national interests are at stake. So there is a presumption here in favour of national sovereignty together with recognition that in practice many decisions may sensibly be delegated upwards.

Perhaps this perspective can better be understood by seeing what it would mean in a few key policy areas. Take national defence first. In a post-imperial world, there seems no reason why defence should not be managed at a supranational level, say in a European context by a collective European defence force. Each nation has an interest in its security, plainly, but no particular interest in that security being provided by its own armed forces as opposed to a collective European force. This is in line with the traditional idea of a confederation, which was that of an alliance for mutual defence and security but with the domestic policy of each member state being left in its own hands.[11] The essential element of state sovereignty here is simply that each state has the right to ensure that it is adequately defended; but this is consistent with entering into a binding pact with others to provide that defence.

At the other end of the spectrum lies social policy. Social policy is both the vehicle whereby common ideals can be expressed and the means whereby a society consciously reproduces its own identity. The latter aspect is particularly clear if one takes the example of public education. What is taught in schools and how it is taught reflects the priorities of a particular culture and tends to instil those priorities in the rising generation. (This should not be understood in a narrowly political sense: consider the case of Japanese children spending long hours learning precisely how to paint the characters of the Japanese alphabet.) As to the former aspect, consider how social policy is bound to reflect common definitions of need which nonetheless may vary substantially across cultures. For these reasons, there is a clear case for national governments retaining direct control over the making of social policy.

Somewhere between these extremes lies economic policy. Or perhaps one should rather say that if we look at economic policy-making there are strong arguments pulling in both directions. In favour of transmitting decision-making powers upward to a supranational authority is the fact that decisions on economic policy taken at state level often appear to place the participants in a prisoners' dilemma. For instance, assuming the standard arguments for free trade as the means of bringing about an efficient global division of labour, each country taken separately may have an incentive to implement policies to protect its own industry, but if all do economic performance falls to a level below that achievable under free trade. This would suggest removing the power to protect from the nation-state, either through some binding pact or through the creation of an international authority. Against this, however, is the fact that economic policy and social policy are intertwined. Consider unemployment levels, which are not only part of an economic equation but have a profound impact on the general character of a society. Or consider agricultural policy, often now regarded as merely a tug-of-war between the vested interests of farmers and the interests of consumers inside and outside the country in question, but also of course a major determinant of the physical shape of the landscape in that country – something in which its members have a very different sort of interest. Most radically, think of a state which for reasons of social justice makes a significant departure from standard capitalist patterns of industry – implementing, say, a scheme of workers' ownership. It is plausible to assume that such an initiative would need sheltering to some degree from international competition, at least in the sense that capital investment could not be left to the free play of market forces.[12] All these examples suggest that the members of a nation-state have a legitimate interest in keeping control of economic policy-making and tell against any transfer of rights in this area in an upwards direction.

I do not know how to escape from this quandary, which indeed seems to me one of the major dilemmas facing the human species at present. The case for a stable international order is strong, not least from the point of view of the poorer nations who need above all open access to world markets and commodity prices that are reasonably predictable in the long term. But who could gainsay the right of a nation to set off along its own path and to set in place the protective institutions that would be needed to make that path feasible – say a nation which decided to adopt a radical environmental policy? The dilemma can perhaps be resolved formally by saying that states should be prepared to make conditional transfers of decision-making rights in this area, while always retaining the ultimate right to opt out of whatever collective arrangements are made. But this does not give much practical guidance.[13]

It is clear at any rate that from the perspective I am developing, there is no reason to make a fetish of national sovereignty. The questions to ask will always be: how much does it matter from the point of view of preserving our national identity and exercising self-determination on questions that concern us that we should retain such-and-such rights of decision? On the other hand, are there real gains to be made by vesting them in a higher authority? Let us turn then to the second issue to be addressed in this section, namely the limits placed by *others'* claims to national self-determination on *our* exercise of rights of sovereignty.

Suppose we have to deal with states embodying claims to

national self-determination that are *prima facie* as good as our own, and suppose that these states are not engaged in acts of aggression or other unjust acts against their neighbours: what obligations ought we to acknowledge towards them? Four obligations of a fairly familiar sort appear to flow directly from the ideas I have so far defended, together with a fifth that is somewhat more problematic. These obligations are as follows:

1 The duty to abstain from materially harming another state either by acts of military aggression or by physical damage in the form, say, of pollution that is exported across national boundaries. States, that is, have a right to territorial integrity which holds against any sort of physical encroachment by other states.

2 The duty not to exploit states which are one-sidedly vulnerable to your actions. This would include the case where a powerful state threatens the use of military force against a weaker state in order to force the latter to change its policies in some respect, but also the more difficult case of economic dependence; that is, the case where state A can devastate the economy of state B by, for instance, suddenly demanding the repayment of a loan or by altering the terms of trade in some commodity that plays a vital role in B's economy. Here there is an obligation to refrain from using the power that the international situation provides you with, however the power imbalance has arisen.[14]

3 The duty to comply with whatever international agreements have been reached, including of course treaties to establish confederal institutions. We need to distinguish what it is right or advisable to undertake by way of international co-operation, and the obligations a state has once it has entered into co-operative arrangements, whether wisely or not. Here I am pointing to the latter; I shall shortly consider what we should say in cases where obligations arising from agreements clash with basic rights of national self-determination.

4 Obligations of reciprocity, arising from practices of mutual aid whereby states come to one another's assistance in moments of need. These obligations arise whether or not there is a formal agreement to provide aid. (If there is a formal agreement, then duties in category 3 plainly supervene on duties in category 4.) An example of what I have in

mind is the emerging convention whereby countries struck by earthquake, flood or certain kinds of famine can count on assistance from other countries in the form of emergency relief. What we have here is essentially an informal scheme of mutual insurance whereby the costs of unforeseeable natural disasters are shared among countries roughly on the basis of each country's ability to contribute to the scheme. Given such a scheme, each country has an obligation to contribute as the occasion arises.[15]

5 More problematically, obligations to ensure the fair distribution of natural resources. The argument for such obligations is fairly straightforward: the current convention whereby states are deemed to have sovereign rights over all the resources found in their territory appears to give resource-rich states a quite arbitrary advantage over resource-poor states. The principle of fairness that it seems natural to adopt here is that each inhabitant of the world has an equal basic entitlement to natural resources, so that states should be entitled to resources in proportion to the number of their citizens.[16] But against this must be set two major complicating factors. First, the value placed on resources by the particular society that has them may depart considerably from their 'global value' as measured (presumably) by the amount they would fetch in an international free market. Second, resources are not simply there for the taking: they need to be discovered, extracted and made serviceable for human use, all at some cost.[17] So there is no straightforward answer to the question how many resources any particular society has. (Do you have coal if it is prohibitively expensive to mine, or if you do not have the technology to extract it?) The apparent simplicity of 'global equality of resources' dissolves in the face of these problems.[18] Yet in a crude way we can still say that there are resource-based inequalities between nations that are plainly unfair – the most obvious being the gulf between those with substantial reserves of oil and those without – and that call for some degree of rectification. So let us say that states which are clearly resource-rich have an obligation to help out states that are clearly resource-poor and economically hard-up as a result. I do not think one can be any more precise here.

Taking this view of the obligations of international distributive justice, one ends up allowing nation-states a considerable degree of freedom to pursue their own social goals. The picture here is very different from that arrived at by Charles Beitz, for instance, who argues for applying the Rawlsian difference principle internationally.[19] It would follow from the Beitz position that states would have an obligation to accept outside economic management in the event that this proved to be the most effective way of raising the living standards of the worst-off members of the poorer states. In the present picture there is no general obligation to help poorer states. (Equally of course there is no *prohibition* on a state deciding to do this on humanitarian or other grounds.) Obligations 1 and 2 amount essentially to a requirement on states that they should respect the autonomy of other states. Obligations 4 and 5 demand redistribution under the specific circumstances cited, not as a matter of general policy. So it would be consistent with these obligations for states to have the freedom to pursue very different economic policies, some growth-oriented, others aiming primarily at resource conservation, and so forth.

Obligation 3 requires a brief comment. My general line has been that nation-states have an underlying right to decide for themselves which rights of sovereignty they should continue to exercise and which rights they can sensibly transfer to some confederal or global agency. What, then, if a state undertakes a binding commitment to transfer a right which it later finds that it wants to reappropriate? (Assume that the confederation is unwilling to restore this element of sovereignty to the state in question.) If the right is vital to continuing national self-determination, then it may be taken back at the expense of the pact. One reason for this is that in international society circumstances may change to the point where the reasons for entering the pact no longer obtain – suppose for instance that at t an alliance is formed to provide security against a common aggressor, but at t_1 this threat has receded, while state S alone faces some new external threat; in these circumstances S seems justified in withdrawing its forces from the alliance if this is necessary to deter the new threat.[20] I do not think this argument is destructive of the very idea of confederation. Confederations are sustained by a sense of mutual advantage and by the sanctions, economic and otherwise, that members can impose on those who default for no good reason. To allow states the residual right to recover their rights of sovereignty in the event that they judge it vital to do so does not imply that the pact has no binding force.

In this section of the argument I have simply presented a set of claims about what international justice consists in with the intention of showing how far they may limit national rights of sovereignty. A critic might argue that, although the picture painted may square with the idea of national self-determination from which I began, there is no reason to think that this is the right place to start. If one wants to understand international justice, should one not begin with the claims of human beings merely as such, and only at a later point in the argument look to see how (if at all) the rights and obligations of states can be fitted in? This question raises basic issues of ethics which cannot be dealt with here.[21] Let me merely state that I believe the onus is on people who adopt the latter approach – starting with global principles such as the difference principle espoused by Beitz – to show that the conditions of international society are such as to make this approach the appropriate one. If one is a Rawlsian, for instance, do the circumstances of justice as Rawls understands them obtain across national boundaries?[22]

IV

Up to now I have been looking at cases in which the boundaries of nation and state coincide, and asking what the principle of national self-determination implies for the issues of sovereignty and confederation. In this final part of the chapter I look at the more difficult problems that arise when the above condition fails to hold; in particular at the question when a national community at present incorporated in a multinational state is justified in demanding secession. An objection that is frequently raised to the principle of self-determination itself is that it cannot possibly be applied to the real world: there is no feasible way of drawing state boundaries that would simultaneously meet all demands for national self-determination. Thus serious attempts to apply the principle would inevitably lead to political chaos.[23]

We can better appreciate the guidance which the principle of national self-determination offers on this question by contrasting it with liberal answers to the same question. It is interesting to observe that liberalism can generate two radically opposed doctrines on the issue of state boundaries.[24] One view subordinates the issue entirely to considerations of individual rights and justice. The state has certain obligations to its citizens, and provided it discharges these obligations in a satisfactory manner, no group can be justified in claiming a right to secede; conversely if the existing state is falling down in this respect, exploiting or oppressing the members of one particular group, and it seems likely that the group could protect its rights more effectively by setting up its own state, then it would be justified in so doing. In classical liberal theory the rights in question were conceived in roughly Lockean terms as life, liberty and property, and this view underlay Lord Acton's defence of the multinational state, recently echoed by Kedourie.[25] Modern liberals take a more expansive view of the state's responsibilities, but they may approach the questions of boundaries and secession in the same way: a group's wish to secede has little or no force unless it can establish that it is receiving unfair treatment from existing political institutions. Birch, for example, lays down four conditions under which a regional group might justifiably claim to secede from a larger state: the prior forcible inclusion of the region within the state; serious failure to protect the rights and security of the inhabitants; failure to safeguard the legitimate political and economic interests of the region; reneging on an explicit or implicit bargain designed to safeguard the essential interests of the region (e.g. by constitutional change).[26] With the possible exception of the first, these conditions reflect an underlying view that each citizen has a range of basic interests which he may expect the state to promote, and it is only in the event that he finds himself in a group which is systematically getting a raw deal that he has a *prima facie* case for opting out. Demands that spring from a wish to preserve cultural identity are quite specifically excluded.[27]

The most sophisticated version of this liberal view can allow culture to stand as one of the things in which individuals may have an interest, along with their liberties and material possessions.[28] This might converge in practice with the nationalist view in circumstances where the policies of the state threaten a minority with cultural destruction. Even here, however, there is a difference: the liberal view may acknowledge a person's interest in having *some* culture, but it finds no particular value in a group's wish to preserve and develop the particular culture into which it was born. In an illuminating metaphor, Buchanan portrays minority groups as clinging to a 'sinking ship' (and demanding timbers and pumps to keep it afloat) when they have the chance to 'board another, more seaworthy cultural vessel'.[29] Why insist on clinging to your old, competitively unsuccessful, culture when nearby there is an alternative to which you can assimilate? To which the nationalist will reply, first, that cultures, unlike ships, are not vessels to be boarded and abandoned at will, but conditions for a person's having an identity and being able to make choices in the first place; second, that the culture in question may not be defective in itself, but merely unable to flourish without the protection that political self-determination can provide.

The first liberal view says in effect that the wishes of a minority community should not count unless it can show that it is not getting a fair deal out of the existing state. The second view makes the wishes themselves paramount. This view also has a Lockean pedigree, for it holds that the boundaries of states should as far as possible depend on individual consent. The practical implication is that any sub-community in any state has the right to vote to secede from that state, provided that it is in turn willing to allow any sub-sub-community the equivalent right, and so on indefinitely.[30] The principle for fixing the borders of states is simply the will of the majority in any territorial area.

This may seem to be nothing more than a recipe for anarchy. Beran attempts to ward off such a charge by laying down a number of conditions that a would-be state should meet if it is to make good its claim to secession: for instance, it must not create an enclave within the existing state, it must not occupy an area which is culturally, economically, or militarily essential, etc. But the effect of this is to substitute a charge of arbitrariness for a charge of anarchy. Consider, for instance, a case like that of Nagorny Karabakh, within which the dominant group is Armenian. Since it would constitute an enclave, it cannot on the principles we are considering vote to secede from Azerbaijan. But it might well turn out to be the case (I haven't checked) that by including a suitably defined corridor strip connecting

Nagorny Karabakh with Armenia a territory could be created in which there was still a majority for acceding to Armenia. Could the inhabitants of the corridor strip then subsequently vote to rejoin Azerbaijan? If they could not, they would seem the arbitrary victims of Armenian cunning in defining the area for the first vote. If they could, then presumably, by the no-enclaves principle, their vote would have the effect of nullifying the first vote and forcing Nagorny Karabakh back into Azerbaijan; in which case the cycle would begin again (always presuming that, contrary to all evidence, the people of that region were prepared to abide by the outcome of majority voting).

Quite apart from the difficulties created by Beran's additional conditions, the original principle that the majority will should determine borders has little intuitive appeal. Consider a state whose population is made up of 60 per cent cultural group A and 40 per cent cultural group B. It includes a small region within which 60 per cent of the population belongs to B and 40 per cent to A (but these populations are closely mingled, so no further division is possible). Suppose the majority in the region vote to secede: we would then have a small state with 60 per cent Bs and 40 per cent As, and a large state with, let's say, 65 per cent As and 35 per cent Bs. Even from the point of view of consent, is this a real gain? The 60 per cent in Small are presumably happy with the outcome, and the 40 per cent are presumably unhappy. On the other hand, the 35 per cent of Bs left in Big may be less happy with the new arrangement than the old (perhaps with the secession of Small important cultural centres are taken away from them, etc.). My point is that it is an illusion to think that, by (repeatedly) applying the majority principle, everyone can end up in the state they would ideally like to be in. Instead, from any redrawing of boundaries there are almost certain to be both gainers and losers, and to assess a proposed redrawing we need to estimate the gains and losses, not merely count heads.

In contrast to these liberal views, the principle of nationality focuses attention neither on material interests nor on individual preferences for boundaries, but on the political conditions for securing national identities. The principle tells us to further the cause of national self-determination wherever possible. So, to begin with, existing boundaries are put in question only where a *nationality* is currently denied self-determination.

This is to be distinguished from the situation of an ethnic group which feels it is currently denied rights of cultural expression, or treated unfairly in some other way, and for which the remedy is reform of existing arrangements and policies within the state. Admittedly the distinction between nationality and ethnicity is not a hard-and-fast one: historically national identities have very often developed out of prior ethnic identities,[31] and where a cohesive ethnic group finds that its legitimate claims are ignored by the state, a natural response is for the group to begin to think of itself as an alternative nationality. But equally such a development is not pre-ordained. It is quite possible for a state to include several groups with separate ethnic identities but a common national identity: Switzerland and the United States are both in their different ways good examples of this. How is this achieved? It is partly a question of ensuring that each ethnic group gets fair material treatment by the state, equal opportunities in economic life, etc. The more difficult issue is the relationship between the group's self-understanding and the nation's. What matters here is on the one hand to purge the national identity of elements that are repugnant to a particular minority group – for instance, by having two or more official languages, or by distancing the institutions of the state from the practice of a particular religion. On the other hand, the state has a legitimate interest in moulding ethnic identities so that they become more closely compatible with the national identity; for instance, it may properly insist that schools teach a national curriculum alongside the subjects required by the culture of the ethnic group.[32] The relationship between ethnicity and nationality is not a static one. They may diverge, but equally through mutual accommodation they may be brought back together.

Once we are clear about the distinction between ethnicity and nationality, we can avoid the error of thinking that the principle of national self-determination requires every cultural group to have its own state. The problem of secession arises only in cases where an established state houses two or more groups with distinct and irreconcilable national identities – irreconcilable because, for instance, each takes a different religion to be constitutive of its identity, or because each includes as part of its historical self-understanding its separation from, and antagonism towards, the other. Let us take it, then, that group G is a group in this position, having national claims that cannot be accommodated by the state in which it is at present incorporated (S). Its representatives demand that G should secede from S and establish its own state. In order to recognize this as a valid demand, we need to be persuaded that what is contemplated is indeed the formation of a nation-state. One condition has already been met: we have established that group G has a national identity that is distinct from that of the remaining members of S, and that cannot be adequately protected and expressed by granting G a limited measure of political autonomy within S. But there is also a second condition: we would need to be convinced that the territory demanded by G did not contain minorities whose own identities were radically incompatible with that of G, so that rather than creating a viable nation-state the secession of G would simply reproduce a multinational arrangement on a smaller scale. Again, this is not simply a matter of the strength of feeling expressed by those minorities. They might resist simply because in the G state they would lose certain privileges they are able to enjoy in the S state. But if they could show, for instance, that their ethnic identity was reasonably secure under S but would be seriously threatened under G, then this would be a good reason for blocking G's demand.[33]

Finally, some consideration must be given to those minority groups who would be left in S when G seceded, particularly members of G who do not live in the seceding territory. The effect of secession might be to destroy a *modus vivendi* and leave these groups in a very weak position. With most of G gone, the majority group in S might no longer feel the need to conciliate G politically, or to attempt to define a common identity in which G might be included. It is, for instance, a strong argument against the secession of Quebec from the Canadian federation that it would effectively destroy the double-sided identity that Canada has laboured to achieve, and leave French-speaking communities in other states isolated and politically helpless. If national self-determination is our governing principle, we need to ask whether the realization of that principle through the creation of the G state is not matched by its weakening in the rump of S.

The principle also suggests a number of further practical conditions that need to be fulfilled before a sub-community could justifiably claim to form its own state.[34] The new state would need to be viable in the sense that it could secure itself territorially; at the same time it should not radically weaken the parent state by, for instance, making it extremely difficult to defend militarily. Another condition sometimes suggested, for instance by Sidgwick, is that the seceding territory should not contain the state's entire supply of some important natural resource.[35] Here I think the following point needs to be made: if a sub-community wishes to secede simply on the grounds that it could do better for itself by hogging all of the resource in question, then by the criterion I am proposing its claim must fail. On the other hand, if its claim to national independence is essentially a good one, then it should not be blocked by the fact that the resource would go with it; not even if the current demand for independence is to some degree fuelled by that perception.[36] As noted in section III, all that it seems realistic to impose in relation to natural resources is a rather general obligation on resource-rich countries to help out countries in economic hardship caused by lack of resources. It was morally arbitrary that state S originally had the resource in question; so members of S have no real complaint against the seceding G that they are taking the resource with them, unless this would leave S itself in the category of breadline states.

If we put the various conditions for justifiable secession together, we can see that the principle of national self-determination is very far from licensing a separatist free-for-all. We can also see that there are cases in which no redrawing of boundaries could implement the principle fully, and we find ourselves in the area of second-best solutions in which the best that can be hoped for is a relatively open regime that allows each community in a given territory some means of political expression (a form of consociational democracy, for instance). In the longer term, we may look towards the building of a new national identity which allows the groups in question to take their place as distinct ethnic groups with a common over-arching loyalty. But we need to be clear that nationality is not the only principle that is at stake in this area. Although I have been resisting cosmopolitan attempts to deal with the issues of sovereignty and state borders entirely in terms of universal principles such as individual rights, individual consent and distributive justice, I should be the first to concede that trade-offs have to be made. The case for the nation-state is not that it spontaneously satisfies all the political ideals we might want to espouse, but that it uniquely embodies a distinct value that has no less a claim on us than these others.

NOTES

1 This is illustrated by the exchange between Kai Nielsen ('World Government, Security, and Global Justice') and Thomas Pogge ('Moral Progress') in S. Luper-Foy, ed., *Problems of International Justice* (Boulder, Westview Press, 1988).

2 The following paragraphs are adapted from my chapter 'In Defence of Nationality'.

3 E. Renan, 'What is a Nation?' in A. Zimmern, ed., *Modern Political Doctrines* (London, Oxford University Press, 1939).

4 See D. Miller, 'The Ethical Significance of Nationality', *Ethics* 98 (1987–8), 647–62; D. Miller, *Market, State and Community* (Oxford, Clarendon Press, 1989), chapter 10; Miller, 'In Defence of Nationality'.

5 This is also stressed in B. Barry, 'Self-government Revisited' in D. Miller and L. Siedentop, eds, *The Nature of Political Theory* (Oxford, Clarendon Press, 1983), reprinted in B. Barry, *Democracy, Power and Justice* (Oxford, Clarendon Press, 1989).

6 I mean this to be a necessary condition for co-operation with the policy, not a sufficient condition; after all, each individual, or each enterprise, will usually have self-interested reasons for defection. My point is that agents will often be prepared to co-operate with policies, in situations where doing so has costs that may put them at a competitive disadvantage unless others co-operate too, *provided* they expect reciprocal co-operation.

7 It may be true, however, that a lesser degree of trust is required to support a nightwatchman state. I have argued elsewhere that redistributive policies of the kind favoured by socialists are likely to demand a considerable degree of social solidarity if they are to win popular consent, and for that reason socialists should be more strongly committed than classical liberals to the nation-state as a institution that can make such solidarity politically effective. See 'In what Sense must Socialism be Communitarian?', *Social Philosophy and Policy* 6 (1988–9), 51–73.

8 I have emphasized the role of nationality in creating trust among the members of large, anonymous societies, but one might also refer to Gellner's argument that industrial societies, if they are to function effectively, require their members to share a high culture transmitted by a common education system, and must therefore organize themselves politically along nationalist lines. See E. Gellner, *Nations and Nationalism* (Oxford, Blackwell, 1983). These two arguments strike me as complementary rather than competitive. Both stress the role played by nationality under specifically modern social conditions.

9 On this aspect see especially A. Margalit and J. Raz, 'National Self-

determination', *Journal of Philosophy*, 87 (1990), 439–61, and Barry, 'Self-government Revisited'.

10 The strengths and weaknesses of this second claim have been sensitively discussed in the context of decolonization by J. Plamenatz, *On Alien Rule and Self-government* (London, Longmans, 1960).

11 See the historical analysis in M. Forsyth, *Unions of States: the Theory and Practice of Confederation* (Leicester, Leicester University Press, 1981), esp. chapters 2–3.

12 For the reasons why this is so, see my 'Market Neutrality and the Failure of Co-operatives', *British Journal of Political Science* 11 (1981), 309–29, and *Market, State, and Community*, chapter 3.

13 What a nation does in practice will no doubt depend on how closely its policies are seen to be aligned with those of the international authority in question. To take a local example, the parties in Britain have performed a small pirouette on the question of Britain's relations with the EEC. For most of the post-war period, the Labour Party, and especially its left wing, has been deeply suspicious of the EEC as a capitalist club, membership of which would seriously inhibit the implementation of socialist policies in Britain. Over the last decade, however, the position has been reversed: Labour has come to see the EEC as a haven of social democracy, whereas the Thatcherite right believes that economic union would prevent the carrying out in Britain of genuine free market policies. At one moment the left is 'nationalist', at another moment the right. I am sure that many other examples of this phenomenon could easily be found.

14 The best analysis of the general principle at stake here is R. Goodin, *Protecting the Vulnerable* (Chicago, University of Chicago Press, 1985).

15 We may expect to see such schemes extended in the future, particularly in response to the impact of large-scale environmental change, where it is likely to be difficult to see in advance how particular countries will be affected. Uncertainty about the future allows such schemes to embrace a certain amount of redistribution between countries in practice, although it is not in their underlying logic that they should be redistributive.

16 For this argument see B. Barry, 'Humanity and Justice in Global Perspective' in *Democracy, Power and Justice*. Barry, however, pulls back from the extremely radical implications of attempting to implement this principle directly in favour of taxes on GDP and on mineral extraction.

17 The extreme view here is that of Israel Kirzner, who argues that in the morally relevant sense, the person who discovers a resource also creates it. 'What no one thought worthy of taking, was something valueless; economically – and morally – speaking, it did not exist. My discovery of the natural resource, my realizing its potential value, has meant that I have brought it into existence.' I. Kirzner, *Discovery, Capitalism, and Distributive Justice* (Oxford, Blackwell,

1989), 155. I do not wish to endorse this view, but to steer a mid-course between it and the manna-from-heaven view which sees natural resources as simply lying available for use in production.

18 Equality of resources is in any case an ideal fraught with difficulties, as I have argued in 'Equality' in G.M.K. Hunt, ed., *Philosophy and Politics* (Cambridge, Cambridge University Press, 1990). Trying to apply it on a global as opposed to a societal basis merely adds to these.

19 C. Beitz, *Political Theory and International Relations* (Princeton, Princeton University Press, 1979), Part III.

20 International lawyers have addressed the general question of when states are justified in renouncing treaties because of radically changed circumstances. The doctrine of *clausula rebus sic stantibus* has been read as holding that a treaty ceases to be binding when a 'vital change of circumstances' has occurred subsequently to its enactment: see J.L. Brierly, *The Law of Nations*, 6th ed. (Oxford, Clarendon Press, 1963), chapter 7. Brierly himself argues that the doctrine should be taken to mean that 'the obligation of a treaty comes to an end if an event happens which the parties *intended*, or which we are justified in presuming they would have intended, should put an end to it (p. 338). This narrower interpretation would apply to the example given in the text, but not to cases where a state reclaims a right of sovereignty because it has since come to believe that the right is vital to national self-determination.

21 I have said something about it in 'The Ethical Significance of Nationality'; the opposite view is developed by R.E. Goodin, 'What is so Special about our Fellow Countrymen?, and by H. Shue, 'Mediating Duties' in the same volume of *Ethics*, 98 (1987–8), 663–86 and 687–704 respectively.

22 For scepticism about this, see Barry, 'Humanity and Justice'.

23 This charge runs throughout E. Kedourie, *Nationalism* (London, Hutchinson, 1966). It is succinctly stated by Gellner, *Nationalism*, 2 (though the remainder of Gellner's book is a powerful attempt to show why the drive to national self-determination is endemic to industrial societies, and for that reason the political problems it brings with it are inescapable).

24 See also here Barry, 'Self-government Revisited', 126–30.

25 Lord Acton, 'Nationality' in *The History of Freedom and other Essays*, ed. J.N. Figgis (London, Macmillan, 1907); Kedourie, *Nationalism*.

26 See A.H. Birch, 'Another Liberal Theory of Secession', *Political Studies* 32 (1984), 596–602; A.H. Birch, *Nationalism and National Integration* (London, Unwin Hyman, 1989), chapter 6.

27 See the concluding page of Birch's article; in *Nationalism* he describes those who argue for self-determination simply on cultural grounds as 'romantics'.

28 See, for instance, A. Buchanan, *Secession* (Boulder, Westview Press, 1991) which sets out what is essentially a liberal view with considerable sophistication. Buchanan makes it clear, however, that he regards arguments for secession based on cultural claims as far

weaker than those alleging 'discriminatory redistribution' of material resources by the existing state.

29 Ibid., 54–5.
30 This position is spelled out clearly in H. Beran, 'A Liberal Theory of Secession', *Political Studies* 32 (1984), 21–31; see also H. Beran, 'More Theory of Secession: A Response to Birch', *Political Studies* 36 (1988), 316–23.
31 See A.D. Smith, *The Ethnic Origins of Nations* (Oxford, Blackwell, 1986).
32 On this topic see further *Market, State and Community*, chapter 11.
33 If G can make out a good case for leaving S in terms of its own identity, but the minorities within G's territory also have a good case against the creation of a G state, then the nationality criterion is plainly indeterminate in application. This is the current situation in Ireland, which represents the case where the G state has been formed. The Protestant majority in Northern Ireland had and still has a good case for separation from a Catholic-dominated Irish Republic, whereas the Catholic minority in the North can reasonably claim that their identity has not been respected in the Protestant state. Until there is movement on one side or the other (and the election of a liberal President in Eire is an unexpected and hopeful sign), neither solution – separation or union – can be preferred on grounds of nationality alone.
34 Some of these correspond to the conditions that Beran proposes in his liberal theory of secession; however I believe that they make better sense from a nationalist perspective than from the perspective of individual consent. Why, for instance, should one insist from the latter perspective that the seceding group should be 'sufficiently large to assume the basic responsibilities of an independent state' (Beran, 'A Liberal Theory', 30)? If a group agrees to set up a political unit that then turns out not to be viable because, for instance, it cannot defend itself adequately, why should that matter if individual consent is our watchword? To prohibit secession on those grounds would be like prohibiting people from marrying when we know they are unsuited to one another, or prohibiting people from setting up business enterprises which we think are too small to compete effectively in the market. On the other hand, if our criterion is the furthering of national self-determination, then it is relevant to ask whether a secessionist group has any prospect of being genuinely self-determining, or whether it is inevitably going to be the puppet of some large neighbouring state.
35 H. Sidgwick, *The Elements of Politics*, 2nd ed. (London, Macmillan, 1897), 228
36 I am thinking, for instance, of Scottish nationalism, where it has frequently been remarked that there is a correlation between the strength of nationalist feeling and the prospect of extracting substantial quantities of oil from what would become Scottish territorial waters.

Chapter 8

The ethics of political restructuring in Europe
The perspective of constitutive theory

Chris Brown

Political restructuring has become a major concern of the post-Cold War era. The collapse of Soviet power in Eastern and Central Europe has seen the re-emergence, or, in some cases, creation *ab initio*, of independent, sovereign, nation-states in that region, and a similar process is now occurring in the republics which once made up the USSR.[1] In Western Europe, partly in response to these changes, especially the emergence of a reunified Germany, the movement towards greater integration which seemed stalled in the early 1980s is now gathering momentum. All told, many political structures and institutions which seemed to be more or less unchangeable a decade ago are now being put in question, their continuing existence no longer a matter simply of inertia, but something that requires a positive defence.

These comments, of course, merely skate across the surface of these momentous changes, but even so it is possible to discern the outlines of a new rift between East and West which may be coming to take the place of the former division between communist and capitalist societies. Whereas in Western Europe the movement of events is clearly in the direction of integration, confederation and an 'ever closer Union', to use the slightly mysterious words of the European Community's Maastricht Treaty of December 1991, in Central and Eastern Europe the trend is clearly in the other direction. The national wars being fought over the corpse of the Yugoslav Republic, secessionist movements in the Czechoslovak republic and, most of all, the disintegration of the Soviet empire into its component republics and their apparent unwillingness to form amongst themselves more than the most tenuous of arrangements for future co-operation all seem to suggest a different direction of change from that prevailing in the West.

What to a political theorist is particularly interesting about this new divide is that it seems, on the surface, to contradict another widely perceived feature of the post-Cold War era, namely the hegemony of the West in the realm of ideas. It is not necessary to subscribe to the (melo)dramatic 'End of History' thesis outlined in a much-maligned but apparently little-read article of Francis Fukuyama in order to recognize this hegemony.[2] It is perfectly clear that ideological contestation between East and West has not ended in some sort of eclectic compromise, or elusive 'middle' or 'third' way – it was at least in part because of his search for this chimera that President Gorbachov was rejected by the Russian people. Instead, the possession of liberal democratic institutions – political and economic – modelled on those of the West has become the *sine qua non* of respectability in the new Eastern and Central European states; such institutions are widely seen in these societies not as pragmatic responses to particular circumstances (circumstances which may in fact not exist in some of these lands) but as part of the 'normality', a revealing locution, which the experiment of communism attempted to ignore, with disastrous consequences. The hegemony of liberalism – widely defined – could hardly be more convincingly demonstrated.

This hegemony, so obvious in the case of the internal institutions of the new political systems, seems singularly absent when it comes to the question of national boundaries and the restructured political geography of Eastern and Central Europe. This is not simply a question of disregarding the trend towards integration and federalism; more basically, it involves a rejection of the cosmopolitan predispositions characteristic of a great deal of modern liberalism – described elsewhere in this volume by Charles Beitz, Onora O'Neill and Thomas Pogge. Oversimplifying somewhat, the stress that most versions of modern liberalism place on individualism is generally seen to imply a high degree of scepticism towards the claims of the nation-state, and a willingness to treat this institution as of essentially second-order importance. This does not seem to be the way that the peoples of East and Central Europe see things; those who *do* see things in this way – often the intellectual 'dissidents' of the old order – have on the whole not done well at the ballot boxes. On the whole an uncompromising belief in the value of the nation-state seems characteristic of the new republics, in spite of the obvious problems this belief throws up, and the apparent benefits of federation or confederation.

Why should this statism be so dominant? It may be that there are uncomplicated and pragmatic answers to this question. One of the features of contemporary politics in Central and Eastern Europe is a wholesale rejection of the legacy of communism, a rejection which, unfortunately, refuses to discriminate; any values promoted under the old regime, including cosmopolitan internationalism, are suspect; any values denigrated, such as bourgeois nationalism, are regarded with favour. This is a tendency which will, presumably, become less important as time passes. Perhaps more to the point is the oft-repeated proposition that nationalism is *functional* for societies facing the sort of transformation required of the successor states of the old Soviet empire.

These societies are faced with the task of reintroducing private property and market forces after their effective absence for periods of half to three-quarters of a century – or, in some cases, of introducing these institutions for the first time – and, moreover, this task will have to be performed in the context of an economic disaster of the first order. Widespread immiser-ation is more or less inevitable in the short to medium run, and social strife if not outright anarchy is a distinct possibility – as is the re-emergence of authoritarian government as a way of coping with these disorders. In these circumstances the higher the degree of fellow feeling and solidarity in the community the better, and given the proven ineffectiveness of socialist accounts of solidarity – for the time being at least – it is understandable that the claims of an alternative, national focus will come to the forefront. There is nothing new here; classic accounts of nationalism as an ideology of mobilization from writers such as Gellner and Nairn tell the same basic story, namely the need to draw upon the resouces of a, possibly imaginary, communal past in order to deal with the, very real, dangers of the present and near future.[3] The felt need to 'catch up' and the awareness of economic and political vunerability promote a tendency to stress the values of the nation and of national self-deter-mination, and an unwillingness to sacrifice sovereignty in a context in which so much else is having to be abandoned.

This is clearly a powerful theory, and one which ties in with a communitarian defence of the nation-state on Millian grounds, exemplified in this book by David Miller's chapter. The more developed fellow feeling is within the community, the easier it is for the community to engage in projects which a purely instrumental approach to membership of a state could not support – projects, for example, which involve redistribution of income or the elimination of privilege. Liberal democratic political institutions require for their survival at least minimal levels of consent, and it is easier to achieve this minimum level of consent from the rich and powerful if a sense of community with the poor and underprivileged is present than if it is not – although still not easy. Whether at the service of democratic socialism or of democratic 'modernization' the functional value of nationalism is not difficult to identify.

From this perspective it can be seen that the commitment to the nation in Central and Eastern Europe, the unwillingness to integrate, and, indeed, the tendencies towards disintegration amongst these states are not simply to be dismissed as a perverse or irrationalist response to the new conditions – even if some manifestations of these tendencies can reasonably be described in this way. However, this functionalist account of the strength of nationalism still leaves the new societies in an intellectually subordinate position – perhaps not atavistic, but still 'backward' by comparison with their West European neighbours whose integration corresponds to a higher level of political and social development, a level which, perhaps with the aid of nationalism as a short-term expediency, the new states will eventually reach. Western confederalism shows the path to the future; adherence to the nation, however understandable, is a short-to-medium-run expedient which will have to be overcome in the long run if the societies of Central and Eastern Europe are to join the mainstream of history.

In this chapter it will be argued that this way of seeing things is more or less inevitable unless the underlying assumptions of liberal cosmopolitanism are challenged. The presuppositions of liberal individualism *do* tend towards cosmopolitan approaches or to a purely pragmatic and correspondingly modest defence of the nation-state, but – and this is the main theme of this chapter – another account of the nature of individuals does not lead in this direction. This account, given classic form by

Rousseau, the English idealists and, pre-eminently, Hegel, stresses the role of communities in *constituting* individuals and thus refuses to grant a privileged position to the latter as opposed to the former.[4] Constitutive theory does not provide instant criteria by which to evaluate the politics of integration and disintegration, federalism and confederalism, but it does offer the promise of an approach to these topics which takes the claims of the nation-state seriously.

CONSTITUTIVE THEORY V. LIBERAL INDIVIDUALISM

A characteristic feature of most liberal accounts of the relationship between individuals and the state is that the latter is deemed to exist in order to solve problems that the former on their own cannot handle, or could only deal with sub-optimally. There are many different versions of this story. Classic social contract theory envisaged individuals contracting with each other (Hobbes), or a ruler (Locke) in order to avoid anarchy; a Kantian version of the contract stressed the need to create a context in which moral choice is possible; a modern political realist, Robert Gilpin, writes of the state providing public goods and solving the 'free-rider' problem, while Rawlsians and other modern contractarians emphasise the need to agree upon principles which will determine the just distribution of the proceeds of social co-operation.[5] Whatever the version, the state is a secondary institution; probably necessary, clearly unavoidable in practice, but secondary in importance to the interests, needs and wills of the individuals who have created it or who live within its jurisdiction – and thus, in principle, a malleable, plastic institution, open to reconstruction whenever its particular forms seem no longer to meet individual needs.

For this family of theories to make sense it is necessary to be able to imagine what pre-social individuals might be like. For the early contract theorists this did not present a real problem. In Book I of *Leviathan*, Hobbes derives human psychology from first principles on mechanistic lines, while Locke's contractors are free-born Englishmen before as well as after creating the state. For Kant individuality is presupposed; all rational beings are capable of making synthetic *a priori* judgments and are subject to the Categorical Imperative by virtue of their rationality. Modern liberal theory is less sure that a rich, 'thick' account of individuality can be reached in this way; instead a 'thin' individuality is offered, most famously by Rawls's account of individuals meeting pre-socially under the 'veil of ignorance', unaware of their sex, race, age, class or intelligence level, knowing only that there are certain 'primary goods' they value, more of which can be produced if they agree upon principles of distribution than otherwise.

A common feature of all constitutive theories of individuality is the belief that none of these accounts of individuals existing pre-socially makes sense. Human beings have always lived in groups of one sort or another and it makes no sense at all to think of individuality as something that can be divorced from this universal experience. Aristotle saw this millennia ago – 'the individual, when isolated, is not self-sufficing' and 'he who is unable to live in society, or has no need because he is sufficient for himself, must be either a beast or a god'.[6] This does not deny the notion of individuality; the point is that individuals are constituted by their social contexts – what it means to be an individual is determined socially. What it *does* deny is the universalism of liberal accounts of individuality. Human beings live in different kinds of groups and these different kinds of groups create different kinds of individuals. There is no such thing as an ahistorical human nature.

Tracy Strong summarizes this communitarian position as '"We" has priority over "I" in contrast to the liberal "I" has priority over "We"' but this is to misstate the case somewhat, or, rather, to use liberal language which makes a clear *a priori* distinction between 'We' and 'I' to describe a position which regards such a distinction as something to be made rather than to be presupposed.[7]

In the constitutive account of individuality, politics and the state play a more important role than in liberal accounts; political structures are unavoidably part of the social context which creates individuals. The kind of political system that exists will be part of the process that determines the kind of individuals who make up the society, and, conversely, the nature of these individuals will impose limits upon the kind of political system that will be viable. Political regimes cannot simply be chosen in accordance with some kind of ahistorical calculus which identifies those political forms which, for ex-ample, best guarantee some set of political rights. The political practices of a society are part of the ways in which individuals are constituted and cannot simply be disregarded in order to achieve some optimum political order – or, if they are so disregarded, the outcome is unlikely to be good. The lack of 'fit' between the nature of individuals and the nature of the political system will lead to permanent crisis. Individuals created by the political practices of one system will not be able effectively to work within the practices of another – as will be argued below, this position can be seen in operation in the problems faced by some of the successor states of the USSR.

However, before moving to the practical application of these ideas it is necessary to pay a bit more attention to the politics implied by the position outlined in the last paragraph. In particular, it may seem on the face of it that the implications of this position are profoundly conservative. If only republicans can make republics work, and if only republics can create republicans, then it would seem to follow that no new republic can be created – a position first recognized by Rousseau, one of the most profound of constitutive theorists, but also one of the most pessimistic. He came to believe that all the existing states of Europe were hopelessly corrupted, and that only in an uncorrupted land – rather implausibly he nominated Corsica as a possibility – would the republic outlined in *Du Contract Social* be foundable.[8]

The same kind of thinking can be found in the work of a number of modern relativists. 'What has to be accepted, the given, is – one could say – "forms of life",' writes Wittgenstein at the end of *Philosophical Investigations,* and Peter Winch's extended meditation on this thought – *The Idea of a Social Science –* is an account of how it is not possible to find a cross-cultural vantage point from which members of one society can judge the practices of another.[9] Communities generate meaning and social practices can only make sense within a 'form of life' – the politics of this relativism are clear; it leads to a modern version of Rousseau's position, but without the value-laden language of corruption. A similar process of reasoning can be found in the work of Richard Rorty, who variously describes himself as a 'liberal ironist' or 'postmodern bourgeois liberal'.[10] What this means is that he feels able to celebrate the values of liberal society, to praise and defend the practices of bourgeois liberalism, while simultaneously accepting both that these practices are ungrounded and that they have no purchase on societies constituted differently. There are no non-relativist reasons for asserting that one set of practices is better than another.

To move beyond this position it is necessary to find a way of refusing to accept Wittgenstein's position that 'forms of life' are a given – and thus introduce a dynamic of change – while at the same time continuing to deny the possibility that this dynamic could employ the idea of an ahistorical pre-social individual as a reference point. This may seem akin to squaring the circle, and it may be that in the end it must be conceded that there is no way of performing the task, but one great thinker claimed to be able to do so, and his claim deserves the most serious attention. Hegel rejected Kantian and Lockean accounts of pre-social individuals combining to form the state but he also rejected Rousseau's account of the way in which the inevitable corruption induced by civilization would shut off the possibility of change and reform. To present Hegel's thought in his own terms would be beyond the scope of this chapter, but it can be rearranged and re-presented as a story about the development of human individuality and the relationship between this development and the development of social and political systems.[11]

Hegel's basic point about human beings is that in order for a full human individual to emerge three different kinds of ethical institution must be present. An ethical family must provide the context within which a human being can begin to develop personality and a sense of security in the world. However, the ethical family is based on unconditional love, and this can only be the starting point in the development of individuality. To become an individual involves making one's own way in the world, earning a living, cutting free from an institution based on love and operating in a context where one is responsible for one's own projects and will be judged on the basis of one's own achievements. This is civil society – the sphere of private property and the market, but also of the political and adminis-trative institutions that enable these economic institutions to flourish by, for example, guaranteeing property rights and adjudicating disputes.

Up to this point many liberals would be happy to go along with the argument even if they would not put things quite in these terms. But Hegel goes further. Civil society leaves individuals in a state of contestation, striving against one another and experiencing the law as an external force; this is not satisfactory. The fully rounded human individual should not have to experience constraint as external, or other individuals as opponents. Laws must be internalized and others experienced as fellow citizens. The role of the rational, ethical, state – based on the rule of law and the separation of powers – is to perform this task.[12]

Full individuality is achievable only when all these institutions are present. Hegel believed that by the beginning of the nineteenth century this condition had been fulfilled, not in the sense that all states were now rational – an obvious absurdity – but in so far as all the elements needed to create each of these institutions were now present. History had reached the point at which the fully free individual could now be constituted. In the past this had not been the case – instead the history of previous societies should be understood developmentally, as the slow emergence of the components which would eventually coalesce in the modern state. The practices of previous societies could not provide the freedom available to all offered by the modern state. These practices – forms of life, perhaps we could say – worked in their own terms and were incorrigible in those terms, but they can now be seen as inferior to those characteristic of our own societies. In the case, for example, of Classical Greece the practices of the *polis* could provide, at best, an unreflective freedom for some – the citizens – and thus were clearly inferior to the practices of the modern ethical state, which could provide reflective freedom for all.

This is not a comparison that could make any sense to an Athenian of the age of Pericles, who would have been bound by the ethical practices of his time and place. However, Hegel does see a dynamic behind change which overcomes the apparent relativism of this position. The ideas that lie behind societies prior to the modern state impose limits on the development of free individuality, and eventually these limits will become intolerable and unsustainable, thus forcing the pace of change. This phenomenon is often marked by the emergence of 'world-historical' individuals who – recognizing the limits of their society – challenge them, and usually suffer as a result, Socrates being the obvious Athenian example. This is the dynamic of history – not, as in the Marxist version, a material contradiction brought about by the full development of a mode of production, which is a strange, indeed metaphysical, notion, but a contradiction that occurs where contradictions do occur, in the realm of ideas. One society succeeds another in sequence, each adding something to the development of the idea of human freedom, until all the components are present – at which point further development is no longer possible.

Although presented in simple terms here this is a complex theory and one that has ramifications which go much deeper than any short essay could investigate. Hegel's ideas rest upon the overcoming of oppositions. His concept of the individual entails as rich an account of freedom as any offered by liberalism, but unlike in liberal thought the free individual is not seen in opposition to state and society. The state is the central ethical institution of modern society, whose claims as against the individual are total yet whose forms are constitutional and limited, circumscribed within the rule of law. He offers an historicist account of rationality and 'forms of life' but also the possibility of making judgments which are not simply Rorty-esque expressions of ironic preference – and the need to make such judgments is the point of this long excursus into political philosphy: only thus can current issues of political restructuring be placed into context.

However, before taking this step back to relevance, there are two points about Hegelian thought which need to be addressed. First, it should be stressed that although Hegel's thought can quite easily be turned into the basis for a defence of whatever *status quo* there may be – a task he himself achieved in the preface to *Philosphy of Right* – it can equally be turned into the basis for a radical critique of the existing order. All the elements exist to enable the rational state to be created, yet it has not happened. A 'left' Hegelian will use the gap between the actual and the possible as the basis for a critique of the existing order. There is nothing inevitably 'right-wing' about Hegel's thought, nor are his criticisms of liberal individualism incompatible with support for liberal political institutions.

A second point is more important. Hegel's thought has been presented here in terms that he would not have accepted. His own account of the emergence of freedom is in terms of the coming to self-awareness of *Geist*, and he does seem to have believed that 'mind' (or 'spirit') is not simply a word that we use as a convenient shorthand for something else but a real entity, indeed the entity that gives reality to everything else. Since this is a claim that it is difficult to take seriously – at least, few people nowadays seem to be able to do so – we are faced with the choice of either (perhaps regretfully) rejecting Hegel's work out of hand or, in the strategy employed here, presenting a 'demythologized' version of his ideas. Obviously the contention here is that such a version works, but readers should be aware of the difficulties.

POLITICAL RESTRUCTURING: STATE AND NATION

Liberal, cosmopolitan, approaches to political restructuring are well developed, but the application of these ideas does not lead to the development of a clear and unambiguous position – and, in any event, the actors involved in this process of reconstruction do not describe what they are doing in cosmopolitan terms, preferring instead the more traditional language of state- and nation-building. Can constitutive (neo-Hegelian) approaches to the relationship between state and individual provide a better guide to the process of political reconstruction, a more clearly defined set of answers to the questions this process is generating? The short answer is, probably not – but what it *can* do is provide a better way of posing these problems, a reason why sometimes answers will necessarily be indeterminate, and an account of recent events which comes closer to the experiences of the participants than non-constitutive theories can offer.

A good starting point here is to look more closely at the notions of 'state' and 'nation' as they pertain to current debates – such an examination will reveal the limits of the neo-Hegelian approach, after which the more positive contribution it can make will come through more clearly. Constitutive theory is resolutely communitarian and, in effect, this means statist. The state is not simply a problem-solving mechanism, it is an essential element in the creation of a fully human individuality, which can only be developed in a constitutional, legal, state. So much is clear – but this high doctrine of the community/state does nothing to answer the practical questions posed by the disintegration of multinational empires and states in Central and Eastern Europe. For example, both Croats and Serbs are resolutely statist in their approach to politics, but they clearly disagree as to which state(s) should exist in the territory that once was Yugoslavia, and as the successor states emerge they will disagree over the boundaries of the new communities. A belief in the value of the state as an institution does not imply an ability to determine what state should exist, within which boundaries, although, in contrast to cosmopolitan approaches, it does imply that this is an important question and one about which the political actors involved are right to be exercised. The concern that Balkan peoples have about the state structure of the region is not irrational or atavistic – they are right to see this as a matter which will determine the success with which they adapt to the post-communist world.

Serbs, Croats, and others of course, see their problems not simply in statist terms but in nationalist terms. It is a *nation*-state that the Croats and Bosnians wish to create. How do constitutive theories stand with regard to nationalism and the nation? Given the general reputation of this approach, it may come as a surprise to some to be told that such theories do *not* offer anything like a blanket endorsement of nationalism, or of the value of the nation. What is important is that the state should be put together in such a way that, along with the family and civil society, it can play its proper role in ethical life. It may be that being a 'nation' is helpful in this respect, but such is by no means necessarily the case – nationalism can be a positive handicap in some circumstances.

It may be helpful to elaborate this point. Hegel wrote in the early nineteenth century and was clearly aware of the strength of French national feeling, and of the emergence of a German nationalism in response. However, he does not give nationalism a role in the constitution of the ethical state – indeed his, rather disreputable, choice of Prussia as some kind of model is significant, since Prussia was most certainly not a *national* state. A hundred years later, Bosanquet, for example, did use the term Nation-state, but more or less synonymously with the term State (his capitals). On pragmatic grounds Bosanquet argues that it is more likely that ethical institutions will thrive amongst those who share a common culture and language, but this is very much a secondary point.[13]

The key issue is the ethical nature of the state – the presence of 'ethical substance', to use the old terminology – and while there may be a slight bias in favour of the state being a national state there are also reasons for concern if nationalism becomes too important. Constitutional government and the rule of law, private property and the market economy, free family relations – all of these are, from a neo-Hegelian viewpoint, of greater significance than the national ideal. If the latter undermines the former, by, for example, curtailing the civil rights of non-nationals, then this is to be deplored. No alleged natural tendency of the world to fall into national groupings can be allowed precedence over the requirements of the ethical state.

It is the ethical quality of the state rather than its national characteristics which make it worthy of support. The statement allegedly made by a senior British politician that he would rather have bad government from Westminister than good government from Brussels is a classic statement of pure nationalism, but if 'good' and 'bad' are understood in ethical terms then this position receives no support from constitutive theory. 'Bad' government cannot be constitutive of human individualism, whether national or not. Thus, from this perspective, claims for national self-determination are not to be regarded as conferring any particular legitimacy on those who make them – or for that matter on those who resist them.

Constitutive theory is for the state, but agnostic towards the nation. This contrasts with liberal cosmopolitanism, which is hostile to both categories, but in neither case do these basic presuppositions lead to much purchase on the big issues of political restructuring. These issues concern which states, which nations, which federations or confederations will, and should, emerge, and in this context neither statism nor anti-statism is particularly helpful. General doctrines must give way to the specific, and the type of question asked needs to be changed. The key issue is not whether the state is good or bad, or whether national self-determination is in itself a worthy goal, but rather, what kind of ethical institutions should be promoted by the processes of political restructuring and which ethical practices are likely to carry forward this task. On this matter neo-Hegelianism has quite firm views.

ETHICAL INSTITUTIONS AND POLITICAL RESTRUCTURING

From the perspective of constitutive theory, human beings do not come into the world as free individuals - they are constituted as such by the operation of ethical institutions at the levels of the family, civil society and the state. It is this basic position that provides criteria by which the *processes* of political change and reconstruction current in the modern world can be judged. It is processes and practices that are critical, and not simply outcomes – as suggested above, *which* states emerge out of this restructuring process is less important than *what kind* of states emerge. Most of the rest of this chapter will be devoted to political institutions in the new states but before moving to this two points need to be made about the family and civil society, because, from a constitutive viewpoint, these institutions are of equal ethical significance to the state.

The first thing that needs to be said about the family and civil society as ethical institutions is that the undermining of communism has, in this respect at least, been more or less entirely to the good. There are many different kinds of family structure that could provide a secure foundation for the development of human individuality but no system that builds a youth cult around the figure of a boy who informed upon his parents to the authorities can fit the bill. The behaviour of Pavlik Morozov – who handed over his parents to Stalin's police during the collectivization of agriculture, was murdered by his uncle, and became a hero of the Pioneers whose portrait hung in classrooms across the nation – is not simply sordid and unpleasant; it offers a role model which, if taken seriously, would undermine any sense of trust and unconditional love.[14] For the most part, of course, it was not taken that seriously, but the cult can stand nonetheless as a symbol of the sort of family relations which have rightly been discredited.

In the same way, the emergence of civil society, private property and the market in Central and Eastern Europe is to be welcomed not simply because these institutions are more economically efficient than those they have replaced, but because they contribute to the development of free human individuality in a way the older system did not. Self-reliance and the ability to make one's way in the world are promoted by civil society and undermined by a system in which the state is the universal provider. The ability to make decisions about one's own fate is critical; communism underdermined this ability. The difficulties even those East Germans who had the initiative to leave East Germany before November 1989 experienced in adjusting to (the then West) German civil society makes the point, as does the apparent inability of employees in state trading firms in Russia to adapt to price liberalization. This is not to be read as a blanket endorsement of capitalism; poverty and gross inequality are as destructive of human individuality as the *dirigisme* of the old regime. As is the case with the family, there are many different ways in which civil society can be formed, and private property and markets are certainly compatible with many forms of social democracy.

The second point that should be made about the family and civil society is that it is important that these institutions should not be undermined by political practices which impairs their ethical functioning. Political violence which damages civil society is not simply economically harmful, because the role of civil society is not simply economic. Economic aid to the new states, while probably necessary, should not be given in ways that undermine the operation of markets. Likewise, when national strife between Croat and Serb, or Russian and Ukrainian, harms the many families which have formed across these divides, this is not simply a personal tragedy for the individuals concerned, it is also subversive of the wider goal of a functioning ethical community. This is one of the features of nationalism that make it suspect in the eyes of the constitutive theorist, that it can work to promote the ethically harmful at the expense of the ethically important.

To the constitutive theorist the role of the ethical state is to complete the process of individuation begun in the family and civil society. The former institution is the site of unreflective, unconditional love, the latter the site of competition and external constraint. The role of the state is to provide a forum within which individuals can relate to one another not as family members or as competitors for scarce resources but as fellow citizens, and within which the constraints necessitated by social life can be internalized, experienced as of one's own creation. This is a tall order, and – *pace* Hegel – no actual state ever has done, or, probably, ever will do, all that is required of it – but setting out the ideal role of the state does have ethical significance, forming as it does the basis for a critique of the existing order.

What kind of state can perform these tasks? Only a constitutional state based on representative institutions, some kind of separation of powers, and the rule of law. Beyond this the theory is unspecific: there is no particular reason to favour unitary as opposed to federal states, presidential as opposed to prime ministerial, or any other such distinction. Different societies have different ways of doing things, and different circumstances require different institutions. What is crucial is that whatever constitution exists it should be clear who are the citizens and how these citizens make law. This requirement of clarity lies in the background of much discussion on the nature of 'sovereignty'. The requirement that the state should be sovereign can be understood not in terms of a largely fictitious freedom of decision which this status is alleged to confer; such a freedom of decison has never existed in practice and the conditions of interdependence in the late twentieth century impose ever greater prudential constraints on states. Rather, the case for sovereignty should be seen in terms of the need of citizens to be able to recognize each other and identify the institutions through which they come together and distinguish themselves from the rest of humanity.

A further point needs to be made here. A constitutional state is not simply a set of institutions which can be described in a legal document. It is also a set of practices and attitudes which cannot be codified but which are critical to the processes of politics. A society based on the rule of law is not simply a society which has the right institutions – a code of laws, a police force and an independent judiciary – it must also be a society which is based on an attitude of respect for the law. Attitudes and institutions are clearly closely related but they are not always synchronized. Similarly, constitutional politics must be based on a willingness to determine policy politically – that is to say, through discussion and debate and not through violence and compulsion. The ethical state must be based not simply on a set of institutions but also on a commitment to the political spirit of those institutions.

With these positions in mind it is now possible to address directly the issues of political restructuring identified in the introduction to this chapter, and in particular the contrasting movements towards integration and disintegration in Western and Eastern Europe. As a generalization it can be said that in Central and Eastern Europe the institutions of an ethical state are emerging from the ruins of communism, and here, especially in Eastern Europe, the problem lies in the practices of politics, the tendencies towards solving political problems by non-political means. On the other hand, in Western Europe the commitment to political means is strong and apparently unshakable, but the institutional structure is beginning to lose the sort of clarity required of an ethical state.

Virtually all the successor states of the old Soviet Union and its empire have gone to some lengths to set up political structures which are constitutional and representative, consonant with the return to ethical family relationships and the (re)establishment of civil society. The attitudes to go with these institutions are less easy to find – a new illustration of the dilemma identified by Rousseau and discussed in the second section of this chapter. Countries such as Czechoslovakia, with a pre-communist constitutional past, and Poland, where civil society was never totally submerged, are faring better than the new republics of the Caucasus or Central Asia which have no such past to draw upon. Within Russia itself there are clear divisions between those who are committed to the rule of law in deed as well as word and those ever willing to resort to extra-legal methods.

Constitutive theory adopts a concerned but ultimately optimistic stance towards these problems. The creation of ethical states requires a change of attitude as well as of institutions but there is no reason to believe that such a change will not come about. On the contrary, the institutions of the constitutional state are actually *better* than those either of the old regimes or of some new hypothetical authoritarianism, and neo-Hegelianism is based on the belief that this qualitative change is, or will be, decisive. In the medium to long run the good will drive out the bad.

One way of bringing the medium run closer might be by stressing the national nature of the new states, on the principle that fellow nationals will find it easier to behave politically as opposed to coercively towards each other. As a general proposition this may be so, but the problems of nationalism are also clear; problems of competing claims to national self-determination and of minority rights come to the fore, both in disintegrating multinational states such as Yugoslavia and the former Soviet Union and within the individual components of these states, as witnessed by the disintegrative tendencies emerging in the new Russian Republic.

The attitude of constitutive theory to issues of national self-determination is based on a concern both with outcomes and with the means employed to reach these outcomes. An abstract right to self-determination makes little sense and cannot be supported. One important issue is obviously whether a particular national grouping has the wherewithal to form the basis of a rational constitutional state – if not its members would certainly be better off remaining within a multinational grouping that does have these resouces. But perhaps more important is the means that are employed to press national claims or to resist them. Groups that employ unlawful and unconstitutional means to assert their independence in circumstances where constitutional, legal means to press their case are available are unlikely to create just institutions within their new boundaries – and this is especially so if these groups persecute or disadvantage their own minorities. Conversely, larger jurisdictions which can only preserve themselves by using violence against those who have expressed a wish to leave are also unlikely to be able to preserve constitutional politics.

Applying these principles to a concrete case may be helpful. Clearly Yugoslavia could not have been preserved as an ethical, constitutional state within its old borders because these borders could not have been maintained by ethical, constitutional means. Seen from the outside, the idea of 'Yugoslavia' as a way of governing the interpenetrated populations of the region seemed to make a great deal of sense, and there are clearly many people who have a genuinely 'Yugoslav' as opposed to, say, a Croat or Serb consciousness – but this is beside the point; the old multinational republic could only have been preserved by the military conquest of (at least) two of its component parts. But, seen from another angle, the possibility that Croatia and Bosnia-Hercegovina will be able to form constitutional states while holding down by force their Serbian minorities – or vice versa – is equally unlikely. This is a case where boundary revisions make sense, and the current prejudice against such action cannot be supported – the alternative of entrenched minority rights, favoured by the European Community, is unlikely to be effective when intercommunal hostility has reached the point that it has in Croatia or Bosnia today.[15]

The same kind of reasoning applies to national problems within the territory of the old Soviet Union. From the angle of constitutive theory the key issue to bear in mind at all times is the desirability of the creation and sustenance of ethical states, and specific issues of political restructuring must be viewed from this perspective. But another thing to bear in mind is that the ability of outsiders to contribute to this process is very limited. Only the peoples of these new states can resolve their own destinies; outsiders can help on the margin, supporting constitutional polities and withholding aid from the unconstitutional, but the best contribution Western Europeans can make to the solution of the problems of the East is to offer models of how functioning constitutional states might work.

This leads into some final reflections on the processes of political restructuring in the West – less violent than some of those of Eastern Europe but in constitutional terms equally dramatic. Here the main problem from the point of view of constitutive theory is the possibility that the new structures which are emerging in the European Community are undermining the state and may, eventually, prevent it from performing the creative function required of it. This point should not be misunderstood by turning it into a defence of national sovereignty in the face of a movement towards federalism; there is no reason to think that a federal Europe could not be designed in such a way as to meet the requirements of an ethical state should the peoples of Europe wish to take this route, as perhaps they do. What is much more problematic is whether the current uneasy mixture of nation-state and supranational bureaucracy can provide the sort of clarity that individuals require if they are to be able to identify their fellow citizens and experience the laws that govern them as of their own creation.

The lack of clarity here is the rational core to complaints often heard in United Kingdom about the 'bureaucracy' of the Community. In fact, Brussels bureaucrats are few in number, generally of high quality, and with very limited powers: the point is that the Commission and its servants are difficult to place within the network of institutions comprehended by constitutive theory. Neither fish nor fowl, they represent an anomaly which ordinary political discourse finds difficult to describe – whence trivializing simplifications such as the picture of an over-mighty, unrepresentative bureaucracy. A similar dislocation leads to the more common continental European combination of a theoretical commitment to the development of central decision-making combined with a practical unwillingness to implement actual decisions made centrally. This is not simply cynicism – it is also a reflection of the doubtful legitimacy of the present institutional structure.

As against this, in the realm of the 'how' as opposed to the 'what' of political institutions, the commitment of the Community to *political* decision-making – to the employment of persuasion rather than coercion – seems firm. The very lack of clarity in the institutions of the Community reflects the spirit of compromise. The processes of decision-making within the Community are designed not to isolate individual member states and are basically consensual, even when in principle based on majority voting. All this is supportive of an ethical approach to politics. The situation here is, thus, the reverse of that in the East, where the institutional structures are increasingly rational but where many political practices remain cast in non-ethical moulds. On the whole the Western combination is healthier on the principle that it is easier for republicans to make a republic than it is for a republic to make republicans, but in both cases there is some reason for concern.

CONCLUSION

The constitutive theory of the relationship between state and individual explains why a particular kind of state is of paramount importance in ethical terms, and from the same starting point other social institutions, the family and civil society, can be assessed. Constitutive theory incorporates some of the positions of other communitarian approaches – such as the pragmatic value to be attached to a sense of community when major and disruptive projects are planned by a society – while rejecting others – such as the proposition that states should always be based on nations. Constitutive theory shares the commitment to human rights, and duties, of many cosmopolitans, while denying that these values can be realized other than in a properly constituted state.

This is a position which has fallen out of favour in the last hundred years, but which, as the century closes, is now receiving closer attention. Constitutive theory employs terminology which is unfamiliar and operates at a high level of generality; however, as is suggested above at a number of points, it is often the case that the terms of everyday political discourse can be translated into constitutive terms. The contention of this chapter has been that in the post-Cold War era these terms offer a more accurate translation of the real processes of political restructuring than their rivals.

NOTES

1 Geographical terms have political import and Eastern Europe will no longer do as a blanket description of these countries. In accordance with their own usage, 'Central' Europe is here used to describe Czechoslovakia, Poland and Hungary. Other countries are termed 'Eastern' Europe.
2 Francis Fukuyama, 'The End of History?' *The National Interest*, Summer 1989.
3 Ernest Gellner, *Nations and Nationalism* (Blackwell, Oxford, 1983); Tom Nairn, *The Break-up of Britain* (New Left Books, London, 1977); Benedict Anderson, *Imagined Communities* (Verso, London, 1983).
4 Another problem of terminology. 'Communitarianism' is too broad a term for the theory espoused here, 'Hegelianism' too narrow, hence the use of the rather clumsy term 'constitutive theory' – taken from *inter alia* Mervyn Frost, *Towards a Normative Theory of International Relations* (Cambridge University Press, Cambridge, 1986) – with neo-Hegelianism as a slightly inaccurate but convenient alternative.
5 Thomas Hobbes, *Leviathan*; John Locke, *Two Treatises of Government*; Hans. J. Reiss, *Kant's Political Writings* (Cambridge University Press, Cambridge, 1970); Robert Gilpin, *War and Change in World Politics* (Cambridge University Press, Cambridge, 1981), p.15; John Rawls, *A Theory of Justice* (Clarendon Press, Oxford, 1972).
6 Aristotle, *The Politics*, ed. Stephen Everson (Cambridge University Press, Cambridge, 1988), p.4.
7 Tracy Strong, 'Introduction' to Strong (ed.), *The Self and the Political Order* (Blackwell, Oxford, 1992), p.1.
8 J-J. Rousseau, 'Constitutional Project for Corsica' in Frederick Watkins, ed., *Political Writings* (Nelson, London, 1953).
9 Ludwig Wittgenstein, *Philosophical Investigations* (Blackwell, Oxford, 1958), 226; Peter Winch, *The Idea of a Social Science* (Routledge, London, 1958).

10 Richard Rorty, *Contingency, Irony and Solidarity* (Cambridge University Press, Cambridge, 1989), and 'Postmodern Bourgeois Liberalism', *Journal of Philosophy* (1983), pp.583–9.

11 Hegel's position is to be found in *Philosphy of Right*, trans T.M. Knox (Oxford University Press, London, 1967). This account rests heavily on Charles Taylor, *Hegel* (Cambridge University Press, Cambridge, 1975); Raymond Plant, *Hegel: An Introduction*, 2nd ed. (Blackwell, Oxford, 1983); John Charvet, *A Critique of Freedom and Equality* (Cambridge University press, Cambridge, 1981), and Mervyn Frost. op. cit.

12 'Rational' and 'ethical' here mean much the same thing, and are used more or less synonymously in the text.

13 Bernard Bosanquet, *The Philosophical Theory of the State*, 4th ed. (Macmillan, London, 1965), chapter XI.

14 For Pavlik's story see Urie Bronfenbrenner *Two Worlds of Childhood* (Allen and Unwin, London, 1971). This is a good illustration of the contradictory nature of totalitarianism – as well as encouraging children to become police informers the socially conservative Stalinist state was also trying to promote patriarchal family structures.

15 Such boundary revisions would have to be on the basis of local referenda. Determining the districts which would be allowed referenda would be difficult, and minorities would continue to exist and still require protection. However, these practical difficulties should not be allowed to prevent sensible boundary changes. The current, almost fetishistic, desire to preserve as many pre-existing boundaries as possible is irrational and indefensible.

Part III

Europe today: nationalism and post-communism

Chapter 9

Notes on the new tribalism*

Michael Walzer

All over the world today, but most interestingly and frighteningly in Eastern Europe and the Soviet Union, men and women are reasserting their local and particularist, their ethnic, religious, and national identities. The tribes have returned, and the dream of their return is greatest where their repression was most severe. It is now apparent that the popular energies mobilized against totalitarian rule, and also the more passive stubbornness and evasiveness that eroded the Stalinist regimes from within, were fuelled in good part by 'tribal' loyalties and passions. How these were sustained and reproduced over time is a tale that waits to be told. The tribes – most of them, at least, and all the minorities and the subject nations – were for several generations denied access to the official organs of social reproduction: the public schools and the mass media. I imagine tens of thousands of old men and women whispering to their grandchildren, singing folk songs and lullabies, repeating ancient stories. This is in many ways a heartening picture, for it suggests the inevitability of totalitarian failure. But what are we to make of the songs and stories, often as full of hatred for neighbouring nations as of hope for national liberation?

The left has never understood the tribes. Faced with their contemporary resurgence, the first response is to argue for their containment within established multinational states – democratically transformed, of course, but not divided. This looks very much like a systematic repetition of the response of early twentieth-century social democrats to the nationalist movements that challenged the old empires. The 'internationalism' of the

* This chapter is reprinted without revision from *Dissent*, spring 1992.

left owes a great deal to Hapsburg and Romanov imperialism, even if leftists always intended to dispense with the dynasties. So many nations lived together in peace under imperial rule: why could not they continue to live together under the aegis of social democracy? So many nations lived together in peace under communist rule: why . . .? When Western Europe is forging a new unity, how can anyone defend separation in the East?

But unity in the West is itself the product of or, at least, the historical successor to separation. The independence of Sweden from Denmark and, centuries later, of Norway from Sweden (and of Finland from Sweden and Russia) opened the way for Scandinavian co-operation. The division of Belgium and Holland, and the failures of French imperialism, made possible the Benelux experiment. Centuries of sovereignty for the great states of Western Europe preceded the achievement of European community. It is important to note that what was achieved first, before community, was not only sovereign statehood but also democratic government. The Swedes could have held Norway indefinitely under one or another form of authoritarian rule. But the practice of democracy, even in its earliest states, made it clear that there was more than one *demos*, and then separation became necessary if democracy was to be sustained. The case is the same in the East. Multinationalism as it has existed there is a function of pre-democratic or anti-democratic politics. But bring the 'people' into political life and they will arrive, marching in tribal ranks and orders, carrying with them their own languages, historic memories, customs, beliefs, and commitments. And once they have been summoned, once they have arrived, it is not possible to do them justice within the old political order.

Maybe it is not possible to do them justice at all. In Eastern Europe today, and in Caucasia, and in much of the Middle East, the prospects don't seem bright, given the sheer number of suddenly raucous tribes and the radical entanglement of their members on the same bits and pieces of land. Good fences make good neighbours only when there is some minimal agreement on where the fences should go. In the West, powerful states were created before the appearance of nationalist ideology and managed to repress and incorporate many of the smaller nations (Welsh, Scots, Normans, Bretons, and so on). The separations I have already noted took place alongside constructive processes that created large nation-states with more or less identifiable boundaries and more or less committed members. Similar efforts in Eastern Europe seem to have failed: there are not many committed Yugoslav or Soviet citizens. The abandonment of these identities is startling in its scope and speed, and it leaves many people who had travelled under their protection suddenly vulnerable: Serbs in Croatia, Albanians in Serbia, Armenians in Azerbaijan, Russians in the Baltic states, Jews in Russia, and so on, endlessly.

There does not seem to be any humane or decent way to disentangle the tribes, and at the same time the entanglements are felt to be dangerous – not only to individual life, which is reasonable enough, but also to communal well-being. Demagogues exploit the hopes of national revival, linguistic autonomy, the free development of schools and media – all supposedly threatened by cosmopolitan or anti-national minorities. And other demagogues exploit the fears of the minorities, defending ancient irredentisms and looking (like the Serbs in Croatia) for outside help. In such circumstances, it is hard to say what justice means, let alone what policies it might require. Hence the impulse of the left, uncomfortable in any case with particularist passions, to cling to whatever unities exist and make them work. The argument is very much like that of a Puritan minister in the 1640s, defending the union of husband and wife against the new doctrine of divorce:

> If they might be separated for discord, some would make a commodity of strife; but now they are not best to be contentious, for the law will hold their noses together 'til weariness make them leave off struggling . . .

The problem, then as now, is that justice, whatever it requires, does not seem to permit the kinds of coercion that would be necessary to 'hold their noses together'. So we have to think about divorce, despite its difficulties. It is some help that divorce among nations need not have the singular legal form of divorce in families. Self-determination for husbands and wives is relatively simple, even when important constraints are imposed upon the separated individuals. Self-determination for the many different kinds of tribes (nations, ethnic groups, religious communities) is bound to be more complicated, and the constraints that follow upon separation more various. There is room for manoeuvre.

II

I doubt whether we can find a single rule or set of rules that will determine the form of the separation and the necessary constraints. But there is a general principle, which we can think of as the expression of democracy in international politics. What is at stake is the value of a historical or cultural or religious community and the political liberty of its members. This liberty is not compromised, it seems to me, by the postmodern discovery that communities are social constructions: imagined, invented, put together. Constructed communities are the only communities there are; they cannot be less real or less authentic than some other sort. Their members, then, have the rights that go with membership. *They ought to be allowed to govern themselves* – in so far as they can do that, given their local entanglements.

Democracy has, of course, no natural units. Self-determination has no absolute subject. Cities, nations, federations, immigrant societies – all these can be and have been governed democratically. The contemporary tribes most certain of their singular identity and culture (the Poles or Armenians, say) are in fact historical composites. If we go back far enough in their history, we will find people's noses being held together (that is one of the methods of social construction). But if the descendants of these people, forgetting ancient indignities, regard themselves now as *fellow* members of a 'community of character', within which they find identity, self-respect, and sentimental connections, why should we deny them democratic self-government?

Except . . . unless . . . were it not for the fact that the self-government of tribe A, happily divorced, makes tribe B a vulnerable and unhappy minority in its own homeland. Locked into an independent Croatia, Serbs believe (not implausibly) that they will live in insecurity. And then, surely, the political unit has to be territorial, not cultural: all the tribes and fragments of tribes that live *here* – noses held together 'til they leave off struggling – must come under the authority of a neutral state and share a characterless citizenship. But these cannot be our only options: the dominance of one tribe or a common detribalization. For the second of the two, if it is not a mere cover for the first, would require coercion of a sort that, as I have already suggested, is neither morally permissible nor politically effective. We would not be worrying about Croatia and its Serbs, after all, if Yugoslavia had succeeded in imposing itself upon its constituent nations; it was, in theory at least, the very model of a neutral state.

Neutrality is likely to work well only in immigrant societies where everyone has been similarly and in most cases voluntarily transplanted, cut off from homeland and history. In such cases – America is the prime example – tribal feelings are relatively weak. But how can one create a neutral state in France, say, where the anciently established French rule democratically over the new immigrants from North Africa (even though the immigrants, many of them, hold 'French' citizenship)? What imperial, bureaucratic, or international authority could detribalize the French? Or the Poles in Poland? Or the Georgians in an independent Georgia? Or the Croats in Croatia? And then the only way to avoid domination is to multiply political units and jurisdictions, permitting a series of separations. But the series will be endless – so we are told – each divorce justifying the next one, smaller and smaller groups claiming the right of self-determination; and the politics that result will be noisy, incoherent, unstable, and deadly.

I want to argue that this is a slippery slope down which we need not slide. In fact, there are many conceivable arrangements between dominance and detribalization and between dominance and separation – and there are moral and political reasons for choosing different arrangements in different circumstances. The principle of self-determination is subject to interpretation and amendment. What has been called 'the national question' does not have a single correct answer, as if there were only one way of 'being' a nation, one version of national history, one model of relationships among nations. History reveals many ways, versions, and models, and so it suggests the existence of many (more or less secure) stopping points along the slippery slope. Consider now some of the more likely possibilities.

III

The easiest case is that of the 'captive', that is, recently and coercively incorporated, nation – the Baltic states are nice examples, since these were genuine nation-states, the nationality ancient even if statehood was only recently achieved and briefly held. The captivity was wrong for the same reasons that the capture was wrong. The principle involved is the familiar one that makes aggression a criminal act. What it requires now is the restoration of independence and sovereignty – which is to say: what principle requires is what practice in this case has achieved. And by a kind of imaginative extension, we can grant the same rights to nations that *ought to have been* independent, where the solidarity of the group is plain to see and the crime of the ruling power is national oppression rather than conquest. I see no reason to deny the justice of separation in all such cases.

Except ... unless ... Conquest and oppression are not merely abstract crimes; they have consequences in the real world: the mixing up of peoples, the creation of new and heterogeneous populations. Suppose that Russian immigrants now made up a majority of the people living in Latvia: would any right remain of Latvian self-determination? Suppose that French colonists had come (by 1950, say) to outnumber the Arabs and Berbers of Algeria: would the right of 'Algerian' self-determination reside with the French majority? These are doubly hard questions; they are painful and they are difficult. The world changes, not necessarily in morally justifiable ways; and rights can be lost or, at least, diminished through no fault of the losers. We might want to argue for partition in cases like the ones I have just described, leaving the 'natives' with less than they originally claimed; or we might want to design a regime of cultural autonomy instead of the political sovereignty that once seemed morally necessary. We look for the nearest possible arrangement to whatever was *ex ante* just, taking into account now what justice requires for the immigrants and colonists, or their children, who are not themselves the authors of the conquest or the oppression.

The case is the same with anciently incorporated nations – aboriginal peoples like the Native Americans or the Maori in New Zealand. Their rights too are eroded with time, not because the wrong done to them is wiped out (it may well grow greater, with ramifying and increasingly deleterious effects on their communal life), but because the possibility no longer exists of the restoration of anything remotely resembling their former independence. They stand somewhere between a captive nation and a national, ethnic, or religious minority. Something more than equal citizenship is due them, some degree of collective self-rule, but exactly what this might mean in practice will depend on the residual strength of their own institutions and on the character of their engagement in the common life of the larger society. They cannot claim any absolute protection against the pressures and attractions of the common life – as if they were an endangered species. Confronted with modernity, all the human tribes are endangered species. All of them, whether or not they possess sovereign power, have been significantly transformed. We can recognize what might be called a right to resist transformation, to build walls against modern culture, and we can give this right more or less scope, depending on constitutional structures and local circumstances; we cannot guarantee the success of the resistance.

IV

The just treatment of national minorities depends on two sets of distinctions: first, between territorially concentrated and dispersed minorities; and, second, between minorities radically different from and those that are only marginally different from the majority population. In practice, of course, both distinctions are really unmarked continuums, but it is best to begin with the clear cases. Consider, for example, a minority community with a highly distinctive history and culture and a strong territorial base – like the Albanians in Kosovo, for example. Their fellow nationals hold the adjoining state; they are trapped on the wrong side of the border as a result of some dynastic marriage or military victory long ago. The humane solution to their difficulty is to move the border; the brutal solution is to 'transfer' the people; and the best practical possibility is some strong version of local autonomy, focused on cultural and educational institutions and the revenues that support them.

The opposite case is that of a marginally differentiated and territorially dispersed community, something like the ethnic and religious groups of North America (though there are exceptions in both categories: the ethnic French in Quebec, say, and the religious Amish in Pennsylvania). By and large, the experience of marginal difference and territorial dispersion gives rise to very limited claims on the state – a good reason for doubting the dangers of the slippery slope. A genuinely equal citizenship and the freedom to express their differences in the voluntary associations of civil society: this is what the members of such minorities commonly, and rightly, ask for. They may also seek some kind of subsidy from state funds for their schools, day care centres, old age homes, and so on. But that is a request that hangs more on political judgments than on moral principles. We will have to form an opinion about the inner strengths and weaknesses of the existing civil society. (A group that has been severely discriminated against, however, and whose access to resources is limited, does have a moral claim on the state.)

Once again, majorities have no obligation to guarantee the survival of minority cultures. They may well be struggling to survive themselves, caught up in a common competition against commercialism and international fashion. Borders provide only minimal protection in the modern world, and minorities within borders, driven by their situation to a preternatural closeness, may do better in sustaining a way of life than the more relaxed majority population. And if they do worse, that is no reason to come to their rescue; they have a claim, indeed, to physical but not to cultural security.

The adjustment of claims to circumstances is often a long and brutal business, but it does happen. We see it today, for example, in the geographically concentrated but only marginally different nations of Western Europe – Welsh, Scots, Normans, Bretons, and so on – whose members have consistently declined to support radical nationalist parties demanding independence and sovereign power. In cases like these, some sort of minimalist regionalism seems both to suit the people involved (small numbers of them – political, not ethnic or religious, minorities – always excepted) and to be politically and morally suitable. The case is the same with small or dispersed but significantly different populations, like the Amish or like orthodox Jews in the United States, who commonly aim at a highly localized and apolitical separatism: segregated neighbourhoods and parochial schools. This too seems to suit the people involved, and it is politically and morally suitable. But no theory of justice can specify the precise form of these arrangements. In fact, the forms are historically negotiated, and they depend upon shared understanding of what such negotiations mean and how they work. The Welsh and Scots have had a hand in the development of British political culture, even if it was not quite the hand they think they ought to have had. Hence their ready adjustment to parliamentary politics. Both the Amish and the Jews have learned, and added to, the repertoire of American pluralism.

Arrangements of these sorts should always be allowed, but they cannot be imposed. What has made *Great* Britain possible is probably the common Protestantism of its component nations. The effort to include the Irish failed miserably. Today, the inclusion of the Slovenes in greater Yugoslavia seems to have failed for similar reasons. The case is the same for the failure of communist internationalism in Poland and pan-Arabism in Lebanon. But I don't mean to argue that the religious differences crucial in all these cases necessarily make for separation. Sometimes they do and sometimes they don't. The differences are different in each case. They have more to do with memory and feeling than with any objective measure of dissimilarity. That's why models like my own, based on such factors as territorial concentration and cultural difference, can never be anything more than rough guides. We have to work slowly and experimentally towards arrangements that satisfy the members (not the militants) of this or that minority. There is no single correct outcome.

V

This experimental work is certain to be complicated by the unequal economic resources of the different tribes. It is obviously an incentive to divorce if one of the partners – a nation, say, industrially advanced or in control of mineral resources – can improve its position by walking away from the existing union. The other partners are left worse off, though some of them, at least, were never involved in any sort of national oppression. They will contest the divorce, but what they are probably entitled to, it seems to me, is the international equivalent of alimony and child support. Long established patterns of co-operation cannot be abruptly terminated to the advantage of the most advantaged partners. On the other hand, the partners are not bound to stay together for ever – not if they are in fact different tribes, who meet the democratic standards for autonomy or independence.

Often enough, separatist movements in the economically advantaged provinces or regions of some established union do not meet those standards. The best example is the Katangan secession of 1961, inspired, it appears, by Belgian entrepreneurs and corporate interests, without locally rooted support or, at least, without any visible signs of national mobilization. In such cases, it is entirely justifiable for unionist forces to resist the secession and to seek (and receive) international support. Obviously, there is such a thing as inauthentic tribalism – here, the manipulation of potential but not yet politically realized differences for economic gain. It does not follow, however, that every wealthy or resourceful tribe is inauthentic. And so there are also cases in which resistance to secession is not justified and should not be internationally supported – so long as some agreement can be negotiated that meets the interests of the people left behind. Their fear of impoverishment must be weighed against the fear of oppression or exploitation on the part of the seceding group or against its desire for cultural expression and political freedom.

VI

The dominant feeling that makes for national antagonism, the most important cause (not the only cause) of all the tribal wars, is fear. Here I mean to follow an old argument first made in Thomas Hobbes's *Leviathan*, where it forms part of the explanation for the 'war of all against all'. Hobbes was thinking of the internal wars of late medieval 'bastard feudalism' but also – more pertinently for our purposes – of the religious wars of his own time. There are always a few people, he writes, who 'take pleasure in contemplating their own power in acts of conquest'. But the greater number by far are differently motivated: they 'would be glad to be at ease within modest bounds'. These ordinary men and women are driven to fight not by their lust for power or enrichment, not by their bigotry or fanaticism, but by their fear of conquest and oppression. Hobbes argues that only an absolute sovereign can free them from this fearfulness and break the cycle of threats and 'anticipations' (that is, pre-emptive violence). In fact, however, what broke the cycle, in the case of the religious wars, was not so much political absolutism as religious toleration.

The two crucial seventeenth-century arguments against toleration sound very familiar today, for they closely parallel the arguments against national separation and autonomy. The first of the two is the claim of the dominant religious establishments to represent some high value – universal truth or the divine will – that is certain to be overwhelmed in the cacophony of religious dissidence. And the second is the slippery slope argument: that the dissidence will prove endless and the new sectarianism endlessly divisive, split following split until the social order crumbles into incoherence and chaos. Certainly, toleration opened the way for a large number of new sects, though these have mostly flourished on the margins of more or less stable religious communities. But it also, and far more importantly, lowered the stakes of religious conflict: toleration made divisiveness more tolerable. It solved the problem of fear by creating protected spaces for a great diversity of religious practices.

It seems to me that we should aim at something very much like this today: protected spaces of many different sorts matched to the needs of the different tribes. Rather than supporting the existing unions, I would be inclined to support separation whenever separation is demanded by a political movement that, so far as we can tell, represents the popular will. Let the people go who want to go. Many of them will not go all that far. And if there turn out to be political or economic disadvantage in their departure, they will find a way to re-establish connections. Indeed, if some sort of union – federation or confederation – is our goal, the best way to reach it is to abandon coercion and allow the tribes first to separate and then to negotiate their own voluntary and gradual, even if only partial, adherence to some new community of interest. Today's European Community is a powerful example, which other nations will approach at their own pace.

But – again – one nation's independence may be the beginning of another nation's oppression. Reading the newspaper these days, it often seems as if the chief motive for national liberation is not to free oneself from minority status in someone else's country but to acquire (and then mistreat) minorities of one's own. The standard rule of intertribal relations is: do unto others what has been done unto you. Arguing for liberation, I have largely ignored the consistent failure of new nation-states to meet the moral test of the nation that comes next, to recognize in others the rights vindicated by their own independence. I do not mean to underestimate the nastiness of tribal zealots. But were not the zealots of the religious wars equally nasty? And their latter day descendants seem harmless enough – not particularly attractive, most of them, but also not very dangerous. Why should not the same sequence, harmlessness following upon nastiness, hold for contemporary nationalists? Put them in a world where they are not threatened, and for how long will they think it in their interests to threaten others?

That at least is the Hobbesian argument. No doubt there are men and women in every tribe – Serbs and Croats; Latvians, Georgians, and Russians, Greeks and Turks, Israeli Jews and Palestinian Arabs – who take pleasure in acts of conquest, who aim above all to triumph over their neighbours and enemies. But these people will not rule in their own tribes if we can make it possible for their fellow tribesmen to live 'at ease within modest bounds'. Every tribe within its own modest bounds: this is the political equivalent of toleration for every Church and sect. What makes it possible – though still politically difficult and uncertain – is that the bounds need not enclose, in every case, the same sort of space.

Religious toleration, however, was enforced by the state, and the godly zealots were disarmed and disempowered by the political authorities. Tribal zealots, by contrast, aim precisely at empowerment; they hope to become political authorities themselves, replacing the imperial bureaucrats who once forced them to live peacefully with their internal minorities. Who will restrain them after independence? Who will protect the Serbs in an independent Croatia or the Albanians in an independent Serbia? I have no easy answer to these questions. In a liberal democracy, national minorities can seek constitutional protection. But not many of the new nations are likely to be liberal, even if they achieve some version of democracy. The best hope of restraint lies, I think, in federal or confederal checks and balances and in international pressure. The nationality treaties of the interwar period were notable failures, but some measure of success in protecting minorities ought to be possible if nation-states are sufficiently entangled with and dependent on one another. Suppose that the leaders of the European Community or the World Bank or even the United Nations were to say to every nation seeking statehood: we will recognize your independence, trade with you or provide economic assistance – but only if you find some way to accommodate the national minorities that fear your sovereign power. The price of recognition and aid is accommodation.

What form this accommodation might take is not a matter to be determined in any *a priori* way. (I have to keep saying this because so many people are looking for a quick theoretical fix.) It will depend on the character of the new states and on a process of negotiation. Secession, border revision, federation, regional or functional autonomy, cultural pluralism: there are many possibilities and no reason to think that the choice of one of these in this or that case makes a similar choice necessary in all the other cases. As the examples I have cited from Western Europe suggest, choices are more likely to be determined by circumstances than by abstract principles. What is required is an international consensus that validates a variety of choices, supporting any political arrangement that satisfies the tribes at risk.

VI

But there is no guarantee of satisfaction and, sometimes, watching the tribal wars, some of us may yearn for the uniform repressiveness of imperial or even totalitarian rule. For was not this repression undertaken in the name, at least, of universalism? And might not it have produced, had it only been sustained long enough, a genuine detribalization? And then we would look back and say that just as the absolutism of early modern monarchs was necessary to defeat the aristocracy and eliminate feudalism, so the absolutism of imperial and communist bureaucrats was necessary to overcome tribalism. Perhaps the bureaucracies collapsed too soon, before they could complete their 'historical task'. But this line of argument repeats again the old left misunderstanding of the tribes. It is no doubt true that particular tribes can be destroyed by repression, if it is cruel enough and if it lasts long enough. The destruction of tribalism itself, however, lies beyond the reach of any repressive power. It is no one's 'historical task'. Feudalism is the name of a regime, and regimes can be replaced. Tribalism names the commitment of individuals and groups to their own history, culture, and identity, and this commitment (though not any particular version of it) is a permanent feature of human social life. The parochialism that it breeds is similarly permanent. It cannot be overcome; it has to be accommodated, and therefore the crucial universal principle is that it must always be accommodated: not only my parochialism but yours as well, and his and hers in their turn.

When my parochialism is threatened, then I am wholly radically parochial: a Serb, a Pole, a Jew, and nothing else. But this is an artificial situation in the modern world (and perhaps in the past too). The self is more naturally divided; at least, it is capable of division and even thrives on it. Under conditions of security, I will acquire a more complex identity than the idea of tribalism suggests. I will identify myself with more than one tribe; I will be an American, a Jew, an easterner, an intellectual, a professor. Imagine a similar multiplication of identities around the world, and the world begins to look like a less dangerous place. When identities are multiplied, passions are divided.

We need to think about the political structures best suited to this multiplication and division. These will not be unitary structures; nor will they be identical. Some states will be rigorously neutral, with a plurality of cultures and a common citizenship; some will be federations; some will be nation-states, with minority autonomy. Sometimes cultural pluralism will be expressed only in private life; sometimes it will be expressed publicly. Sometimes different tribes will be mixed on the ground; sometimes they will be territorially grouped. Since the nature and the number of our identities will be different, even characteristically different for whole populations, a great variety of arrangements ought to be expected and welcomed. Each of them will have its usefulness and its irritations; none of them will be permanent; the negotiation of difference will never produce a final settlement. What this also means is that our common humanity will never make us members of a single universal tribe. The crucial commonality of the human race is particularism. With the end of imperial and totalitarian rule, we can at least recognize this commonality and begin the difficult negotiations it requires.

Chapter 10

The moral basis of political restructuring

Zarko Puhovski

There can be no doubt that political actions – especially such major actions as the destruction of existing political communities or the construction of new ones – are often legitimated on strictly moral grounds, and if it is accepted that a (modern) political construction really needs to be based on an acceptance of certain moral goods, it follows that some kind of moral discourse ought to precede every concrete political discussion about the fundamentals of a given community. This may seem a somewhat abstract proposition, but with the decline of 'really-existing socialism' in Eastern and Central Europe the reconstruction of political communities is once again an actual, acute, political problem, the urgency of which should not mislead analysts – in the way in which, apparently, it has the principal actors – into neglecting its moral basis. This latter is the subject of this chapter, but, first, it may be helpful to examine the ways in which the problems of reconstruction are actually being posed.

SOVEREIGNTY AND POLITICAL RECONSTRUCTION

It is clear that there are two basic types of reaction to the aforementioned decline; on the one hand, there is the search for a 'new' foundation for the community in its past, on the other there is the ambition to replace the totalitarian order with democratic procedures in the hope that this will provide some kind of panacea for all past (and maybe even some future) political and social ills. The key word for both these orientations is sovereignty. In the first case, sovereignty is understood as the sovereignty of an ethno-national state, in the second, as the sovereignty of the people, i.e. of citizens constituted by the political processes of a democracy. And yet, ironically, the modern politics of Europe – to become part of which is the most important goal of all the political forces emerging in the former communist countries – is *not* based on sovereignty. The supranational politics, and policies, of European unification – with some elements of statehood already present and much more to come in the next few years – suggest that a high standard of living and a satisfactory level of freedom is attainable in states which are not sovereign in the traditional sense of the term.

From a political as well as a moral point of view, the most important consequence of post-war developments in Europe is the fact that free and wealthy individuality has proved to be possible in a community which is *not* a sovereign nation-state. There is, of course, nothing unfamiliar in this to modern political philosophy (at least from Locke onwards), but the existence of some kind of empirical proof of the point makes it, to say the least, politically complicated to argue that the 'strong sovereign state' (as defined by international law) is the only proper replacement for the communist party state characteristic of Eastern (and a part of Central) Europe for decades.

Traditionally, sovereignty has had to do with state power, and could be used for purposes of legitimation only as sovereignty within the international community – i.e. as external sovereignty. This is, in fact, the way in which sovereignty, as the permanent formalization of the superiority of the ultimate power in the state, became important for modern political thought. Hobbes puts it in quite a direct way: sovereignty (both by acquisition and by institution) arises from fear, the passion which inclines men most to peace[1] – but this is certainly not a position that could be applied to the enthusiastic 'fight' – literally as well as figuratively – for sovereignty in the states succeeding the former communist countries. There is in these countries an emotional relationship towards sovereignty incompatible with the Hobbesian concept; however, it is also the case that even if on some occasions the expression 'popular sovereignty' is employed it is only rarely in the forefront of actual political discussion in the former communist countries.

'External' sovereignty is therefore the concept which clearly prevails in the political context sketched above. However, external sovereignty is only a possible focus if some kind of external enemy can be perceived, and if there is some kind of certainty about 'our side'. The constitution of 'our community' must therefore contain some indisputable presuppositions which allow the identification of a collectivity which defends 'our' position against the other side. The European tradition is that such a collectivity must be ethnically based. The political processes characteristic of European history, especially in the second half of the nineteenth century, held the construction of a national state for every ethnic group to be an aim which was, almost, natural. That the repetition of such a process can nowadays be observed in Eastern Europe has, of course, its roots in the fact that the countries of that region, with some exceptions, were not able to follow the mainstream of European development in this earlier period. But it is also substantially connected to the very nature of the regimes of really-existing socialism, and the 'socialist construction of reality'.

It is obvious now that, in a process neither observed, nor understood nor analysed at the time, the communist Leviathan had already, some years ago, gradually transformed itself into Behemoth. Its rulers acted as if their citizens (or, more accurately, their subjects) were minors; government acted *in loco parentis*, creating a patriarchal power structure instead of a modern political leadership. As a consequence, the quasi-parental socialist rulers had to feed, dress, educate, socialize, and house their 'youngsters', as well as provide them with a moderate amount of pocket money. As in the case of families, such relations cannot be economic – there was, for better or worse, as Franz Neumann formulated fifty years ago in his analysis of the National Socialist order, 'an economy without economics'.[2] It was only when such a type of social organization became clearly impossible to maintain that the real crisis of these regimes emerged.

THE ROLE OF IDEOLOGY IN THE SURVIVAL OF THE COMMUNIST ORDER

But this description – or rather analytical hypothesis – cannot explain the main problem, which is why the communist system was able to survive throughout the past decades. In order to understand this we have to focus our attention on the global construction of 'socialist reality' as a whole, not just on the construction of, say, the party, state, 'economy', or culture, and the key methodological question is to identify the crucial difference between this system and previous social orders. The communist regimes differed substantially from all other characteristic historical constitutional orders. All previous orders have been marked by a common feature – namely that traditional forms of social, private, group, or class existence (whether kinship, slave-based or feudal) had outlived their usefulness. New forms of community (for which there was a perceived widespread need) began in each case with a radical intervention (often violent) into the previous, inherited, form of existence.

Contrary to these historical precedents, the communist order was constituted independently of the obsolescence of the historically actual social, political, or cultural state of affairs; indeed, it was constituted with the consciousness that the contemporary world had already shown convincingly that some of the basic features of the original socialist programme could be realized. Contrary to the schema outlined above, the inherited (local) reality offered no opportunity for the new order to make a radical intervention, instead it had to construct its own reality, its own foundations, developing a 'social' context in which its original anti-bourgeois programme would make sense in the absence of any real possibility of interference in the actual 'bourgeois world'.

How could this be possible, how could such an order construct its own reality? In only one way – the route actually taken – by creating a reality of a substantially different quality, incommensurable with the reality characteristic of the modern type of production of social life. This new kind of reality, the 'socialist' reality, is, of course, an ideological reality, which is to say, a reality which is possible only as a mediated state of affairs – with the result, of course, that the systematic mediation itself then takes the place of reality. In order to preserve its incommensurable status – to prevent the very possibility of comparison with its environment – the regime needed an ideological veil.

Ideology is here used not only as a term which denotes 'false conscience', but, more generally, as a term which signifies any idea put to the production of action, regardless of its truthfulness as such. Communist ideology tends to action, but the medium of the action – the society as a whole – is not of epistemological or sociological interest, but of ideological, fundamentally mediated interest. Its reality deals with the concept of society as a work of art, with society as a medium of theory and not of practice.

The real 'material' out of which such a kind of society is constructed is, despite its aggressively materialist ideology, the idea or, to be more precise, ideologically activated ideas. Thus, ideology takes the place of the 'productive forces' of which Marx spoke. Since Lenin, the constructors of communist order have learnt that their first task has to be to take ideologically creative control over the 'means of production', and over the 'productive forces', employing behaviour that looks political but is, in fact, pre-political. It is in respect of this last point that terms like 'dictatorship' or 'tyranny' do not describe the essence of the system; much more helpful is the notion of power as a productive relation, developed – of course, in quite another theoretical and political context – by Michel Foucault.[3]

Since all the relations recognized in such a society existed only through ideological mediations, they could also only be realized when mediated by power – which was not only the instance of control (as it is in the modern political tradition in general), but also the most important productive instance of the system. And so the productive formula for these systems was not the production of surplus value – characteristic of modern civil society in general – but the production of surplus power, even the production of power for the sake of power as some kind of symbolic communication with the subjects of the regime. This explains why the regime built, organized and preserved much more power than was required for its own protection, function or even prolongation.

At the same time, such an immense concentration of power was not really of practical use in any circumstances other than those of major, open, armed revolt against the government, the only situation in which the rulers would be able to risk mass killing. This is why they could not really act at the time of the final challenge to these systems, in the year 1989 – at least, elsewhere than in Romania, a strange mixture of really-existing socialism and a sultanic regime. And this is also why, in a unified Germany, police forces from West Berlin have to help their colleagues in the Eastern part of the city in the face of large-scale street riots. The reason is quite simple; the police of the former police state were not even able to control effectively skinhead tumults or leftists' demonstrations – it was a police force which had been organized to create cases for its further (political) use, not to control the streets of the town.

In short: politics – the ideological command structure – was the actual base of the social order, while so-called material production was, according to the logic of the system, some kind of superstructure. In practice, these regimes relinquished the possibility of real intervention in the underlying social reality, but in order to preserve the impression of revolutionary change in progess, they found it necessary to formulate already existing relations in a new way every now and then. This produces an ideologically mediated reality which is constructed in such a way that the principle of power is established as the leading principle of an illiberally constituted political 'sphere'. This power was legitimated by the idea of preserving a revolutionary government – but a government which was revolutionary only in its origin (in the Soviet Union and few other countries) or, at second-hand, by its origin in the country from which it was actually imported.

Internally, 'really-existing socialism' was designed to be measured only by the standards of its own self-understanding. It was an order basically content with itself, an order which had no systematic space available for essential improvement. So the official revolutionary ideology was intrinsically able to tolerate only quantitative changes. Paradoxically, behind the public commitment to the idea of the revolution there was an evolutionist idea *sub specie aeternitatis*, and a purely idealistic ideological formation. This order considered its most important aim to be the creation and maintenance of (ideologically mediated) social relations; the production of goods was, therefore, of secondary importance. It failed to improve any of the forms of material or cultural production through the decades of its existence – indeed, it quite often tried to prevent radical changes in these areas. As a consequence the communist system was really good only in the production of weapons and of professional athletes, and that was definitely not good enough!

Stalin, probably the most important dogmatic thinker of our age, was the first to give up the Marxian and traditionally socialist concept of world revolution – the most widely accepted dogma of leftist culture. As a result, first the Soviet Union, and then, with time, the whole world communist order lost the possibility of comparison with equal entities (since there was none available). The communist 'world' was understood as surrounded by societies of a different basic quality, i.e. by bourgeois societies, and this was the 'logical' excuse for the claims that there is no general notion from which any type of critique of 'really – existing socialist' order could be legitimated, since it was supposed to be an order original in itself. In fact, 'socialist reality' was basically of the same kind as 'bourgeois reality' except that it was 'turned upside down', and less developed in all relevant respects.

NATIONALISM AND THE END OF THE COMMUNIST ORDER

The very moment at which comparison of the communist order with its relevant social environment became not only possible but inevitable – with results which were evident to practically the whole population of these countries – saw the end of the whole system. With the removal of the ideological veil which protected these systems – and of the concrete border with all the 'necessary' surveillance that surrounded them – this comparison became the essential aspect of all critiques of the system. The very basis of the self-legitimation of the system was the claim that it could not be compared with other systems; once the fear and disorientation created by this ideological veil were removed, it was unable to create once again the context in which all 'measures', including force, could be used for its maintenance.

The political methods – even more generally, the shape of the political landscape of former communist countries – have still much in common with their pre-communist past. As is well known, practically none of these countries has a democratic or liberal legacy (with the exception of Czechoslovakia, none of them had a tradition of free elections), and all have inherited from communism illberal political structures and patriarchal social relations.

In so far as the new constructions seem to begin with abstract notions of democracy and the market economy, it is only logical that traditional values – especially nationalistic ones – tend to fill the newly constituted political spaces. There are basically three origins of post-communist nationalism which can be traced back to the old system, which was based on an illiberal ideology which was collectivist and antagonistic – these three elements are, equally, at the heart of contemporary nationalist ideologies.

The system was based on ideology; it was a fundamentally political construction, a kind of dictatorship over society. This type of dictatorship was strictly political in the sense that only politics had the possibility not only to control, but also to produce basic relations within the society taken as a whole. In such a situation, all attempts to act politically or socially without the omnipresent control of the dominant 'ideological apparatus of the state' had to rely upon the constitution of a group of independent actors not subject to ideological mediation by this apparatus. This constitution could not take place on the basis of an ideology which has to be overtly (i.e. publicly) chosen by its adherents, but only on the basis of a kind of belonging which could identify the members of the group more or less automatically. Such a belonging is, indeed, ethnic, since this is a kind of belonging which can be shown simply by speaking one's language (or dialect) or by pronouncing one's name (or family name) – something that could not be easily stopped or mediated. Thus, ethnic membership became a kind of 'natural' context of the activities of almost all dissidents, with the consequence that, in many cases, a transformation that was meant to be the (re)birth of civil society turned out instead to be the renaissance of an ethno-national community.

The fact is that the enormous authority created by the illiberal constitution of the communist political 'sphere', supported by the dominant ideology, functioned as a kind of huge refrigerator which froze solid all the political actions that were part of the history of the states which became communist. The disintegration of these systems led almost directly back to the same political situations which had characterized these countries before communist rule, and in the ethnically mixed states of Eastern and Central Europe that was a political situation characterized by the rivalries of nationalist factions. And yet there is worse to come. For the 'historical' reasons discussed above, which led to the very constitution of ethnic groups, each believed – and still believes – that it was the major victim of the communist system, and that its rival groups were beneficiaries. Since the dominant ideology of the old system was the ideology of class struggle, for decades ideological rhetoric had been cast in collectivist terms. From a methodological point of view it is not too complicated to switch the public 'sphere' from one collectivist basis to another – even one quite distant in its ideological content. Thus, ethno-national collectivism was almost tailor-made to replace the old ideological schema. And another element of the ideological universe which cultivated an important role for nationalism in post-communist states was the element of struggle in the official ideology of the previous system. It worked to constitute ideologico-political life in existentially interpreted terms of 'friend or foe', which, of course, also suits the nationalist world view.

From a methodological point of view, actual nationalisms in these countries tend to act in a revolutionary way, especially against 'national enemies', and this presents a special problem for the period of transition from communism. Thus it is that such movements act against the spirit of the events in 1989 in former communist Europe although they have, beyond any doubt, emerged out of these events. The events of 1989 were based on the spontaneous assumption of the methods of counter-revolution, i.e., in other words, on a revolt against the very notion and practice of the principle of (permanent) revolutionary change.

In the countries which were living with basically ideologically and politically mediated relations, there was, of course, no civil society as a modern autonomous and self-reproducing sphere, and, therefore, no economy in the contemporary sense of the term. The consequence of this in terms of political and social strategies of transition is very important, namely, that it is not possible to reconstruct an economy which did not exist in the first place; instead the economy had (or, better, still has) to be prepared and organized from first principles. In the meantime, political and ideological events are still the most important and formative ones: every day news broadcasts show that in practically every one of the former communist countries symbolic (and not concrete, everyday) political questions, especially those which can be reduced to ethno-national relations, are to the fore.

Moreover, when finally the question of a new (which means modern market) economy does come to be considered to be the most pressing problem, other inheritances of the former system will, unfortunately, remain. But even this is, and not only for the countries of the former Yugoslavia and the USSR which are involved in post-communist wars, very much a future perspective. The very fact that there is no systematic orientation towards an individual subject of political life (because of the domination of ethno-national collectivist orientations characteristic of post-communist situations) is going to make it extremely hard to effectuate the process of privatization and to enact the market economy. Moreover, this lack will make it especially difficult to live in the economic, social, psychological, even anthropological context created by competition – not to speak of the problems arising from the necessity to impose the social measures required to bring this about.

In any event, the 'new' construction of society will have to deal with the old Hobbesian contractual formula, only this time in reverse. According to Hobbes, the political community begins when people are ready to risk a part of their liberty in the state of nature in order to obtain more security, but, in the present-day situation, the inhabitants of former communist countries have to be ready to risk a part of their inherited security – albeit guaranteed only at a very low level – in order to obtain more freedom.

THE REBIRTH OF CIVIL SOCIETY

The (re)birth of civil society was – and still is – the essential precondition for political reconstruction in the former socialist countries. But this is exactly the point where the mere search either for an, at least partly, ideologically invented tradition, or for a formal procedure is not, and cannot be, enough. First experiences of the 'post-socialist' situation suggest that social problems are emerging as the most important, and that the only possibility of avoiding them for some time lies in the sentimentalization of politics, which, once the initial enthusiasm for post-communism is over, can be achieved most easily through fear.

The fear (re)produced in post-communist societies has two main elements: the fear of economic (and therefore social) insecurity (discussed above) and a strictly political fear. This latter fear is not reducible simply to the direct fear of competition, as is the case in the field of economics. But this is part of what is involved, along with its inheritance of some of the traditions of the ideology of 'really-existing socialism'. In reaction to communist collectivism, which set the modernizing working class as the privileged subject of the system, post-communism seeks to rehabilitate pre-communist traditions, but to do so in a collectivist, ethno-nationalist sense, thereby aiming to reduce the fear of individualist politics set out above.

The political problems raised by the central position of nationalist political movements and parties in practically all the post-communist countries can be understood in terms of the political use of fear of other, traditionally rival ethnic groups as an element of unification, forced solidarity, and as a substitute for collective spirit among persons who are otherwise not devoted to such an ideology. Supposed enemies are the (political) reason for 'oneness' within the ethnic group, for avoiding the real 'internal' competition, for not discussing some moral issues (if such a public discussion could 'make the other side stronger'), in general for forced – and internalized – discipline.

There is, however, one other element of the prevailing nationalist ideology which makes the political foundations of the new communities doubtfully democratic from the very beginning. This is the fact that nationalism involves an increased emotionalization of political life following from the fact that it always deals with the (group) identity of persons – and with an identity established pre-politically. About identity one cannot bargain, nor even negotiate in the modern political sense; compromises are, in principle, not possible as long as it is believed that political relations (or struggles) are about ethnic identity. This makes the presidents of newly constituted states often more leaders (not to say Führers) than elected servants of the people – and, interestingly, almost all these leaders have imposed some kind of presidential system. The emotional-ization of politics means that every negotiation with one's neighbours (beginning, usually, with the Russians) is possible only if leaders do not inform the public that they, in fact, have to bargain about some issues previously regarded as sacred to the nation as a whole.

For the future of liberal democratic politics, the most import-ant (and dangerous) problem arises with the question of ethnic minorities, who come to be seen as the real opposition to the very notion of the nation. 'The victory of democracy' was often interpreted literally as the victory of a (usually ethnic pre-constituted) majority over a minority which was often treated as part of a larger ethnic group surrounding the majority, and not as a minority as such. This strategy – plausible, since ethnic groups are usually mixed together in the territories of European countries – can be seen clearly in operation in, for example, the Baltic states, where, even in the Western media, the actual Russian minorities were almost never treated as such.

Moral arguments are commonly used, in the circumstances described above, with reference to groups. This is, quite simply, a misuse of ethical categories and argument which results in a kind of anthropomorphic interpretation of whole groups, sometimes with millions of members. Real individuals play the role of members, elements, limbs of already presupposed wholes. The space for personal 'sovereignty' is systematically limited. Such individuals are, therefore, in principle not regarded even by themselves as entirely responsible for their acts, but instead tend to locate such responsibility in the leadership, which is, in turn, legitimated by elections, even though it was already present – sometimes mediated by the Church – before any such elections were held.

This is why the whole context of moral behaviour in the political field has to be established in the countries in Eastern Europe which are, at present, undergoing reconstruction. Legal and political guarantees of the independence of the individual can, however, be established only within a community based on a consensus as to the basic political processes and institutions. And this consensus is, in the circumstances, possible only on the basis of a presupposed common past. Modern democratic communities act as if they are based on a consensus which cannot be questioned in everyday political life. But, in an actual situation in which reconstruction is both necessary and urgent but consensus is both actually and technically not possible, and where there is no uninterrupted tradition of original consensus in the geographically and ethnically given political community, only a nationalist programme could pretend to take the place of original consent. Of course, this political process has no regular procedure, and therefore no formal rules, which is why the formality of democratic decision-making has to be involved in such transitional processes – in order, that is, to formalize a perfectly new political experience, an experience that all modern democratic communities claim to have had somewhere in the past, albeit an experience which was not as democratic as their legends describe.

The problem is especially complicated in situations in which former states are to be dissolved, in which, that is, there are popular political orientations towards the constitution of several new (or 'renewed') states on the territory of former federal systems (e.g. the USSR, Yugoslavia, and, perhaps, Czechoslovakia). The questions raised by the necessity of forming a new type of political government are thus complicated by the will to establish new (or 'renewed') territorial entities. Political processes must then deal with the division of both territory and institutions, and also wealth and debts – there are other divisions which directly involve the relations of civil society, and private relations, and which are, of course, also extremely important and sometimes painful, but they are not subject to this type of analysis.

In situations like this the question of original consensus becomes even more important. According to the natural-right tradition, original consensus is the real basis of a political community, and especially of a democratic community. If previously existing states are to be divided, a referendum is therefore generally required, but its political consequences are often interpreted in practice in terms of nationalist notions of ethnic liberation, and only marginally in terms of the democratic rights of the majority (and the limits of such rights) which follow the primary decision to found a new state.

A referendum is, of course, a necessary precondition for the establishing of a new community in a democratic way and for its subsequent democratic development. But, contrary to the situation which characterizes practically all the former communist countries, to perform this task it would have to be a referendum with certain essential procedural characteristics. In the first place, there should be public space which is open for the arguments of all sides – but in the referenda which have occurred in the former communist countries there was such an excited atmosphere that only one side, 'our' side, had a real opportunity of making its case. In such a public discussion some objective, international indicators should be available, especially regarding the economic costs and benefits of independence. There should also be a discussion about minority and individual rights; this also has only been partially present in actual referenda, which is why not one among the new states founded in the process of the dissolution of the USSR and Yugoslavia has proclaimed the automatic right of every citizen of the former federal state, living permanently on the territory of the new state at the moment of independence, to the citizenship of the new state regardless of his or her ethnic, religious or social background. Finally, there has been no discussion about the present and future of disputed territories (with minority populations, or with special strategic positions) which would be created by the process of forming a new state. Therefore, while these referenda have been an appropriate way to show the prevailing feelings of the people in the emerging states, they have not been entirely up to the task of creating a rational foundation for new democratic communities.

In these circumstances, referenda organized to show support for the foundation of a new state are destined to result in a rather high (sometimes extremely high) percentage of votes for independence. The reason is quite obviously the popular belief that a new state means a new start, and better chances to achieve the desired quality of life which was impossible under the former regime – in ethnically mixed states the regime being, almost always, identified with the former, larger political unit. But such large percentages are also a consequence of the fact that there is usually no really substantial discussion about the conditions and prospects for the new state. Even in situations in which leaders have directly said that the independence will bring – 'in the first months' as they usually put it – a declining standard of living, the answer in the referendum has been practically the same – economic or other questions suitable for rational debate have not been important in the highly emotional atmosphere characteristic for those events.

The first political consequence of forming a new nation-state (interpreted strictly in ethnic terms) on a part of territory of a former ('transnational') state lies primarily in the fact that the ethnic majority and minority change places. This was, and is, understood as the only realistic solution because nobody believed in the possibility of fair treatment for minorities, with the result that every group tended to try and overcome its minority position, to create itself as a majority, which means creating a new state, new borders, a new economic and cultural situation and so on. But the psychology of being a minority, which was, through decades, even centuries in some cases, built into the self-understanding of the group, remained still part of everyday political reality. The crucial aspect of such a self-understanding is the assumption that one has no power (or, at best, only irrelevant power). And a subject who is powerless has no logical obligation to be tolerant, since only the powerful can be tolerant, toleration meaning, as is well known, a deliberate choice not to prohibit, hinder or interfere with conduct of which one disapproves, which implies that one has both the requisite power and the requisite knowledge. Such a 'minority' group – now in the majority, having power which is more or less democratically legitimated – still believes that it has no power, and is therefore under no obligation to act tolerantly. Moreover, within such groups there is still the habit of insisting on strong discipline. There is still a readiness to interpret the new situation in old terms, especially in the old terms of majority/minority relations. Therefore, there is no requirement of tolerance, fairness, not to speak of 'generosity' towards the newly powerless group in the new state. This is, once again, not the best perspective for a democratic community.

EUROPE DIVIDED

Europe is divided again, and it is impossible to say how long the new wall will stand. The split is no longer between a communist East and a capitalist, democratic West. The division now rests, as has been shown, on the role and importance of ethno-national sovereignty.

Defining sovereignty in ethnic terms necessarily means exclusion: the exclusion of ethnic minorities by majorities; the exclusion of democrats – who are cast as traitors because they argue for a participatory politics; the exclusion of women, because ethnic nationalism is almost always based on patriarchal traditions and values; and the exclusion of critical intellectuals, who were often the first activists against the old regime but who refuse to be limited to a propagandistic role. From the muting of public discussion to policies of active repression, nationalistic pressures have affected all aspects of political life.

Recent events in post-communist Yugoslavia and (parts of)

the former USSR have led Europe into a perverse stage of 'post-politics' – into civil war accompanied by regular war in the form of aggression against those former republics which wished to establish new states. The most peculiar aspect of the whole process has been the speed with which the pre-political situation characteristic of the first period of post-communism (inevitable, given the absence of real political life, of political traditions and culture in the societies in question) turned into these post-political, warlike events, simply bypassing modern political types of activity. Ethno-national sovereignties have collided over territorial claims, and thus ethno-national sovereignty did not simply involve exclusion (of 'extrinsic' minorities), but also a programme of inclusion (of territories 'temporarily' under foreign control).

But the battle over sovereignty has led, paradoxically, to the relativization of the very notion of sovereignty. The wars in Croatia or Azerbaijan have shown that the old states (or, rather, their federal governments) were unable to guarantee their citizens any kind of security. Yet many former republics (and new states) have been equally powerless to provide such protection (and sometimes not even willing to proclaim it for the whole population). So, after only a few weeks of war, it became increasingly obvious (not, of course, to everyone) that, ironically, the only solution to these problems was international intervention. European (and US) foreign ministers almost took on the role of Yugoslav interior, or Soviet finance, ministers. Thus, although the sovereignty of the old federal states was abolished, emerging ethno-national sovereignties were also, at least temporarily, set aside.

But it seems obvious that this cannot be simply an interim, wartime, arrangement. The (political) reasons for the war(s) can be rescinded only by the political and legal construction of an institutional context in which solutions can be found. Since nobody in these ethnically mixed countries is ready to believe in the objectivity of local institutions, only international institutions (even, in some cases, foreign administration) can, for the time being, provide such a context. Significantly, the solution suggested by the EC representatives for the former Yugoslav republic of Bosnia-Herzegovina points in this direction. The projected establishment of a supreme ('constitutional') court – with ultimate jurisdiction over the protection of human and civil rights – made up of three members from Bosnia-Herzegovina and four members from abroad is a clear example of intervention by the international community and international law in matters traditionally held to be exclusively internal. The original aim of sovereignty was to prohibit foreign interference in such affairs, but this comes up against the fact that human rights have been for decades subject to supranational regulation and the due processes of international law – especially within the European Community.

THE FUTURE OF POST-COMMUNIST SOCIETIES

The hopes which led intellectuals and activists, thousands of dissidents, and then, in the first elections, millions of voters to put an end to the decades of 'really-existing socialism' were directly connected with the ideals of democracy, the free market and the 'European way of life'. And yet – even bearing in mind the very important differences among those Eastern and Central European countries – it is already quite clear that the actual problem lies not in the fact that these ideals have yet to be realized (which is easily explicable in terms of the short time span involved) but in the fact that the present situation shows many characteristics pointing in the opposite direction, towards pre-modern, even quasi-totalitarian politics.

Nationalism is the key to the interpretation of this situation, regardless of the political or the ideological context. It is quite obvious, even at the phenomenological level, that nationalism is the essential political ideology, basis for historical interpretation and source of legitimacy of the governments of these various states. A key question nonetheless is why nationalistic tendencies have this role in the immediate post-communist environment, and not in other European countries – which are accepted as political and social ideals for the former communist states. And another important problem is to account for the differences among post-communist countries – even if nationalism is present in all these societies, in some it has led to wars, in others, simply to additional problems in the transition period.

The first post-communist elections – which were held mostly in the latter countries – showed even so that nationalist ideologies were clearly predominant. This meant a continuing concentration on politics and thus the assigning of only secondary importance to social and economic problems. But this had further implications in terms of the very constitution of the new communities. It was already the case that these communities inherited many technical elements from the old system, but these were now to be organized according to a 'new' ideology – claiming, of course, to be an old one – which itself was ready and able to show totalitarian tendencies. And yet there seems to be an essential difference. What we now have are states which are democratically legitimated; the people have finally chosen their leaders. Reversing the trend of decades of 'really-existing socialism', in the last two or three years there has been a major change, demonstrated by a headlong rush towards a democratic political system and a market-oriented economy. The practice – and, even more, the self-image – of the developed Western states has provided a kind of guidance for this part of the post-communist world; for the first time fundamental political changes were to be directed by the image of something already existing and functioning rather than inspired by a utopian vision.

Unfortunately, there was a catch (or two). The socio-economic and cultural prerequisites for democratic rule had not been analysed in any depth. Society did not really exist as an independent element; all there was was a common will to 'join Europe' – but the actual image of 'Europe' held by the population of these countries merits a study of its own; suffice it here to say that it was not a realistic image. It was an image composed of dreams, hope and television, with Albanian viewers of Italian television as only the most extreme example of this unreality. The changes seemed like radical reforms with popular support but the reality was reform from above – inevitably, given that the only way to the desired changes was via the old political forms. Democracy had to be implemented as a political process, with all the attendant risks.

In this context yet another problem presents itself, namely the question of the ends in the name of which democracy is to be actuated – a question the answers to which were taken for granted before it had even been publicly posed. Implicitly or explicity, the well-being of the prevailing ethnic group in the state was the end in the name of which democracy was installed – the very subject of democratic order – and thus 'the people' could only be interpreted as this ethnic group, which, of course, puts the question of minorities into a very specific context.

On this basis, minorities are divided into native minorities (who live on the territory of other states and can be used to show how strong 'our' case for bringing these territories back to the homeland is) and alien minorities (who live in 'our' state and therefore are regarded as a threat to national security, since they could be used in the same way that 'we' are ready to use our native minorities, as grounds for territorial revision). And, of course, another result of this atmosphere of political suspicion is to increase pressure on other, differently con-stituted minorities – democratic activists, leftists, peace-move-ment activists, feminists and so on.

At best – in Hungary, for example – such an environment can produce democracy for almost everyone. But, even in such cases, some inhabitants are excluded from the possibility of collaborating with the system, even from the possibility of living normal lives within it. At worst this environment leads directly to war as in the case of the former Yugoslavia, and in the former USSR – with the huge difference that while there was, and still is, an inter-ethnic war going on in the former USSR, in the Yugoslav case inter-ethnic civil war has been overshadowed at every stage by the crucial aggressive role of the federal army.

Yet democratic institutions are still – more or less – present in the post-communist states, and this, doubtless, is a substantial improvement on the conditions of the recent past. But do they really function? Or is this an improper question since there clearly has not been enough time for democracy to establish itself? If so, is the direction of events the right one, towards actual democratization?

Before answering this final and crucial question, we must deal with the two commonest critiques of the post-communism situation. First, there is that critique which is so alarmed by the fact that nationalist ideologies and leaders could come to power after communism that it is unable to see the equally important fact that this took place through democratic processes, however imperfect. Millions of inhabitants of the former 'really-existing socialist' regimes actually chose nationalism as the way out of the old system. There is, thus, no democratic way of eliminating nationalism, and the consequences of employing non-demo-cratic means are there in these societies for all to see.

Another critique starts from the premiss that there has been nationalistic manipulation of democratic institutions – indeed, of the very concept of democracy – in these post-communist countries. As has been shown above, this is clearly so, partly because the concept of democracy in question has relied on the procedural formalities which have to be fulfilled rather than on a political content which, it was assumed, could be left to emerge once these formalities were in operation. Even so, these formalities have, to some extent, limited the aforementioned consequences of nationalist ideology.

Bearing all this in mind, the only way to deal with the problems outlined above is through democratic self-discipline. This is, as is well known, not a very efficient or quick way to solve all these problems, but it is the only way which does not lead back to a communist future. The rule of the majority, based on individual rights and on strict respect for the rights of minorities of all kinds, is the oldest, but still the best, or the least bad, prescription for the actual situation of post-communist states. Anything else would imply the paternalistic belief that one knows better than the people in these countries what is good for them – and all the unbearable political consequences of such a position in the actual post-communist situation have been the real subject of this analysis.

NOTES

1 See Thomas Hobbes, *Leviathan*, ed. Michael Oakeshott (Blackwell, Oxford, n.d.), Part I, Ch. XIII, and Part II, Ch. XX.
2 Franz Neumann, *Behemoth: The Structure and Practice of National Socialism 1933–1944*, 2nd ed. (Octagon, New York, 1944).
3 See, e.g., Michel Foucault, *Power/Knowledge: Selected Interviews and Other Writings 1972–1979*, ed. Colin Gordon (Harvester Wheatsheaf, Hemel Hempstead, 1980).

Part IV

Conclusions

Chapter 11

Cosmopolitans and communitarians
A commentary

Ryszard Legutko

Most of the papers collected here represent, not surprisingly, one of two contrasting views – individualism (cosmopolitanism) or communitarianism. The debate between individualists and communitarians which has been going on among Anglo-American political theorists for some time could not fail to re-emerge when the issues under discussion became the current controversies over sovereignty, the legitimacy of the nation-state, the future of Europe and a new international order. What we are witnessing today in Europe and even beyond its boundaries – and this diagnosis both individualists and communitarians tend to share – are two processes which apparently lead in opposite directions. On the one hand, we have a movement towards international integration, on the other, movements for local ethnic autonomy. It is important to note at the outset that this divergence cannot be seen in terms of a simple dichotomy of progressive and regressive forces. Both movements are progressive (in the common sense of the term), as they seem to undermine the traditional structures that have been with us for some time and of which the basic constituent was the nation-state, and to lead to some form of new world order, whether unified or pluralistic, or both. But looked at from a different angle, both movements may be regarded as partly conservative: the trend towards integration is an expression of the triumph of Western liberal democracy – it perpetuates and reproduces, on an international scale, the ideology and structures that are deeply embedded in the Western tradition; on the other hand, the trend towards local, ethnic, religious and national autonomies is, in fact, the triumph of pre-modern forms of social bonds that were supposed to have disappeared long ago – or to be reduced to a politically harmless folklore – not only in the ideologically homogeneous Soviet Bloc, but also in the more or less spontaneously developing Western countries.

A question thus arises about the ambitions the authors of these chapters – as spokesmen of one or other of these orientations – have as regards the restructuring of the new world. Formulated more precisely, the question reads as follows: what changes do individualism and communitarianism legitimize in the present processes; how far do they transcend the *status quo* and encourage a certain type of restructuring while discouraging other types; to what extent do they limit themselves to expressing an appeal for caution, or to restating basic criteria to which all restructuring must conform, or to sketching moral boundaries beyond which the new order, whatever form it takes, cannot trespass, and to what extent do they stimulate the changes in a certain direction, provide inspiring visions for citizens and politicians, and describe positively what the new order ought to be?

COSMOPOLITANS

Let us start with the first orientation – individualism – which is explicitly espoused by three writers, O'Neill, Beitz and Pogge, and which they term 'moral cosmopolitanism'. It is defined as an ethical system where the central idea 'is that every human being has a global stature as an ultimate unit of moral concern' (Pogge, p. 90). The expression 'moral concern' appears in all three authors. Beitz's definition is almost identical with that of Pogge. O'Neill takes a weaker stand on cosmopolitanism – although equally critical of communitarianism – satisfying herself with the less apodictic, less abstract and metaphysical formula of agents 'sharing a world'.

This attitude – regardless of possible disagreements among the authors – is universalist, that is, it aims to establish universally valid criteria with which we can evaluate institutions and processes. The obvious criterion that follows from moral cosmopolitanism is that all restructuring of boundaries or of institutional frameworks should be assessed in the light of 'the human values they advance as compared with the human values they deny or threaten, for all persons affected' (Beitz, p. 125). This seems to be a very commonsensical approach. Whenever changes occur, it is always individuals who are most affected by the imperfections of ill-conceived or badly executed reforms. The criterion merely states that what happens to individuals – irrespective of their national, religious, or political affiliation – tells us to what degree the restructuring is defensible; it is they who primarily count, not groups, nations, tribes, ethnic communities, or other collectives. The boundaries between states or communities – as O'Neill argues – cannot be the limits of justice.

The most obvious reading of this criterion would be in terms of conceptual nominalism as contrasted with conceptual realism. The implication of political nominalism (that is, of suspending the authority of collectives as separate moral agents or entities) would be the advocacy of a policy of moderation. The message it would convey is the following: we should be careful with sweeping political decisions; the bolder the decision (secession, for example), the more it will affect people; we should therefore make more modest plans and follow piecemeal policies. There is a trace of conservatism in this: since every decisive move we make in the name of a community may threaten the 'human values' of some group within this community or in its neighbourhood, and since the overall calculus of possible gains and losses in those values is, in such situations, usually precarious, there is always a danger of a stalemate and a likelihood of a very slow rate of restructuring. This paradox of the conservative – or rather mutually limiting – conditions of Western freedom was, to my knowledge, first noticed, and obviously deplored, by Nikolai Byerdyayev, who maintained there should be more room for reformers determined to work energetically for the improvement of the human lot.

But this self-limiting and cautious approach is not what the authors of the individualistic and cosmopolitan persuasion in fact argue. If they do, it is predominantly in the context of exclusivist, self-assertive movements, that is, with reference to the emancipatory tendencies of ethnic groups and nationalities. The razor of conceptual nominalism which the cosmopolitan individualists employ effectively undermines the unconditional right to self-determination or to secession. Such a right, the authors argue, can never be unconditional. If exercised unconditionally, it encourages local tyrannies to sacrifice individual human rights for the sake of the obscure general good, or even more obscure national sovereignty. This is usually accompanied by the rejection of universalist criteria, a convenient excuse to justify the violation of individual rights on the basis of a relativist ethic which is in fact a smokescreen for sheer arbitrariness. Moral cosmopolitanism is thus a form of 'sceptical humanism' (Beitz, p. 125) which debunks or, in more moderate versions, simply makes us wary of, local collectivisms. Applied to the current situation, this attitude is concerned mainly with developments in Eastern Europe, in the former Soviet empire, and in all areas where national movements for independence define themselves in exclusivist and relativist terms; it has, evidently, less relevance to most of the movements for local autonomy in the Western world, where the danger of collectivism is considered smaller.

But does moral cosmopolitanism express equal scepticism towards inclusivist, i.e. integrationist processes? Does the spirit of moderation which goes with conceptual nominalism and its insistence on the well-being of concrete individuals also undermine the radicalism of those who want to unify the whole world by a common system of institutions or common criteria of justice? Here the answer is not as unambiguous as before. To be sure, all three authors write critically of world government, none seeing it as a desirable institution. They are not, however, unsympathetic to the idea that animated the world government project and this is perfectly understandable: whoever considers himself a cosmopolitan cannot completely disavow his support for global organization, whatever its defects. Pogge aims at no less than a global project, free – as he hopes – of the defects of the world state. Beitz writes explicitly that 'the widely alleged undesirability of world government is not a good reason to reject the ethical aspiration', and that the advocacy of world government 'exibits political naivety [rather] than philosophical error'(p. 126). O'Neill restricts herself to stating that reasons against a world state seem 'serious reasons' to her, and she opts for 'justice across borders', which means that individuals have equal claim to just treatment regardless of which side of the state boundary they happen to live; this does not necessarily imply (though it very well may) a common set of supranational institutions.

This seems to suggest that the cosmopolitans tend to be less sceptical and less cautious towards the inclusivist projects. Here a case in point may be Beitz's chapter, where the author explicitly formulates a programme of scepticism and indeterminacy towards all political restructuring, whether confederation, self-determination or consolidation: 'political arrangements and rearrangements [should] be evaluated impartially in terms of their impact on the basic human rights and interests of all those affected' without 'prejudg[ing] the outcome of this evaluation' (p. 135). It is, however, symptomatic that Beitz concerns himself mostly with showing the conditionality and instrumentality of self-determination, naturally enough for someone who espouses moral cosmopolitanism. Yet it is less obvious that equal scepticism towards inclusivist policies on the same cosmopolitan grounds is shown: while it is true that moral cosmopolitanism need not necessarily imply institutional cosmopolitanism (a point Beitz repeats several times), it is no less true that the former favours cosmopolitan solutions rather than exclusivist ones. True, a moral cosmopolitan would support a liberal democratic nation-state rather than a tyrannical world state, but the natural disposition would be to work for the creation of cosmopolitan institutions, or for the improvement of existing ones, rather than for the creation of a new nation-state or for the improvement of a nation-state *qua* nation-state.

One cannot fail to notice that those who fear an exclusivism which is most often embodied in local collectivisms, and who therefore wish to limit the right to self-determination, usually seek the support of cosmopolitan institutions. One can see this in Beitz too: 'The likelihood of continuing pressures for political realignment makes it all the more urgent that we invent international institutions with the capacity and legitimacy to play constructive roles in accommodating these pressures'. (p. 135). In other words, to make self-determination conditional on universal criteria and instrumental to universal objectives we need cosmopolitan institutions through which moral cosmopolitanism can express itself. A world without such institutions would be exposed to the abuses of the right to sovereignty or to self-determination against which Beitz and like-minded thinkers warn.

One of the consequences – or possibly presuppositions – of this conscious or unconscious preference for inclusivism is a lack of sympathy for the nation-state, the institution which has always seemed a major stumbling block on the way to a cosmopolitan world. It is not that cosmopolitan individualists proclaim open revolt against the nation-state. A more accurate statement would be that in their interpretations this institution loses the privileged position it has occupied for centuries, and enjoys a rather limited legitimacy. Cosmopolitan individualists do not question the necessity for individuals to have group loyalties; indeed, they believe that their institutional solutions will serve those group loyalties better than the nation-state. What they question is its claim to closed territoriality. People should have maximum access to their own communitarian values, but this does not require a sovereign state having fixed boundaries. An absolutely homogeneous state is impossible (and indefensible) and heterogeneity, along with the international connectedness which is an essential characteristic of the modern world, is said to have dealt a mortal blow to the aspirations of the nation-state. Nation-states may continue to exist in one form or another, but – so cosmopolitan individualists argue – there is nothing natural, sacred or optimal about them. With the nation-state partly delegitimized, institutional cosmopolitanism seems an irresistibly favoured outcome.

This position is a reversal of the standard established by Aristotle, who maintained that a state (*polis*) is a natural entity and constitutes an optimal political order. This naturalness and optimality is justified by the position it occupies between two extremes which fail to satisfy man's political nature – on the one hand, family and other local communities, which were said not to be sufficient and self-sustaining, and on the other, humanity (empire), with which, it was claimed, no person can identify himself politically. The cosmopolitan individualists seem to be arguing that a good order should consist primarily of organized local communities having political autonomy (though not complete sovereignty) and of supranational institutions. The mean element – the state – which for Aristotle was the natural and ultimate area of politics – loses its central role, though of course it need not be entirely dispensed with. If the cosmopolitan individualists were to express their ideas in Aristotelian terms, more tinged with essentialist metaphysics, they would probably say that local communities and supranational institutions are more natural than a state, and more in accord with man's political nature, which is determined by the experience of 'sharing a world' even with people living in distant lands.

From the penchant for political inclusivism one could draw the inference that cosmopolitan individualists support the integrational processes that are going on in the post-Cold War world. But such an inference would not be totally accurate. A possible explanation is that explicitly articulated support for those processes would make them less cosmopolitan and more 'perspectival': they would be liable to the charge of being the partisans of Western ideology and Western institutional hegemony. But there is more to it than that, particularly in Pogge's chapter (O'Neill and Beitz being reticent on this issue).

Pogge's project for global reform – which, roughly speaking, amounts to economic centralization plus political decentralization – stems from the conviction that the current world order is unjust and should be changed. The presupposition is that, whatever the merits of spontaneous (or designed) developments in the modern world, deprivation and misery are widespread and appalling and that ongoing processes as well as existing structures, if unchanged or left to their current dynamics, promise no substantial improvement. This position is far bolder than a warning against the collectivist implications of sovereignty, or scepticism about the essentialist interpretation of the state, or sympathy for institutional inclusivism and cosmopolitan politics. All these things could be more or less validly deduced from the assumptions of moral cosmopolitanism. Global reform is something that cannot be so easily inferred, unless some other assumptions are added, whose connection with moral cosmopolitanism is at best incidental. Here are some of them (the full list is, of course, much longer).

1. There is, in the modern world, such a thing as a global regime. To make this assertion one must have at one's disposal a theory which explains how a regime of such magnitude may have come into being, and how diverse human actions tend to unify in one structure. It is clear that moral cosmopolitanism has nothing explicit to say about this, although, at the same time, there is little in cosmopolitanism that would prohibit the acceptance of such a theory. The best-known theory which explains the birth and existence of a global regime is, of course, Marxism, whose traces are easily identifiable in Pogge's chapter. Whether Marxism as such can be reconciled with moral cosmopolitanism is a complex issue – there is a significant element of

communitarianism in Marx's philosophy – but I see no obvious reason why some aspects of this philosophy could not be so incorporated.

2. A global regime is a deliberate human construction. This assumption stands in glaring opposition to a well-known conservative thesis that the institutions which organize social life emerge in a mysterious way – that is, they come into being not by conscious and deliberate design but out of countless individual and collective actions, which means we cannot prescribe good institutions without facing the problem of unintended consequences. For Pogge's global project, the rejection of this conservative thesis is necessary; without this step he cannot postulate the removal of the existing framework and the introduction of the new one. The fact that the existing framework was deliberately constructed is proof that it can be deliberately replaced without fearing unanticipated results. Obviously such a constructivist assumption must be substantiated by an additional theory; Marxism can be helpful here, but in a rather more specific version than was needed for the first thesis. The question whether this is reconcilable with moral cosmopolitanism is also more complex. Moral cosmopolitanism itself is silent on the issue. Only indirect arguments are possible: since moral cosmopolitanism is not easy to harmonize with a conservative interpretation of institution-making (which favours conceptual realism in its insistence that institutions are a sort of corporate persons, not to be understood simply in functionalist terms) it may indeed be more akin to constructivism.

3. There are feasible alternatives to the existing global regime. This is a very bold statement. It requires a lot of additional theoretical assumptions, and rather controversial ones, to produce a feasible account of the mechanisms of change (which is not to be confused with a moralistic imperative to replace allegedly unjust structures). What seems particularly difficult to explain here is the contradiction between the integrationist processes that are actually going on and the hypothetical social acceptance of the alternative global order, without which there can be no question of its feasibility. In other words, whether the world is just or unjust, the more integrated it becomes the more difficult it is to envisage a feasible alternative to the existing framework of institutions. A possible solution would be radical opposition to this frame-

work, an open proclamation of a revolution against the ongoing West-dominated process of integration, with the intention of establishing an entirely new set of institutions – but this is a step which, understandably, Pogge does not seem inclined to take.

The statement that an alternative global regime is feasible is also hard to reconcile with moral cosmopolitanism. The latter is primarily an ethical position, useful for the criticism of existing institutions or for providing axiological guidelines for future ones. But to assert that an alternative cosmopolitan regime is feasible we must presume more than this. We must presume that moral cosmopolitanism has become a cultural fact, that is, that the overwhelming majority of people have become moral cosmopolitans, ready to part with their institutions in their current form and embark on a great reforming mission. As an empirical statement this seems plainly false, regardless of our wishes. What is more important, it also seems to contradict the initial message of moral cosmopolitanism, which was that of prudence and caution in political restructuring. In a way, the assumed feasibility of alternative global regimes seems to provide what, according to Byerdyayev, Western culture lacked: scope for well-meaning and energetic reformers.

COMMUNITARIANS

We should now turn to communitarianism, the second orientation represented in the volume, exemplified by two writers, Miller and Brown. At the beginning one should remove one possible misinterpretation. Whatever the differences between those orientations, there is one point where they seem to be in perfect agreement. Like individualism, communitarianism does not imply an unlimited right to self-determination; it does not condone nationalistic *sacro egoismo* or a totalitarian collectivism which would unconditionally subject the individual to the good of society; nor does it lead to political adventurism by undermining existing structures and justifying every form of secession under the false pretence that national sovereignty constitutes the supreme objective of a community. Whoever fears chauvinism, collectivism, political irrationalism and the tyranny of groups over individuals, or of one group over another, should not regard communitarianism as a potential vehicle for these phenomena. This reservation is important because one of the standard arguments for cosmopolitanism has always been the 'slippery slope' tendency of communitarian theories, allegedly bound to degenerate, sooner or later, into some variant of collectivism. The flaw which was said to make this degeneration almost inevitable, or at least predictable, is the inherent relativism of those theories: since all norms are matters of the community's culture and history there is, allegedly, no universalist defence against arbitrariness.

The communitarian reluctance to allow unlimited secession and unqualified self-determination as supreme values is not something extrinsic and inessential to the theory. To prove this one can propound four arguments, three of which are found in Miller and Brown:

1. A communitarian individual is not a person totally malleable by the cultural environment, having no properties other than those supplied or determined by the society in which he or she lives. Communitarianism only states that an individual cannot be conceived of unless we take into account his political (in the Aristotelian sense) existence: an individual deprived of his political and historical ramifications is a fiction and as such cannot provide any basis for political theory. The individual human person is not lost sight of in the communitarian perspective, and this forms an intractable barrier to what cosmopolitans fear most: the supremacy of a group over an individual.

2. Among various communities there is a logic and a hierarchy. The logic – comparable to that among individuals – imposes various more or less stable forms of coexistence, which express themselves in practices, international agreements, collective instincts of self-preservation, and formal and informal checks and balances; thus, unlimited rights to self-determination and to absolute sovereignty, for example, are self-defeating because they would lead either to continuous disintegration of all communities into smaller and smaller organisms, or to the petrification of existing hegemonies. Hierarchy (which is not to be confused with a differentiation between superior and inferior nations, for example, in a version popular in the nineteenth century, between nations that make history and those that do not) makes it possible to distinguish, however provisionally, between communities that are nations and those that are ethnic groups, the former having more profound and

more permanent cultural identities than the latter. There is therefore no danger of the chaos which would occur if all groups, whether of weak or strong identity, sought independence: a spontaneous accommodation is certain to prevail. Elements of this argument can also be found in Michael Walzer's chapter; the latter's position, however, stems from different assumptions.

3. The political identity of a community does not express itself only in non-rational or pre-rational sentiments. A well-developed political community contains everything that is necessary for the harmonious coexistence of individuals within this community and for harmonious coexistence with other communities: civic culture, basic freedoms, law, civil society, good institutions, religious and ethnic associations, traditional communities such as the family, and so on. A nation oppressing its own citizens, including ethnic minorities, and subjugating neighbouring communities deserves, in the light of communitarian theory, condemnation as severe as in the light of cosmopolitan individualism. This form of communitarianism was formulated by Hegel and is here reiterated by Brown.

4. The inherent relativism of communitarianism – a basis for political arbitrariness and consequently for collectivism – can be even further reduced if we follow Aristotle and say that over and above the practices of communities, which are necessarily different from one another, there exist absolute metaphysics and theology, accessible to those who value theory more than practice. Speaking in Hegelian terms, one can assert that the objective spirit of a community tolerates some forms of arbitrariness but that they cannot be the carrier of ultimate meanings and judgments; such meanings and judgments are the prerogatives of a higher tribunal (in fact, the highest) – Absolute Spirit – which Hegel associated with art, philosophy and religion. It should be observed, however, that such a defence of communitarianism which links moderate political relativism with non-political (metaphysical and theological) absolutism is entirely absent in the volume. In fact it is one of those ideas which, regrettably, have almost completely disappeared from modern consciousness and modern political philosophy in the West. Absolutist metaphysics and theology have recently received heavy blows from postmodernists who saw in them the last ominous stronghold of political hegemony. It is char-

acteristic, for example, that Brown, who employs the Hegelian notions of subjective and objective spirit to defend the ethical state, leaves out Absolute Spirit as if this concept did not matter for Hegel's vision of human existence, and as if neo-Hegelianism could very well do without it.

The last point is important not only because it reveals modern philosophical preferences; it is important also because it shows that the cosmopolitanism–communitarianism dichotomy need not exist. Aristotle and Hegel were both cosmopolitans *and* communitarians; their philosophies contained elements of universalism and localism, of individualism and collectivism. True, they could be interpreted as representatives of anti-individualist authoritarianism, but such interpretations, although popular, seem inadequate. The fact that a dichotomy exists today, and that cosmopolitans and communitarians accuse each other of misrepresenting human existence in the world of politics, suggests that both sides agree to the following alternative: either we accept cosmopolitanism and interpret human individuals in universalist terms as beings devoid of culture, history, and tradition; or we accept communitarianism and then fall into some form of relativism, since cultures, histories, and traditions are so different that no meaningful universalism is attainable.

Communitarianism, as we have seen, has tried to limit its relativism, and it has succeeded in avoiding two dangers: the sanctification of the *status quo* (conservatism) and the justification of an absolute right of any and every community to self-determination (anarchism). The question now arises whether communitarians accept the post-Cold War processes. The cosmopolitans – it will be recalled – had mixed feelings about them: on the one hand, they welcomed the disintegration of communism, and on the other, they feared the spectre of nationalism on its ruins; on the one hand, they welcome integration, on the other, since integration falls short of cosmopolitan standards, they search for better solutions. Communitarians also have mixed feelings about those processes but for different reasons.

An Aristotelian justification of the *polis*, applied to the post-communist world, leads communitarians to the conclusion that the tendency of newly liberated societies to create nation-states is a natural course of development and should not be regarded as a symptom of political immaturity. This also seems to be a conclusion shared by many East European political commentators. Their reasoning is more or less as follows. Although – given the weakness of civil culture and the lack of republican traditions in many of those societies – there is much to be feared in the processes that are going on in this part of Europe, it is unreasonable to expect that there is some other and better route for the new republics to take. If we agree with Miller that communities may be more successful when they are self-governing, then the process of state-building in the former Soviet bloc becomes, indeed, a natural one (not necessarily in the metaphysical sense of the word). All the dangers and complications that accompany this process (and sometimes jeopardize it) cannot change this overall positive assessment.

The Aristotelian argument in Brown's chapter has additional force in this context. The state (more Hegelian than liberal) is an obvious environment in which political culture can develop and where individuals can master the art of self-government. All Western countries – whatever the future of European integration – have passed through this stage of institution-building, and there is no reason why the new countries should avoid it. There will be no peace in the region and no chance for those countries to join the Western community if they do not achieve and learn to practise sovereignty, not in the absolute sense of having an unlimited freedom of decision but in the sense which Brown, following Hegel, gives to this concept. Sovereignty should be thus understood 'in terms of the need of citizens to be able to recognize each other and identify the institutions through which they come together and distinguish themselves from the rest of humanity' (p. 178). The function of such a sovereign state is 'to provide a forum within which individuals can relate to one another not as family members or as competitors for scarce resources but as fellow citizens, and within which the constraints necessitated by social life can be internalized' (p. 177). This forum – it should be emphasized – cannot be provided either by local communities or by supranational organizations, that is, by the two categories of political institutions to which the anti-Aristotelian theorists of a cosmopolitan and individualist persuasion are inclined to attach a higher value than they attached to nation-states.

The alternative that individualists and the communitarians

propose for the newly liberated societies is the following. The individualist perspective stems from a universalist conception of human rights, equality and justice: individuals are defined as right holders; the value of institutions is objectively determined by the degree to which they respect human rights: the main problems of the community are, largely, negative – to neutralize and remove everything that stands in the way of these rights, i.e. intolerance, nationalism, discrimination, exploitation. On the positive side, this orientation opts for some form of international regulation and institutionalization (not necessarily as comprehensive as those suggested by Pogge) that secures the maximum realization of human rights. The second orientation defines individuals as members of a community and as citizens; the value of institutions is determined by the degree to which they constitute a well ordered and well-functioning republic ('an ethical state'); the main problems of the community are positive – to create an institutional, legal and moral system; human rights are seen as useful and important correctives in these processes, but they are never the core of republican politics or the republican mentality; international institutions are also important but never gain the primary loyalty.

Which of these two options is better for the new republics is of course an open question, much debated in those countries. The strong point of the individualists is that the dangers against which they warn are real. Generally, however, the communitarian republicans seem to occupy safer ground. Republican experience appears to draw more from the traditions of those countries than does the cosmopolitan project. Besides, a society that skips or neglects the republican phase in its development, aiming at a larger and more ambitious objective, has little chance to become a reliable member of the international community. This also solves, for the time being, the problem of European integration with which those countries are confronted. The developing of republican practices and institutions will certainly bring the newly liberated countries closer to Europe, but whether or not they will participate in the integration process when, in the future, their economy and political systems become stabilized remains to be seen. From today's point of view it seems undeniable that the successful construction of European institutions within those countries – by no means an obvious prospect – would be, in itself, a remarkable achievement and a major contribution to the stability of Europe, even if eventually these new republics decided to refrain from becoming formal members of the European Community.

The communitarian attitude towards integrational processes in the West is less clear. Authors like Miller who defend the nation-state will certainly be extremely reluctant to subscribe to these processes (though Miller's chapter does not contain any explicit statement to this effect). There is no theoretical possibility of combining support for the nation-state as a basic political institution with support for integration which would lead to Europe as a common fatherland. More, there is no possibility of ascribing any degree of spontaneity to such an integrational process, since this would imply either the concession that the nation-state is not an optimal institution or the conclusion that the decline of nation-states is a symptom of a serious crisis. Neither implication would be welcomed by communitarians, though, of course, the second is not damaging to communitarian assumptions. All this does not mean that the defenders of nation-states are against international co-operation. They certainly favour all types of co-operation, including international help for poor countries, as long as it is, precisely, co-operation, and not the creation of a political organism which is meant to replace the nation-state.

The position of the defenders of an 'ethical state' (Brown) is more complicated. They do not reject integration, or, at least, they refrain from making a definite statement on this issue. Brown makes three points in this context. (1) There is a possibility that the ethical state will decline as a result of integration and will cease to perform the creative function required of it. (2) Integration may lead to federalism and 'there is no reason to think that a federal Europe could not be designed in such a way as to meet the requirements of an ethical state should the peoples of Europe wish to take this route, as perhaps they do' (p. 181). (3) But he expresses some doubts 'whether the current uneasy mixture of nation-state and supra-national bureaucracy can provide the sort of clarity that indi-viduals require if they are to be able to identify their fellow citizens and experience the laws that govern them as of their own creation'(p. 181).

These statements are divergent in some respects but not

contradictory. It would be hard, however, to express them in a single general formula and to pin down their author to any specific standpoint. What they seem to amount to ultimately is a conviction that the current changes are real and irreversible, and, in spite of all imperfections (which should not be underrated on an impulse of European euphoria), there is a chance that the new political form that may emerge, a federal Europe, will preserve a certain modus of the republican spirit and thus a comparable framework for the functioning of the ethical community or communities. In short the author believes in the power of the Hegelian *Aufhebung* (a concept he does not make explicit use of): some aspects of the state will perish but some of their qualities will survive in new political structures. This idea has some commonsense support: in the current developments there should be a strong and deeply felt element of continuity – otherwise we fall into a utopianism which is always dangerous, no matter how lofty and desirable our ideals.

Chapter 12

Comments and conclusions

Hidemi Suganami

Political/moral philosophers often remark that, apart from insisting that the constitution be ethically acceptable, which usually means liberal democratic, they cannot say much about which territorial space should come under one national constitution, or whether it be federal or whatever, since, they say, these are *instrumental* questions. Beitz says this from the cosmopolitan viewpoint; Brown says it from the constitutive viewpoint; and Walzer also says it from the communitarian viewpoint.

Sunstein argues, however, that at least one thing can be said, instrumentally, about the desirable content of any constitution: a constitution must not recognize the right to secede even where secession is plausibly justifiable, as in some parts of contemporary Eastern Europe. There, debates over the right to secede have already played an extraordinarily important role in discussions of new institutional arrangements, Sunstein notes, because Eastern European countries are deciding about the contents of proposed constitutions in the context of profound cultural and ethnic divisions, both often defined at least roughly in territorial terms. Such divisions concern all the contributors to this volume.

In some cases, Sunstein acknowledges, a right to secede will be fully justified as a matter of political morality. But the existence of occasionally powerful moral claims, he insists, supplies insufficient reason for *constitutional* recognition of the right to secede. A nation that recognizes this right in a founding document, and is prepared to respect it, would, he argues, increase the risks of ethnic and factional struggle; raise dramatically the stakes of day-to-day political decisions; introduce irrelevant and illegitimate considerations into those decisions;

create dangers of blackmail, strategic behaviour, and exploitation; and, most generally, endanger the prospects for long-term self-governance, and may well find that it has thereby endangered ordinary democratic processes.

Even where as in Eastern Europe there is good reason to secede, there are, Sunstein notes, generally more direct means of accomplishing the desired goals, such as local self-determination through federalism, firm protection of civil rights and civil liberties, and institutional and substantive guarantees against economic exploitation. Where such more direct means are inadequate, he suggests, the proper remedy is to reach a negotiated solution, to exercise the unwritten right to revolt, or to apply the pressure of domestic and international law, rather than to create a constitutional right to secede. Further, even in cases of sub-units absorbed through aggression, such as the Baltic states in the former Soviet Union, Sunstein's preferred remedy is a system of international law, including an internationally recognized right to restore original borders when sufficient time has passed and when the exercise of that right would not unduly disrupt existing arrangements.

In developing the position outlined above, Sunstein does not ask whether the division of the world into sovereign states, and consequently into a plurality of constitutions, is itself a justifiable move: he takes this for granted. O'Neill, however, challenges such uncritical acceptance of a basic assumption, and criticizes certain standard arguments in support of the division of the world into sovereign states. She is a cosmopolitan (some of her contentions are similar to those of David Mitrany and Johan Galtung[1]), and she disagrees with communitarians in particular, holding that an argument for *nation* statehood is spurious. This can be contrasted with Miller's contribution, to be considered later. None the less, O'Neill concedes that certain boundaries may after all be justified.

O'Neill maintains, however, that 'plurality', 'finitude' and 'sharing of a world' are necessary *and sufficient* for moral considerations to become operative. Although the most familiar case of a world shared by a plurality of finite agents is that of a community whose members interact a great deal, she observes, interaction now hardly ever stops at political or other boundaries. We trade, we broadcast, we travel, we negotiate. For practical purposes we are already committed to viewing both nearby and distant and unknown others as agents like ourselves. Hence if we think that there are ethical principles – principles of justice – whose scope includes all with whom we interact, we cannot exclude distant others, O'Neill asserts. Although the notions of 'global community' or 'global society' may be no more than a sentimental rhetoric of cosmopolitanism, the weaker relation of 'sharing a world' is one that agents today cannot consistently deny.

It follows that a territorial boundary should not be interpreted as an absolute one, as a boundary of morality. Since therefore boundaries should not interfere with the operation of moral considerations across the boundaries, O'Neill concludes, state A need not and must not refrain from concerning itself with human rights violations in state B merely because B is a separate sovereign state. Thus legitimate claims of nations cannot be to impermeable boundaries, but may be to a political order through which each can secure and hand on its specific ways of life and sense of identity.

But then, it would be a mistake to assume that communitarians necessarily regard the boundaries of traditional communities as those of morality: communitarians, too, may and do concede that there are at least *international* (though not necessarily *transnational*) obligations, as will be seen later in Miller's work.

Pogge is also a cosmopolitan, and supports an institutional (as opposed to interactional) form of moral (as opposed to legal) cosmopolitanism. This form of cosmopolitanism, he shows, leads us to aim for the feasible global institutional scheme that produces the best pattern of human rights fulfilment. For example, according to Pogge, our present global economic regime produces a stable pattern of widespread malnutrition and starvation among the poor, and there are likely to be feasible alternative regimes that would not produce similarly severe deprivation. In such a case of avoidable deprivation, we are confronted not merely by 'persons who are poor and starving' (as will be suggested by the interactional version of cosmopolitanism), but by 'victims of an institutional scheme' (as is claimed by Pogge, who adopts institutional cosmopolitanism). There is an injustice in this economic scheme, which it would be wrong for its more affluent participants to perpetuate.

Pogge's broadly consequentialist variant of institutional cosmopolitanism accords, he notes, with how the concern for human rights is understood in the Universal Declaration of Human Rights: 'Everyone is entitled to a social and international order in which the rights and freedoms set forth in this Declaration can be fully realized.' In Pogge's judgment, such an aim would necessitate a global order in which sovereignty is widely distributed vertically, i.e. not a world state, but in effect what Hedley Bull calls 'new mediaevalism':[2] persons should be citizens of, and govern themselves through, a number of political units of various sizes, without any one political unit being dominant and thus occupying the traditional role of the state. Their political allegiance and loyalties, Pogge adds, should be widely dispersed over these units: neighbourhood, town, county, province. People should be politically at home in all of them, without converging upon any one of them as the lodestar of their political identity, in his view.

One great advantage of his proposed multi-layered scheme, Pogge remarks, is that it can be reached gradually from where we are now. This requires moderate centralizing and decentralizing moves involving the strengthening of political units above and below the level of the state. This, according to Pogge, leads us to the question: what principles ought to govern the geographical separation of political units on any level? Pogge answers in a somewhat lawyer-like manner by formulating detailed procedural principles based on the need to respect the will of a majority of inhabitants in any contiguous territory without sacrificing the will of the minority. However, these principles seem relatively unimportant in a fully multi-layered world, since territorial boundaries would have lost their current significance.

Pogge is clearly in agreement with Beitz in believing that cosmopolitanism need not be indifferent to particularistic values such as the loyalties and affiliative sentiments characteristic of membership in cultural or national groups. However, as O'Neill had also argued, normative reasoning, according to cosmopolitanism, is incomplete if it fails to take account of the interests of everyone affected; and it is, at best, distorted if it privileges proximity in space or time for its own sake. It follows that we would be justified in recognizing the entitlement to statehood of a communal group only if doing so was not only best from the point of view of the group but also best overall. This, Beitz observes, significantly qualifies the responsiveness of cosmopolitanism to communitarian values.

Beitz reminds us that from a moral cosmopolitan point of view whether self-determination is acceptable is an instrumental question. It involves a hypothesis that the group could not prosper without political independence, or it would suffer persecution otherwise. A cosmopolitan argument in favour of either confederation or disaggregation will also be instrumental in form. Accordingly, a cosmopolitan analysis of confederation or disaggregation will depend heavily on the facts of each case. It will not always be true therefore that the communal interests of members of a group would be enhanced if the group were separated off from other groups and provided with greater communal autonomy. In any case, as with self-determination, it is essential, Beitz stresses, to consider the impact of political rearrangement on everyone involved – not only the groups whose interests recommend it, but also anyone else affected.

In short, on a cosmopolitan view, whether a group is entitled to separate from a larger entity to form its own state, and if so on what terms, is a complicated question that is not easily resolved by resort to simple abstract principles. It is, Beitz observes, a classic case for informed political judgment, and for some form of creative mediation as well. Beitz adds, however, that the likelihood of continuing pressures for political realignment makes it all the more urgent that we invent international institutions with the capacity and legitimacy to play constructive roles in accommodating these pressures. The shape of such international institutions would in turn be a matter of informed political judgment.

A political, and instrumental, judgment to the effect that on the whole it is more sensible for a state to consist of a nation, and for a nation to constitute a state, is offered by Miller. Of course, a tricky question of defining a nation must be faced, and he suggests the following: a nation is a community constituted by mutual belief, extended in history, active in character, connected with a particular territory, and thought to be marked off from other communities by its members' distinct traits. These, he suggests, serve to distinguish nationality from other collective sources of personal identity, including perhaps subnational ethnicity.

But to say that national solidarity is good for a state and that statehood is good for a nation does not show (1) that a state should exercise its sovereignty (the term is used here roughly to mean 'exclusive control') over all its national affairs, (2) that there is no international obligation, or (3) that national self-determination, rather than human rights, is an appropriate starting point for the discussion of international political morality.

As regards (1), Miller asserts that 'defence' need not be, but 'social and economic policies' need to be, kept in the hands of national governments. This part of Miller's argument seems a little rudimentary, if not arbitrary. As regards (2), he enumerates a number of moral restrictions upon the sovereign freedom of the state: the duty not to violate the territorial integrity of another state (entailing, interestingly, the duty not to export pollution); the duty not to abuse one's national power against another; the duty to observe treaties, subject to the proviso that circumstances remain substantially the same (this proviso in Miller's view would allow a group to withdraw from confederation if its national identity were at stake); the duty of mutual aid in cases of emergency; and the duty of states which are clearly resource-rich to help out states that are clearly resource-poor and economically hard-up as a result. As regards (3), Miller merely states that in his belief the onus is on people who adopt the cosmopolitan approach to *show* that the conditions of international society are such as to make this approach an appropriate one. O'Neill would reply that she has *argued* this in her piece (although, presumably, not to Miller's satisfaction).

On the question of secession, Miller notes that there are two liberal views: a sub-community may secede only when it is not getting a fair deal; a sub-community may secede if it so wishes provided that it is in turn willing to allow any sub-sub-community the equivalent right, and so on indefinitely. The latter we saw in Pogge. In contrast to these liberal views, says Miller, the principle of nationality focuses attention neither on material interests nor on individual preferences for boundaries, but on the political conditions for securing national identities. The principle tells us to further the cause of *national* self-determination wherever possible. So, to begin with, existing boundaries are put in question only where a *nationality* is currently denied self-determination. This is to be distinguished from the situation of an *ethnic* group which feels it is currently denied rights of cultural expression, or treated unfairly in some other way, and for which the remedy is reform of existing arrangements and policies within the state. Accordingly, it is Miller's view that the problem of secession only arises in cases where an established state houses two or more groups with distinct and irreconcilable *national* identities.

Thus in order justifiably to secede, group G (wanting to secede) must have a national identity which is distinct from that of the remaining members of S (the state), and which cannot be adequately protected and expressed by granting G a limited measure of political autonomy within S. We would also need to be convinced, Miller adds, that the territory demanded by G did not contain minorities whose own identities were radically incompatible with that of G, so that rather than creating a viable nation-state the secession of G would simply reproduce a multinational arrangement on a small scale. If the sub-sub-community could show, for instance, that its ethnic identity was reasonably secure under S but would be seriously threatened under G, then this is a good reason for blocking G's demand, Miller reasons.

Beitz argued that a group can be permitted self-determination only if it could not prosper without political independence or would suffer persecution otherwise, and, additionally, if self-determination of the group is best for everyone affected by it. By contrast, according to Miller, no groups but only a nation (as defined by his criteria and distinguished from an ethnic group) can seek self-determination. Despite this difference, Miller would not go so far as to suggest that a nation, just because it constitutes a nation, can seek self-determination *selfishly*. Thus Miller says, for example, that some consideration must be given to those minority groups who would be left in S when G secedes. Further, the new state would need to be viable. It should not radically weaken the parent state. Perhaps the seceding territory should not contain the state's entire supply of some important natural resource. Walzer, another communitarian, suggests this in his contribution to this volume. But Miller is somewhat sceptical of this last condition: it was morally arbitrary that state S originally had the resource in question; so members of S have no real complaint against the seceding G that they are taking the resource with them, unless this would leave S itself in the category of 'breadline' states. To this, a more radical cosmopolitan would reply: if it is (rightly) admitted that it was morally arbitrary that state S originally had the resource in question, then it must also be acknowledged that G's taking it away would be just as morally arbitrary, and thus morally unacceptable.

Walzer, as a communitarian, is inclined to support separation whenever separation is demanded by a political movement that, so far as we can tell, represents the popular will. Walzer's style is informal but eloquent, and his argument is quite judicious. Let the people go who want to go, he says. Many of them will not go all that far. And if there turn out to be political or economic disadvantages in their departure, they will find a way to re-establish connections. Indeed, if some sort of union – federation or confederation – is our goal, the best way to reach it is to abandon coercion and allow the 'tribes' first to separate and then to negotiate their own voluntary and gradual, even if only partial, adherence to some new community of interest. Today's European Community is a powerful example, which other nations will approach at their own pace. As we shall see later, such a positive assessment of the EC is not shared by Brown.

Walzer notes, however, that one nation's independence may be the beginning of another nation's oppression. Reading the newspaper these days, he remarks, it often seems as if the chief motive for national liberation is not to free oneself from minority status in someone else's country, but to acquire (and then mistreat) minorities of one's own: Puhovski would regard this as an apt remark. But Walzer remains optimistic: put a threatened nation in a world where they are no longer threatened, and for how long will they think it in their interest to threaten others?

But *who* will protect the Serbs in an independent Croatia or the Albanians in an independent Serbia? Walzer concedes that he has no easy answer to these questions. In a liberal democracy, national minorities can seek constitutional protection. But not many of the new nations are likely to be liberal, even if they achieve some version of democracy. The best hope of restraint lies, he thinks, in federal or confederal checks and balances, and in international pressure. What is required, he says, is an international consensus that validates a variety of choices, supporting any political arrangement that satisfies the tribes at risk. Interestingly, this is not very different from Beitz's position noted earlier.

Puhovski is a good deal more pessimistic than Walzer, and deplores that, in post-communist Eastern Europe, nationalism tends towards pre-modern quasi-totalitarian politics. He contends: millions of the inhabitants of the former 'really-existing' socialist regimes actually chose nationalism as the way out of the old system; there is thus no democratic way of eliminating nationalism, and the consequences of employing non-democratic means are there in these societies for all to see; implicitly or explicitly, however, the well-being of the prevailing ethnic group in the state was the end in the name of which democracy was installed, and thus 'the people' could only be interpreted as this ethnic group, which, of course, puts the question of minorities into a very specific context. Puhovski's faith is in democratic self-discipline. This, he says, is the only way, not very efficient, but the only way that will not lead back to communism. The rule of the majority, based on individual rights and on strict respect for the rights of minorities of all kinds, is the oldest but still the best or the least worst prescription for the actual situation of post-communist states.

In abstract terms, all the essays in this volume are concerned with one central question: how ought individuals and communities of individuals to organize themselves and relate to one another? They discuss this question from various angles, having in mind more or less explicitly the current political predicament of Eastern and, to a lesser extent, Western Europe. Brown's essay is exemplary in its very explicit effort to apply an answer to the abstract question to the concrete context of contemporary Europe. His approach, which he calls 'constitutive', derives from Hegel, and the context to which this is applied is a process of disintegration in the East and integration in the West.

Constitutive theory, as Brown admits, does not provide instant criteria by which to evaluate the politics of integration and disintegration, federalism and confederalism; but, he maintains, it does offer the promise of an approach to these topics which takes seriously the claims of the nation-state – not in opposition to the claims of the individual, but on the basis that it is not possible to be an individual in the first place without the presence of a political community to give content to individuality.

Constitutive theory is thus resolutely communitarian and, in effect, statist. The state, according to this theory, is not simply a problem-solving mechanism, but an essential element in the creation of a fully human individuality, which can only be developed in a constitutional, legal, state. But this high doctrine, Brown notes, does nothing to answer the practical questions posed by the disintegration of multinational empires and states in Central and Eastern Europe. A belief in the value of the state as an institution does not imply an ability to determine what state should exist, within which boundaries, although, in contrast to cosmopolitan approaches, it does imply that this is an important question.

There is no blanket endorsement, however, of nationalism, or of the value of the nation, on the part of constitutive theory, Brown notes. What is important, according to constitutive theory, is that the state should be put together in such a way that, along with the family and civil society, it can play its proper role in ethical life. As Brown rightly remarks, the key issue therefore is the ethical nature of the state – the presence of 'ethical substance', to use the old terminology – and while there may be a slight bias in favour of the state being a nation-state, there are also reasons for concern if nationalism becomes too important. Constitutional government and the rule of law, private property and the market economy, free family relations – all of these are, from the viewpoint of constitutive theory, of greater significance than the national ideal. If the latter undermines the former, by, for example, curtailing the civil rights of non-nationals, then this is to be deplored. No alleged natural tendency of the world to fall into national groupings can be allowed precedence over the requirement of the ethical state. Cosmopolitans, such as O'Neill and Beitz, to the extent that they allow states to exist, would agree with this last pronouncement; communitarians, such as Miller, to the extent that they do not endorse national selfishness, would probably also agree with it.

To the constitutive theorist, the role of the ethical state is to complete the process of individuation begun in the family and civil society. The former institution, Brown notes, is the site of unreflective, unconditional love, the latter the site of competition and external constraint. The role of the state is to provide a forum within which individuals can relate to one another not as family members or as competitors for scarce resources but as fellow citizens, and within which the constraints necessitated by social life can be internalized, experienced as of one's own creation. This, as Brown notes, is a tall order, and – *pace* Hegel – no actual state ever has done (or will do) all that is required of it – but supplies the basis for a critique of the existing order.

Only a constitutional state based on representative institutions, some kind of separation of powers, and the rule of law can do this, Brown remarks. But beyond this the theory is unspecific. In any case, Brown observes with some satisfaction that the breakdown of the Soviet system has somewhat enhanced the hitherto suppressed role of the family and civil society. A constitutional state is not simply a set of institutions, it is also a set of practices and attitudes which cannot be codified but which are critical to the process of politics. This, Brown reminds us, means that the ethical state must be based not simply on a set of institutions but also on a commitment to the political spirit of these institutions. Brown observes that, broadly speaking, in Central and Eastern Europe the institutions of an ethical state are emerging on the ruins of communism, and here, especially in Eastern Europe, the problem lies in the practices of politics. On the other hand, in Western Europe, the commitment to political means is strong and apparently unshakable, but, he maintains, the institutional structure is beginning to lose the sort of clarity required of an ethical state.

So what can and ought to be done in practical terms? One suggestion, which Miller will endorse, will be to stress the national nature of the new states, on the principle that fellow nationals will find it easier to behave politically as opposed to coercively towards each other. As a general proposition this may be so, Brown agrees, but, he is quick to add, the problems of nationalism are also clear, the problems which Walzer seems to hope will eventually decline, and which Puhovski seems to think can only be controlled to a limited extent by democratic self-discipline.

One important issue, from the viewpoint of constitutive theory, is whether a particular national grouping has the wherewithal to form the basis of a rational constitutional state – if not its members would certainly be better off remaining within a multinational grouping that does have these resources. But, Brown argues, perhaps more important is the means that are employed to press national claims or to resist them. Groups that employ unlawful and unconstitutional means to assert their independence in circumstances where constitutional, legal means to press their case are available are unlikely to create just institutions within their new boundaries. Conversely, he says, larger jurisdictions which can only preserve themselves by using violence against those who have expressed a wish to leave are also unlikely to be able to preserve constitutional politics.

This line of reasoning can be applied to the case of Yugoslavia. Brown thus notes: the old multinational republic could only have been preserved by the military conquest of at least two of its component parts, i.e. it could not have been contained within an ethical state. The possibility that Croatia and Bosnia-Hercegovina will be able to form constitutional states while holding down their Serbian minorities by force is equally unlikely. According to Brown, this is a case where boundary revisions make sense, and the current prejudice against such action cannot be supported.

It may be recalled that Beitz noted the importance of international institutions, and Walzer that of international pressure, in accommodating the stresses of political rearrangements in Eastern Europe. Brown agrees that outsiders can help at the margin, supporting constitutional polities and withholding aid from the unconstitutional. In his view, however, the best contribution Western Europeans can make to the solution of the problems of the East is to offer models of how functioning constitutional states might work: this is similar to Puhovski's conclusion that only democratic self-discipline, learnt from past experience, can be of some help to the Eastern problem of nationalism.

Brown, however, is sceptical of the European Community, not, he hastens to add, because it is becoming federal. What is much more problematic, he remarks, is whether the current uneasy mixture of nation-state and supranational bureaucracy can provide the sort of clarity that individuals require if they are to be able to identify their fellow citizens and experience the laws that govern them as of their own creation. Unfortunately, Brown does not articulate his claim satisfactorily, pointing only to 'the doubtful legitimacy of the present institutional structure'(p. 182). Brown appears to be rather fond of schematic juxtapositions, but there is hardly any doubt that, compared with the problems faced in Eastern and Central Europe, those facing the members of the European Community are minor, if not insignificant.

What is striking about the contributions to this volume is that they are remarkably similar in their substantive contentions. A consensus is relatively easily reached, therefore. Apart from Pogge, who on cosmopolitan grounds favours a move towards a multi-layered structure, all the contributors to this volume accept, in some cases perhaps reluctantly, that sovereign states must continue to coexist in Europe. Moreover, all the contributors more or less explicitly endorse liberal democracy as appropriate to the states of Europe even though some of them are relatively pessimistic about the speed with which former communist countries can adopt liberalism in practice. Furthermore, all the contributors pay attention to the persistent fact of nationalism, while unanimously making a case against national selfishness. Even Miller, who defends national self-determination and is sceptical of cosmopolitanism, argues for a good deal of international moral constraint upon the sovereign freedom of nation-states. There are of course some differences in detail among the contributors regarding the circumstances under which secession is legitimate, but they agree that secession as such is not much of a sin, at least in the context of post-communist Eastern and Central Europe. As for the precise international and domestic institutional arrangements which should operate in Europe, East, West or Central, a consensus appears to be that they cannot be worked out in the abstract: what is required is a sensible political judgment grounded in the facts of each case. As for the role of Western European countries in particular, the contributors are on the whole modest in their expectations: these countries can supply models of democracy and perhaps also of international co-operation, although Brown appears sceptical with respect to the latter; they can encourage democracy to take root by refraining from aiding anti-democratic movements; but not much more. Conspicuously, no one advances an argument for massive economic or technological aid to the former communist countries. Perhaps the contributors believe that the problems are too enormous for this to be of much use.

NOTES

1 See David Mitrany, *A Working Peace System* (Chicago, Quadrangle Books, 1966); David Mitrany, *The Functional Theory of Politics*, introduced by Paul Taylor (London, Martin Robertson/LSE, 1980); Johann Galtung, *The True Worlds* (New York, Free Press, 1980).

2 See Hedley Bull, *The Anarchical Society: A Study of Order in World Politics* (London, Macmillan, 1977).

Select bibliography

and guide to further reading

Anderson, B. *Imagined Communities*, Verso, London, 1983.

Avineri, S. and de-Shalit, A. (eds) *Communitarianism and Individiualism*, Oxford University Press, Oxford, 1992.

Barry, B. 'Humanity and Justice in Global Perspective' in Pennock, J. Roland, and Chapman, John W. *Nomos*, XXIL 1982.

Barry, B. *Democracy, Power and Justice: Essays in Political Theory*, Clarendon Press, Oxford, 1989.

Barry, B. and Goodin, R. E. (eds) *Free Movement: Ethical Issues in the Transnational Migration of People and Money*, Harvester Wheatsheaf, Hemel Hempstead, 1992.

Beitz, C. R. *Political Theory and International Relations*, Princeton University Press, Princeton N.J., 1979.

Beitz, C. R. 'Cosmopolitan Ideals and National Sentiment', *Journal of Philosophy* 80, 1983.

Beitz, C. R., Cohen, M., Scanlon, T. and Simmons, A. J. (eds) *International Ethics*, Princeton University Press. Princeton N.J., 1985.

Brilmayer, L. 'Secession and Self-determination', *Yale Journal of International Law* 16, 1991.

Brown, C. 'Ethics of Co-existence: The International Theory of Terry Nardin', *Review of International Studies* 14, 3, 1988.

Brown, C. 'Hegel and International Ethics', *Ethics and International Affairs* 5, 1991.

Brown, C. *International Relations Theory: New Normative Approaches*, Harvester Wheatsheaf, Hemel Hempstead, 1992.

Brown, P. and Shue, H. (eds) *Boundaries* Rowman and Littlefield, Totowa N.J., 1981.

Buchanan, A. *Secession*, Westview Press, Boulder, 1991.

Buchheit, L. C. *Secession: The Legitimacy of Self-determination*, Yale University Press, New Haven, 1978.

Bull, H. *The Anarchical Society: A Study of Order in World Politics*, Macmillan, London, 1977.

Bull, H. (ed.) *Intervention in World Politics*, Clarendon Press, Oxford, 1984.

Charvet, J. *A Critique of Freedom and Equality*, Cambridge University Press, Cambridge, 1981.

Ellis, A. (ed.) *Ethics and International Relations*, Manchester University Press, Manchester, 1986.

Elster, J. and Slagstad, R. (eds) *Constitutionalism and Democracy*, Cambridge University Press, Cambridge, 1988.

Forsyth, M. *Unions of States: The Theory and Practice of Confederation*, Leicester University Press, Leicester, 1981.

Frost, M. *Towards a Normative Theory of International Relations*, Cambridge University Press, Cambridge, 1986.

Fukuyama, F. 'The End of History?' *The National Interest*, Summer 1989.

Gellner, E. *Nations and Nationalism*, Blackwell, Oxford, 1983.

Hegel, G.F.W. *Philosophy of Right* (translated with notes by T.M. Knox), Oxford University Press, Oxford, 1967.

Held, D. (ed.) *Political Theory Today*, Polity Press, Cambridge, 1991.

Kymlicka, W. *Liberalism, Community and Culture*, Clarendon Press, Oxford, 1989.

Luper-Foy, S. (ed.) *Problems of International Justice*, Westview Press, Boulder 1988.

Margalit, A. and Raz, J. 'Self-determination', *Journal of Philosophy* 87, 9, September 1990.

Mayall, J. *Nationalism and International Society*, Cambridge University Press, Cambridge, 1989.

Miller, D. *Market State and Community*, Clarendon Press, Oxford, 1989.

Miller, D. and Siedentop, L. (eds) *The Nature of Political Theory*, Clarendon Press, Oxford, 1983.

Nardin, T. *Law, Morality and the Relations of States*, Princeton University Press, Princeton N.J., 1983.

Nardin, T. and Mapel, D. (eds) *Traditions of International Ethics*, Cambridge University Press Cambridge, 1992.

Navari, C. (ed.) *The Condition of States*, Open University Press, London, 1991.

O'Neill, O. *Faces of Hunger: An Essay on Poverty, Justice and Development*, Allen and Unwin, London, 1986.

Plamenatz, J. *On Alien Rule and Self-government*, Longmans, London, 1960.

Plant, R. *Modern Political Thought*, Blackwell, Oxford, 1991.

Pogge, T. *Realizing Rawls*, Cornell University Press, Ithaca, N.Y. 1989.

Rawls, J. *A Theory of Justice*, Oxford University Press, Oxford, 1971.

Rawls, J. 'Kantian Constructivism in Moral Theory', *Journal of Philosophy* 27, 1980.

Rorty, R. *Contingency, Irony and Solidarity*, Cambridge University Press, Cambridge, 1989.

Sandel, M.J. *Liberalism and the Limits of Justice*, Cambridge University Press, Cambridge, 1982.

Smith, A.D. *Theories of Nationalism*, Duckworth, London, 1971.

Stront, T. (ed.) *The Self and the Political Order*, Blackwell, Oxford, 1992.

Twining, W. (ed.) *Issues of Self-determination*, Aberdeen University Press, Aberdeen, 1990.

Vincent, R.J. *Nonintervention and International Order*, Princeton University Press, Princeton N.J., 1974.

Vincent, R.J. *Human Rights and International Relations*, Cambridge, 1986.
Walzer, M. *Just and Unjust Wars*, Penguin, Harmondsworth, 1980.
Walzer, M. *Spheres of Justice*, Martin Robertson, Oxford, 1983.

Index